HELLBOY

AND THE

BUREAU FOR PARANORMAL · RESEARCH AND DEFENSE ·

1953

Created by MIKE MIGNOLA

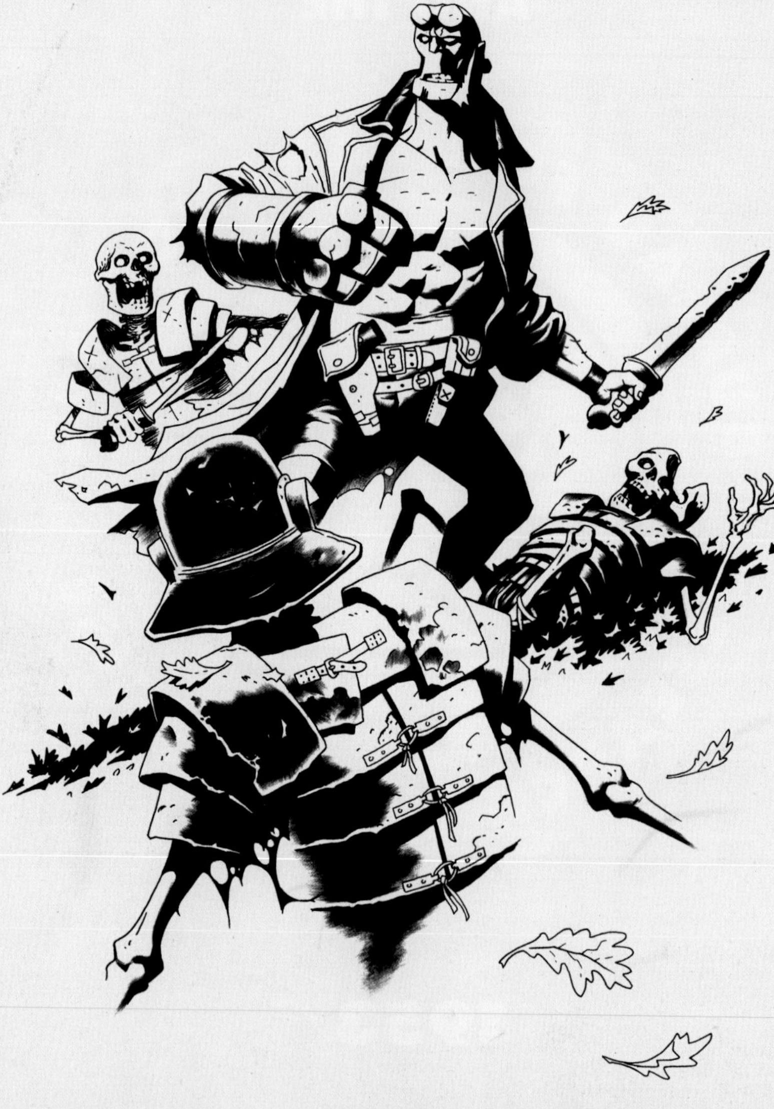

MIKE MIGNOLA'S

HELLBOY
AND THE B.P.R.D. 1953

THE PHANTOM HAND	WANDERING SOULS	BEYOND THE FENCES
RAWHEAD AND BLOODY BONES	✠	✠
THE WITCH TREE	*Story by*	*Story by*
THE KELPIE	MIKE MIGNOLA	MIKE MIGNOLA
	&	&
✠	CHRIS ROBERSON	CHRIS ROBERSON
Story by		
MIKE MIGNOLA	*Art by*	*Pencils by*
	MICHAEL WALSH	PAOLO RIVERA
Art by		
BEN STENBECK		*Inks by*
		JOE RIVERA

✠

Colors by
DAVE STEWART

Letters by
CLEM ROBINS

Cover art by
MIKE MIGNOLA WITH DAVE STEWART

Series covers by
MIKE MIGNOLA, PAOLO RIVERA, MICHAEL AVON OEMING & DAVE STEWART

Publisher MIKE RICHARDSON ✧ *Editor* SCOTT ALLIE
Associate Editor SHANTEL LaROCQUE ✧ *Assistant Editor* KATII O'BRIEN
Collection Designer CINDY CACEREZ-SPRAGUE ✧ *Digital Art Technician* CHRISTINA McKENZIE

DARK HORSE BOOKS

Published by Dark Horse Books
A division of Dark Horse Comics, Inc.
10956 SE Main Street
Milwaukie, OR 97222

DarkHorse.com
International Licensing (503) 905-2377
Comic Shop Locator Service (888) 266-4226

First edition: August 2016
ISBN 978-1-61655-967-0

1 3 5 7 9 10 8 6 4 2
Printed in China

This book collects Hellboy and the B.P.R.D.: 1953—The Phantom Hand & The Kelpie, Hellboy and the B.P.R.D.: 1953—The Witch Tree & Rawhead and Bloody Bones, Hellboy and the B.P.R.D.: 1953—Beyond the Fences *#1–#3, and "Wandering Souls" from* Hellboy Winter Special 2016.

Library of Congress Cataloging-in-Publication Data

Names: Mignola, Michael, author. | Roberson, Chris, author. | Stenbeck, Ben, illustrator. | Walsh, Michael (Comic book artist), illustrator. | Rivera, Paolo, 1981- illustrator. | Rivera, Joe, illustrator. | Stewart, Dave, illustrator. | Robins, Clem, 1955- illustrator.
Title: Hellboy and the B.P.R.D., 1953 / story by Mike Mignola, Chris Roberson ; art by Ben Stenbeck, Michael Walsh ; pencils by Paolo Rivera ; inks by Joe Rivera ; colors by Dave Stewart ; letters by Clem Robins.
Other titles: B.P.R.D. 1953 | 1953
Description: First edition. | Milwaukie, OR : Dark Horse Books, 2016.
Identifiers: LCCN 2016008184 | ISBN 9781616559670 (paperback)
Subjects: LCSH: Comic books, strips, etc. | BISAC: COMICS & GRAPHIC NOVELS / Fantasy.
Classification: LCC PN6727.M53 H374 2016 | DDC 741.5/973--dc23
LC record available at https://lccn.loc.gov/2016008184

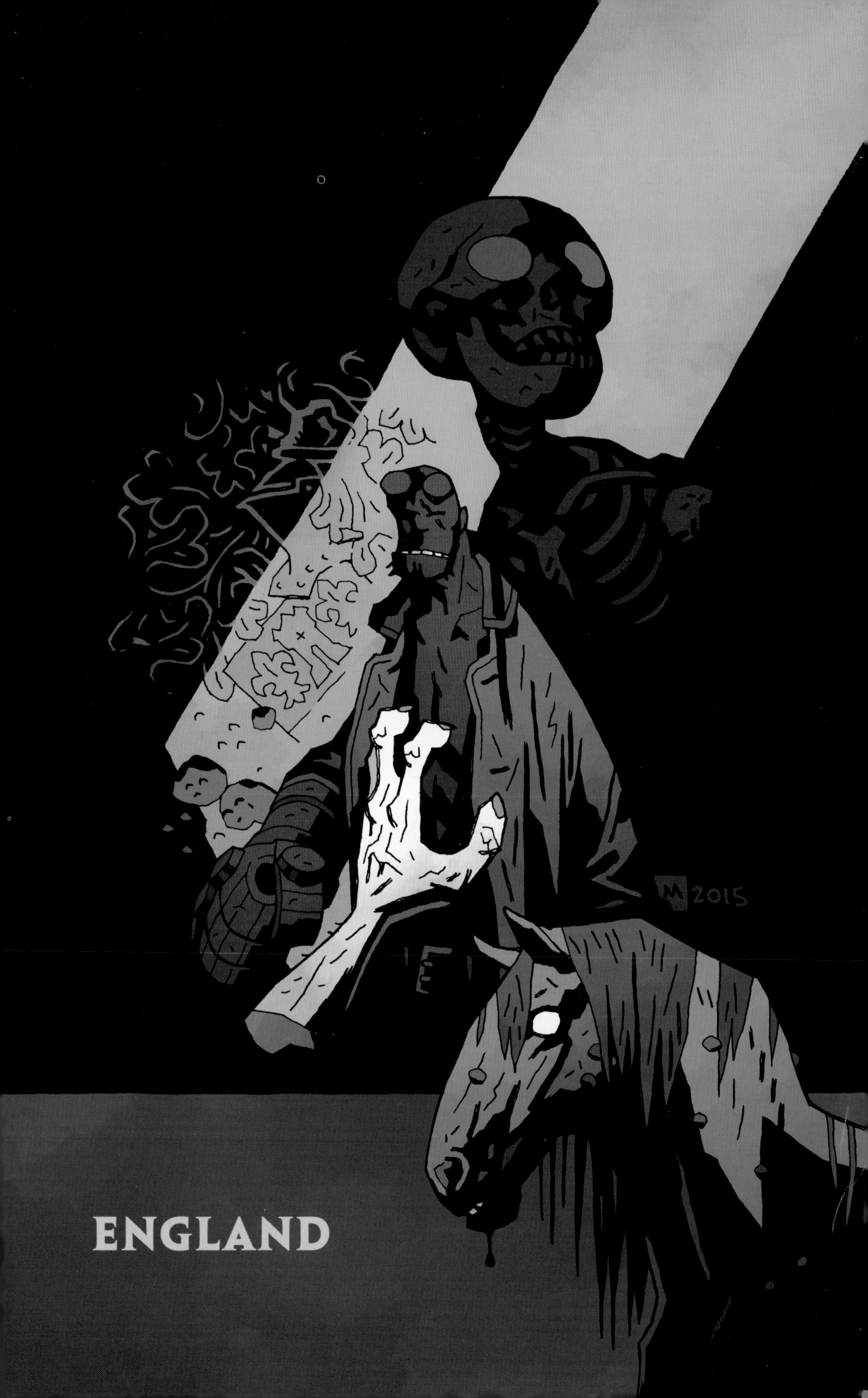

ENGLAND

The Phantom Hand

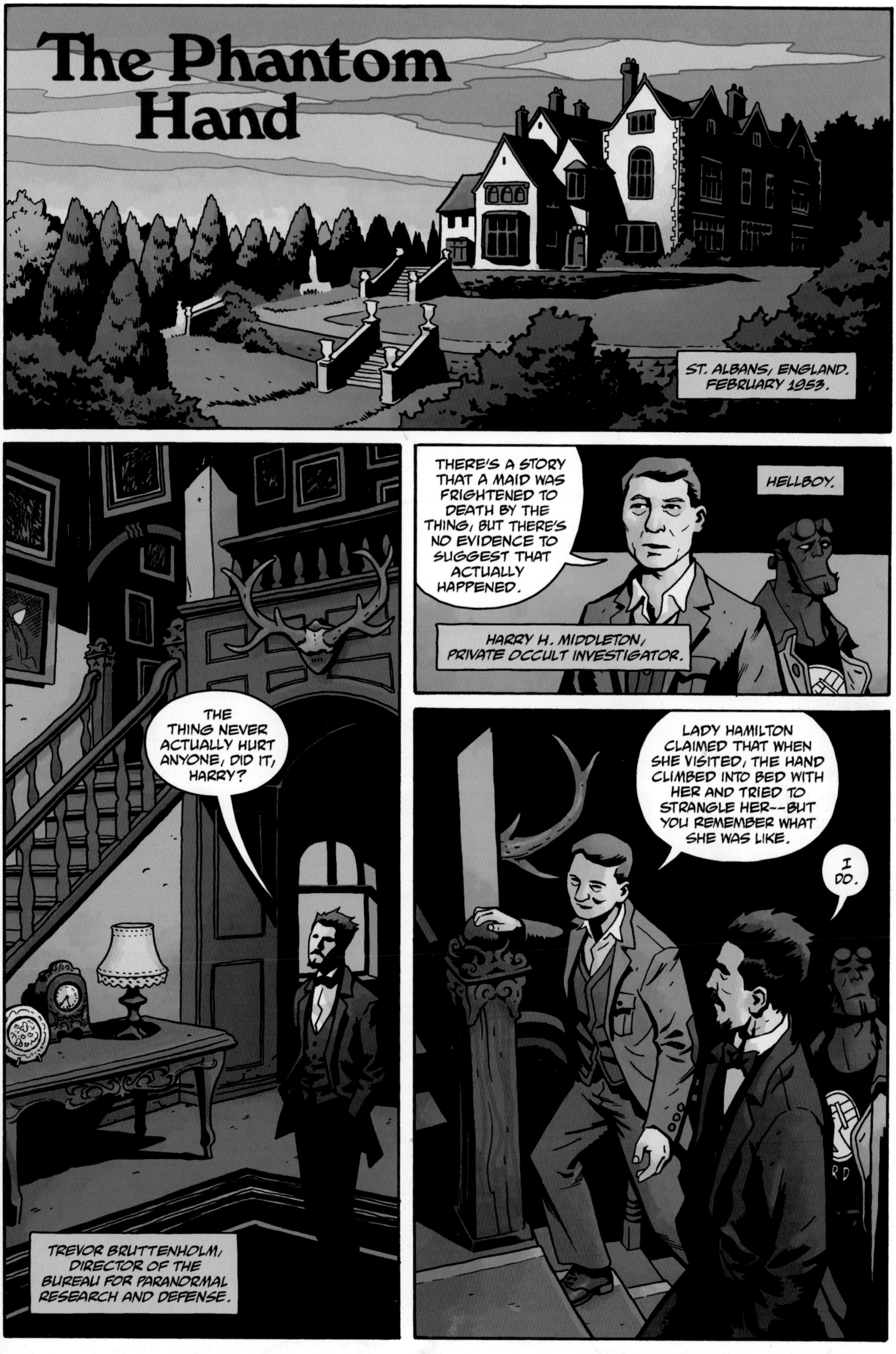

ST. ALBANS, ENGLAND. FEBRUARY 1953.
THERE'S A STORY THAT A MAID WAS FRIGHTENED TO DEATH BY THE THING, BUT THERE'S NO EVIDENCE TO SUGGEST THAT ACTUALLY HAPPENED.
HELLBOY.
HARRY H. MIDDLETON, PRIVATE OCCULT INVESTIGATOR.
THE THING NEVER ACTUALLY HURT ANYONE, DID IT, HARRY?
TREVOR BRUTTENHOLM, DIRECTOR OF THE BUREAU FOR PARANORMAL RESEARCH AND DEFENSE.
LADY HAMILTON CLAIMED THAT WHEN SHE VISITED, THE HAND CLIMBED INTO BED WITH HER AND TRIED TO STRANGLE HER--BUT YOU REMEMBER WHAT SHE WAS LIKE.
I DO.

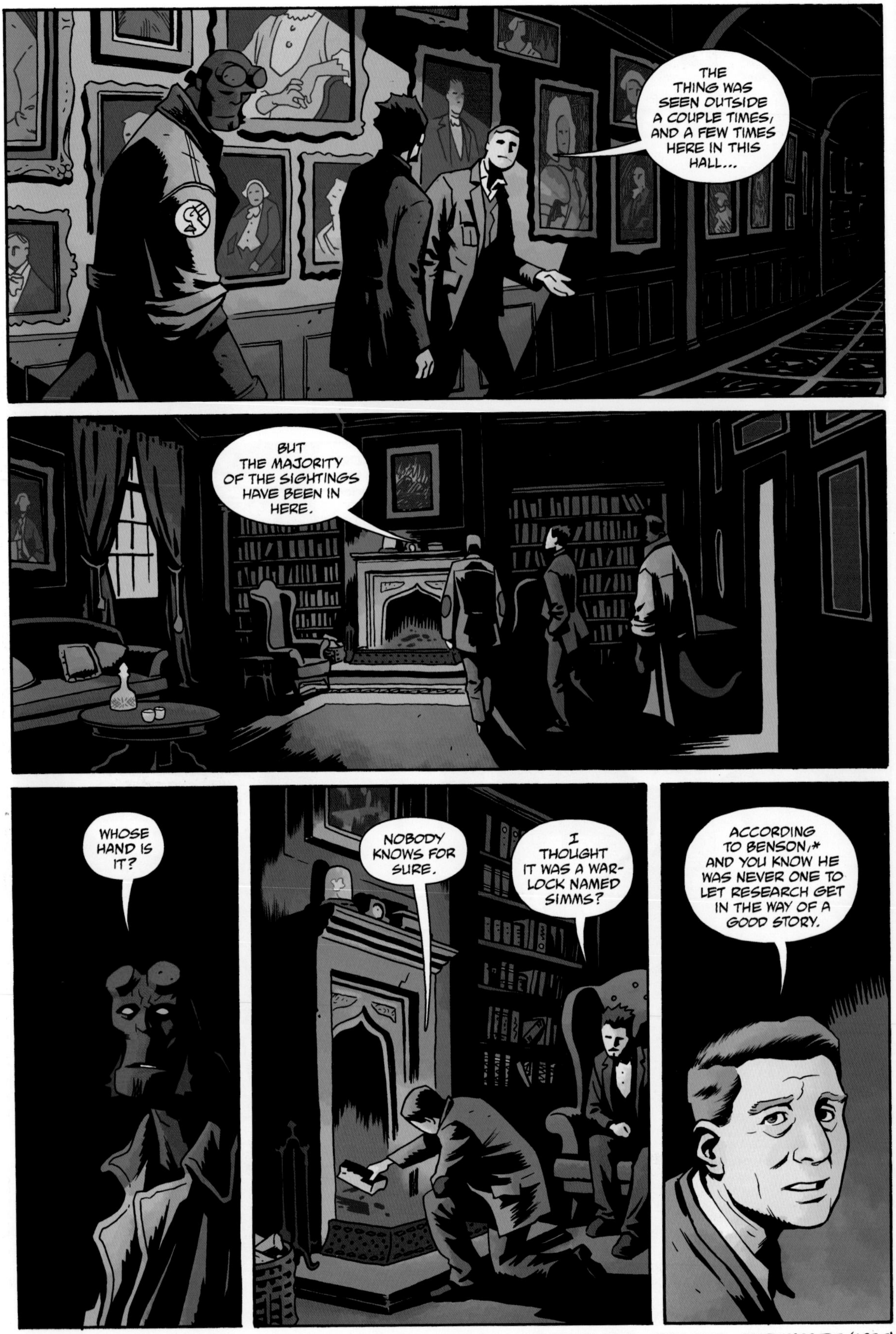
THE THING WAS SEEN OUTSIDE A COUPLE TIMES, AND A FEW TIMES HERE IN THIS HALL...
BUT THE MAJORITY OF THE SIGHTINGS HAVE BEEN IN HERE.
WHOSE HAND IS IT?
NOBODY KNOWS FOR SURE.
I THOUGHT IT WAS A WAR-LOCK NAMED SIMMS?
ACCORDING TO BENSON,* AND YOU KNOW HE WAS NEVER ONE TO LET RESEARCH GET IN THE WAY OF A GOOD STORY.

*F. T. BENSON (1882–1947), AUTHOR OF ***OUR HAUNTED HOUSES OF ENGLAND, IRELAND, AND WALES*** (1936)

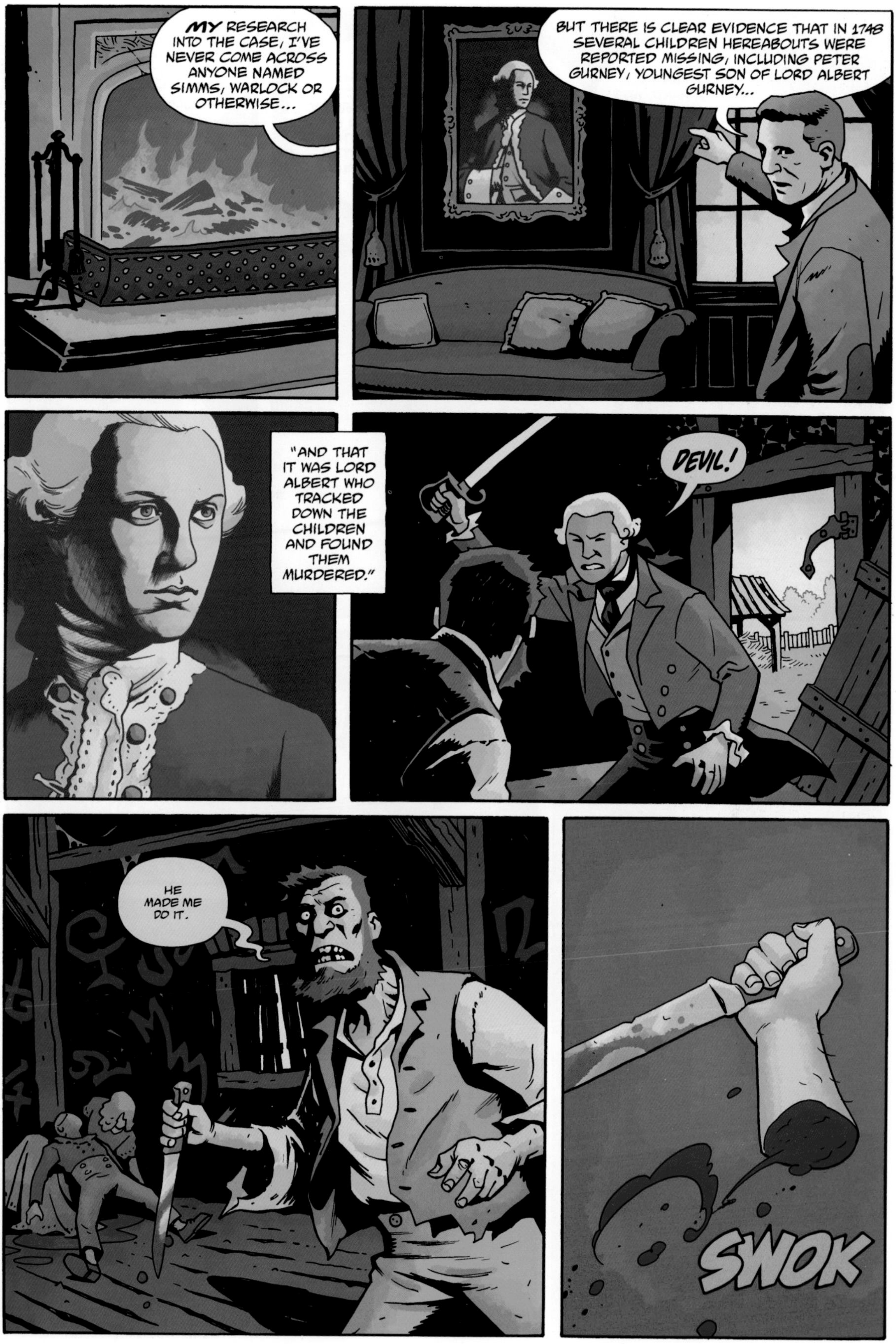
MY RESEARCH INTO THE CASE, I'VE NEVER COME ACROSS ANYONE NAMED SIMMS, WARLOCK OR OTHERWISE...
BUT THERE IS CLEAR EVIDENCE THAT IN 1748 SEVERAL CHILDREN HEREABOUTS WERE REPORTED MISSING, INCLUDING PETER GURNEY, YOUNGEST SON OF LORD ALBERT GURNEY...
"AND THAT IT WAS LORD ALBERT WHO TRACKED DOWN THE CHILDREN AND FOUND THEM MURDERED."
DEVIL!
HE MADE ME DO IT.
SWOK

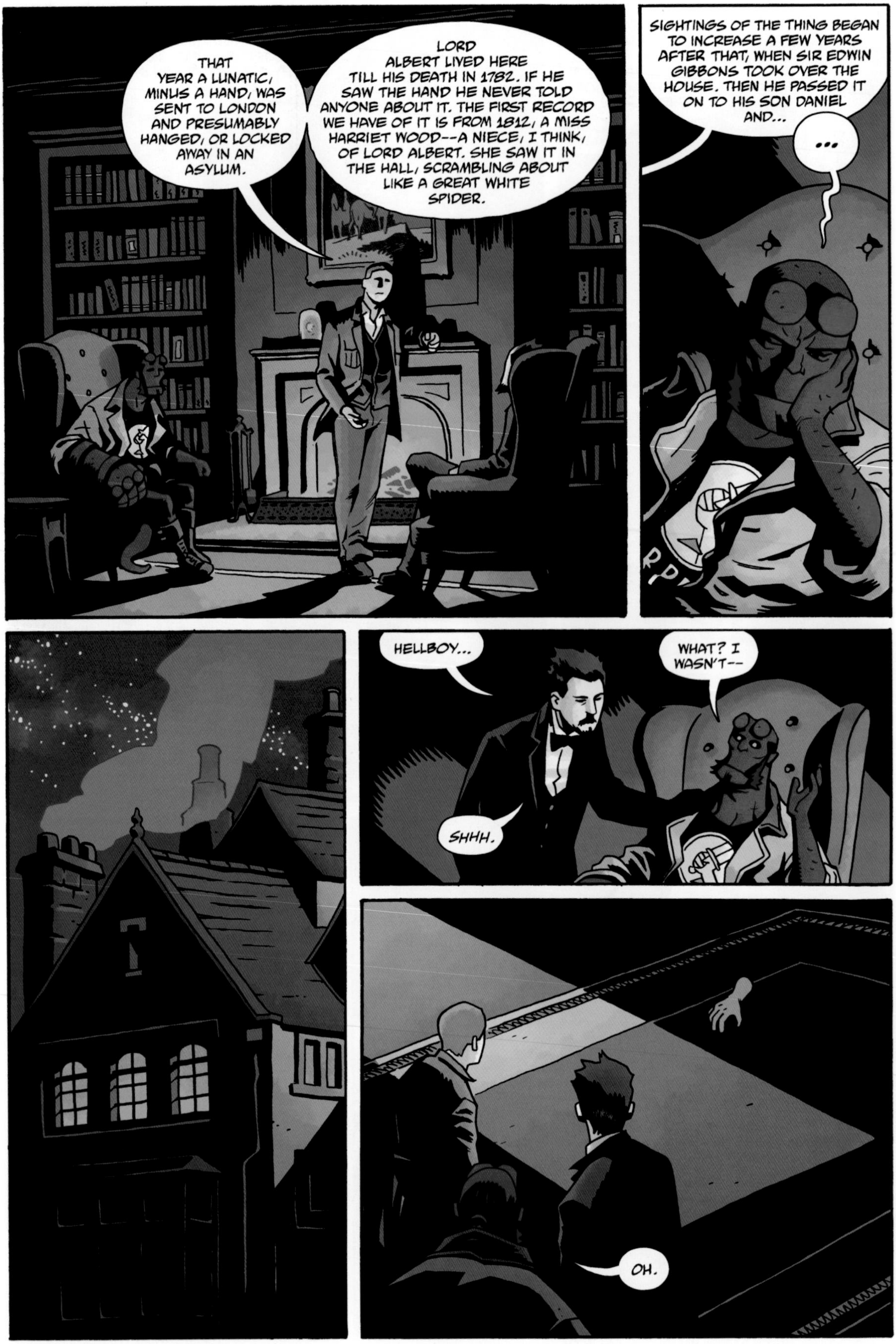
THAT YEAR A LUNATIC, MINUS A HAND, WAS SENT TO LONDON AND PRESUMABLY HANGED, OR LOCKED AWAY IN AN ASYLUM.
LORD ALBERT LIVED HERE TILL HIS DEATH IN 1782. IF HE SAW THE HAND HE NEVER TOLD ANYONE ABOUT IT. THE FIRST RECORD WE HAVE OF IT IS FROM 1812, A MISS HARRIET WOOD--A NIECE, I THINK, OF LORD ALBERT. SHE SAW IT IN THE HALL, SCRAMBLING ABOUT LIKE A GREAT WHITE SPIDER.
SIGHTINGS OF THE THING BEGAN TO INCREASE A FEW YEARS AFTER THAT, WHEN SIR EDWIN GIBBONS TOOK OVER THE HOUSE. THEN HE PASSED IT ON TO HIS SON DANIEL AND...
...
HELLBOY...
WHAT? I WASN'T--
SHHH.
OH.

CREEK

SON OF A--

WAIT! WHAT ARE YOU--?

AHH!

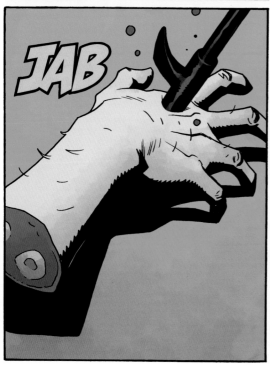

JAB

HORRIBLE THING!

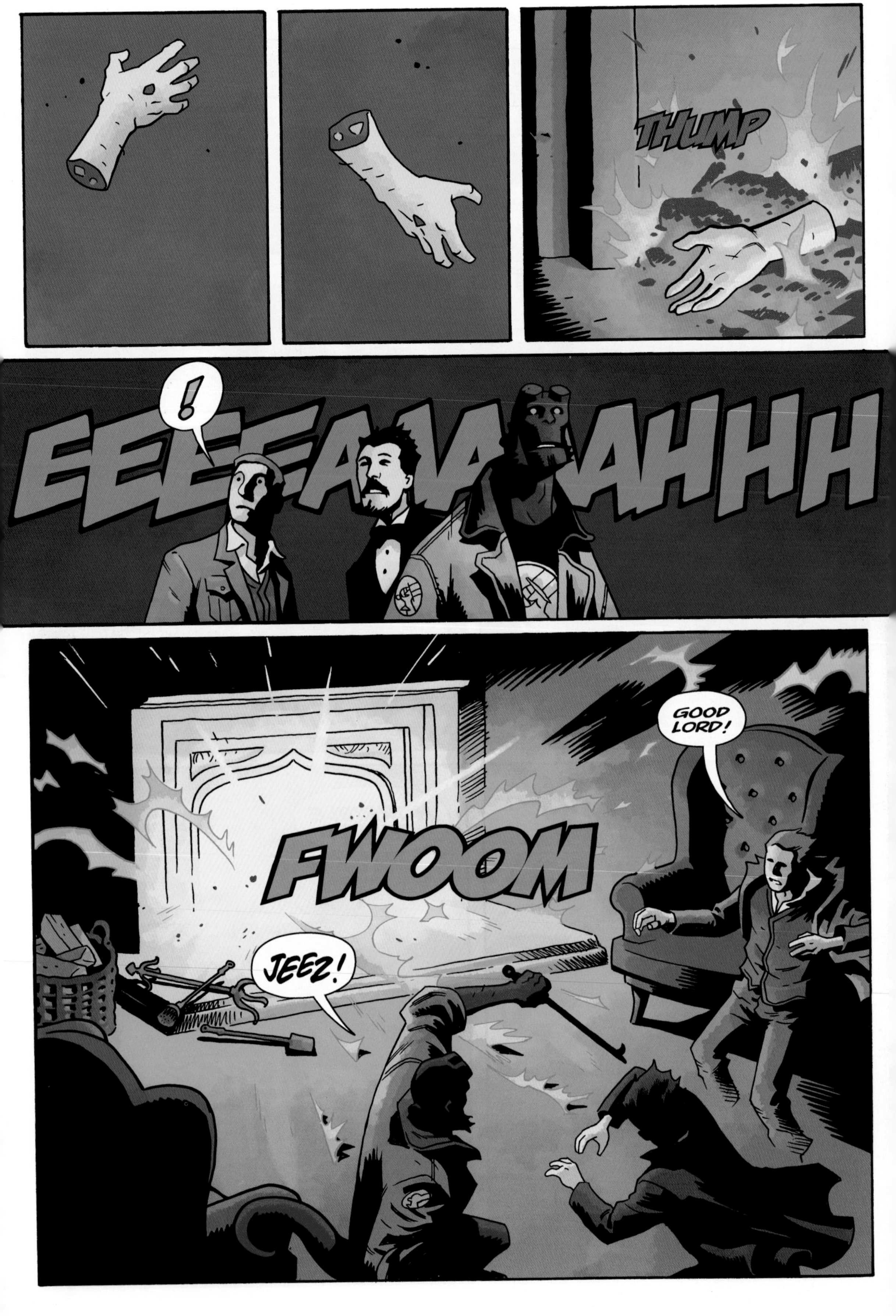
THUMP
!
EEEAAAAAHHH
GOOD LORD!
FWOOM
JEEZ!

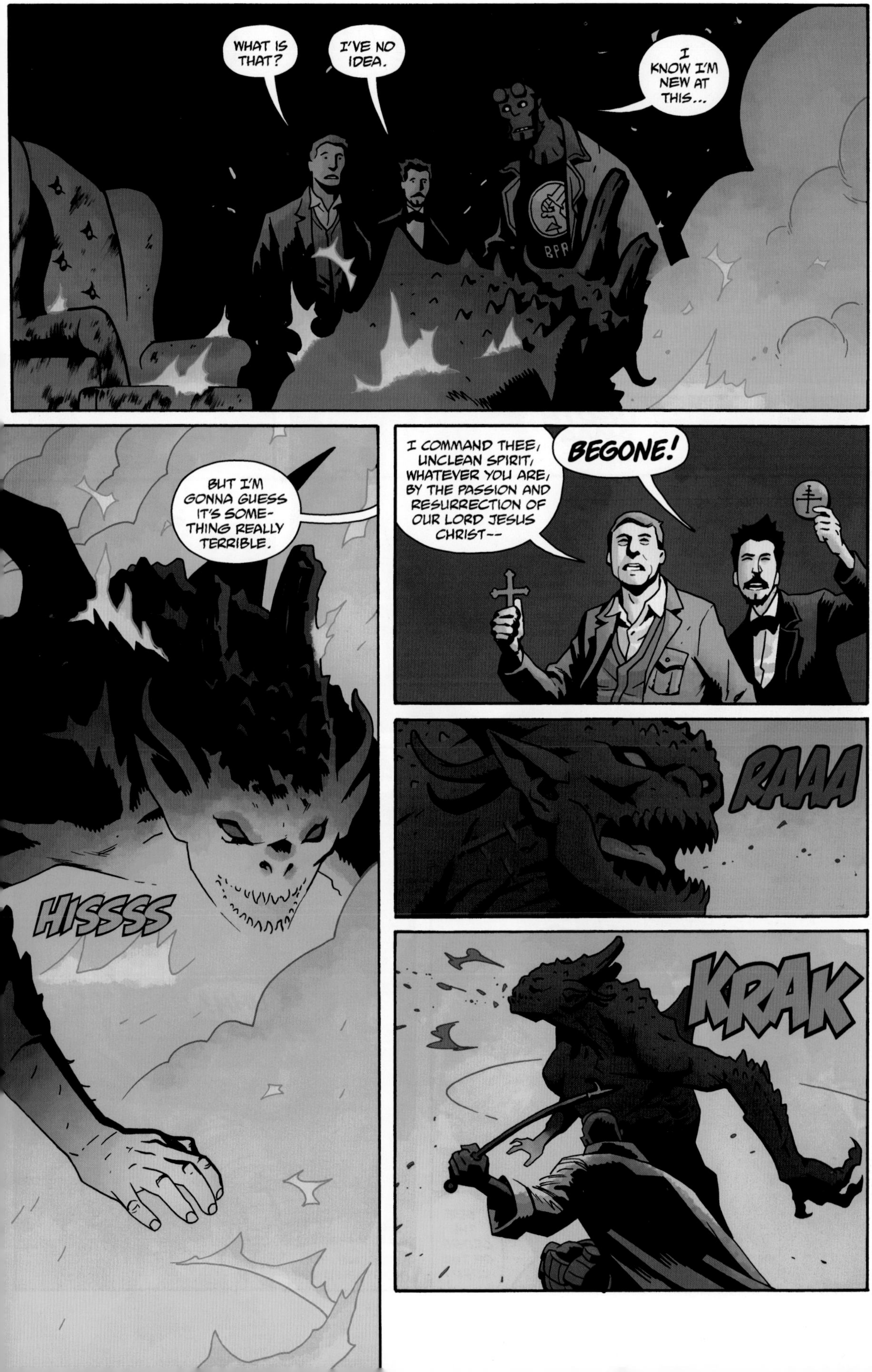
WHAT IS THAT?
I'VE NO IDEA.
I KNOW I'M NEW AT THIS...
BUT I'M GONNA GUESS IT'S SOME-THING REALLY TERRIBLE.
HISSSS
I COMMAND THEE, UNCLEAN SPIRIT, WHATEVER YOU ARE, BY THE PASSION AND RESURRECTION OF OUR LORD JESUS CHRIST--
BEGONE!
RAAA
KRAK

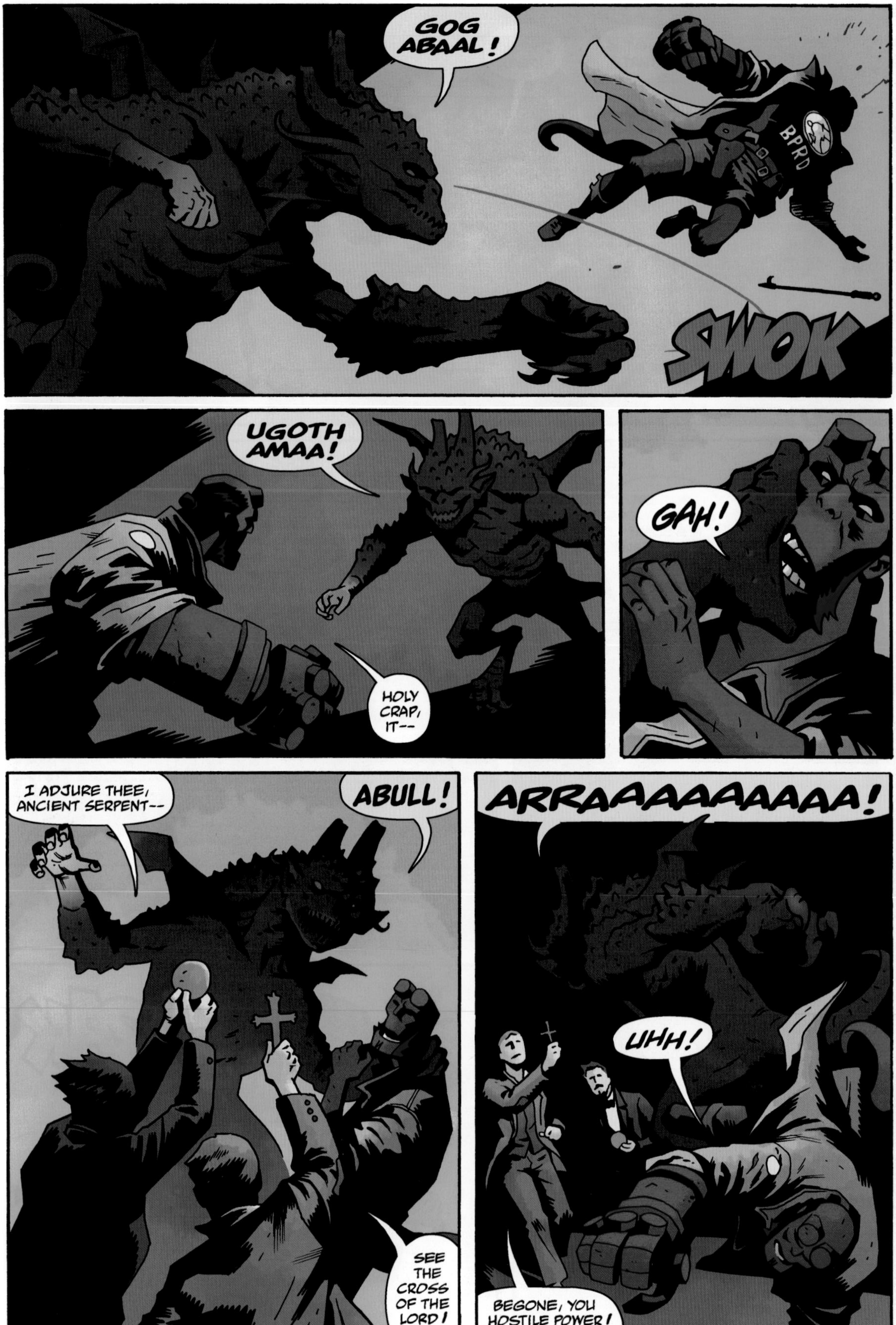
GOG ABAAL!
SWOK
UGOTH AMAA!
HOLY CRAP, IT--
GAH!
I ADJURE THEE, ANCIENT SERPENT--
ABULL!
SEE THE CROSS OF THE LORD!
ARRAAAAAAAAAA!
UHH!
BEGONE, YOU HOSTILE POWER!

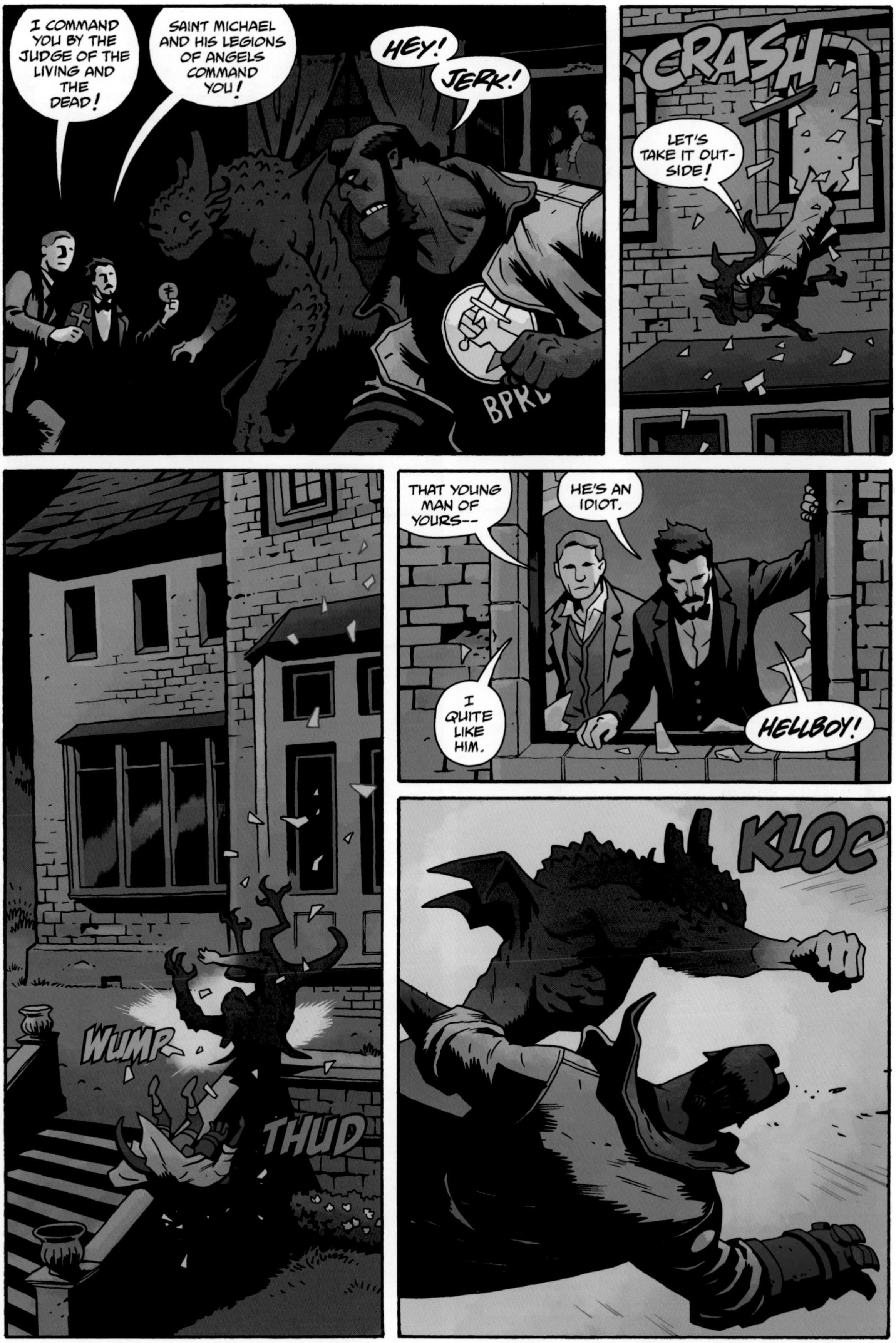

I COMMAND YOU BY THE JUDGE OF THE LIVING AND THE DEAD!
SAINT MICHAEL AND HIS LEGIONS OF ANGELS COMMAND YOU!
HEY!
JERK!
BPRD
CRASH
LET'S TAKE IT OUT-SIDE!
THAT YOUNG MAN OF YOURS--
HE'S AN IDIOT.
I QUITE LIKE HIM.
HELLBOY!
WUMP
THUD
KLOC

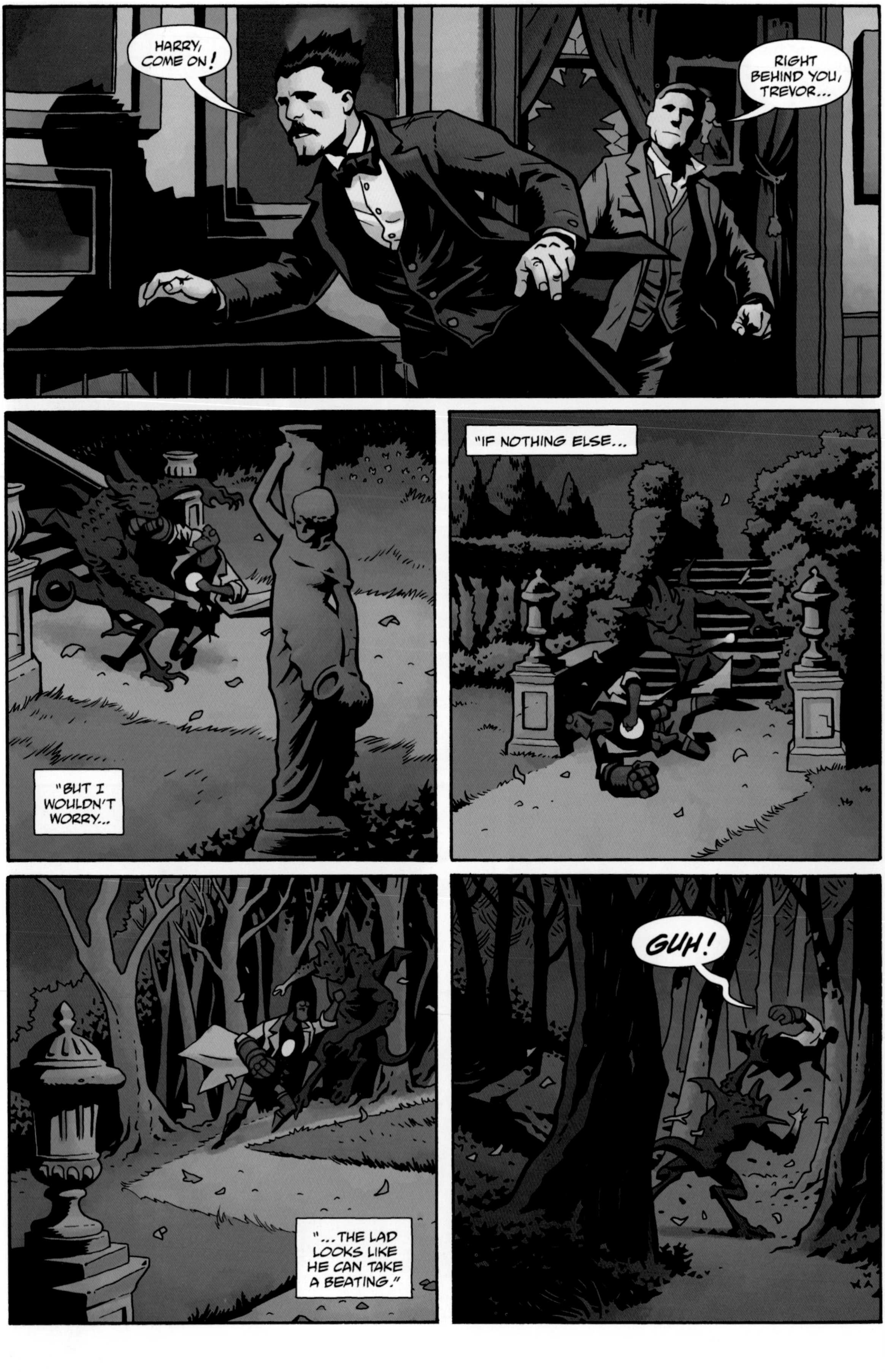
HARRY, COME ON!
RIGHT BEHIND YOU, TREVOR...
"BUT I WOULDN'T WORRY...
"IF NOTHING ELSE...
"...THE LAD LOOKS LIKE HE CAN TAKE A BEATING."
GUH!

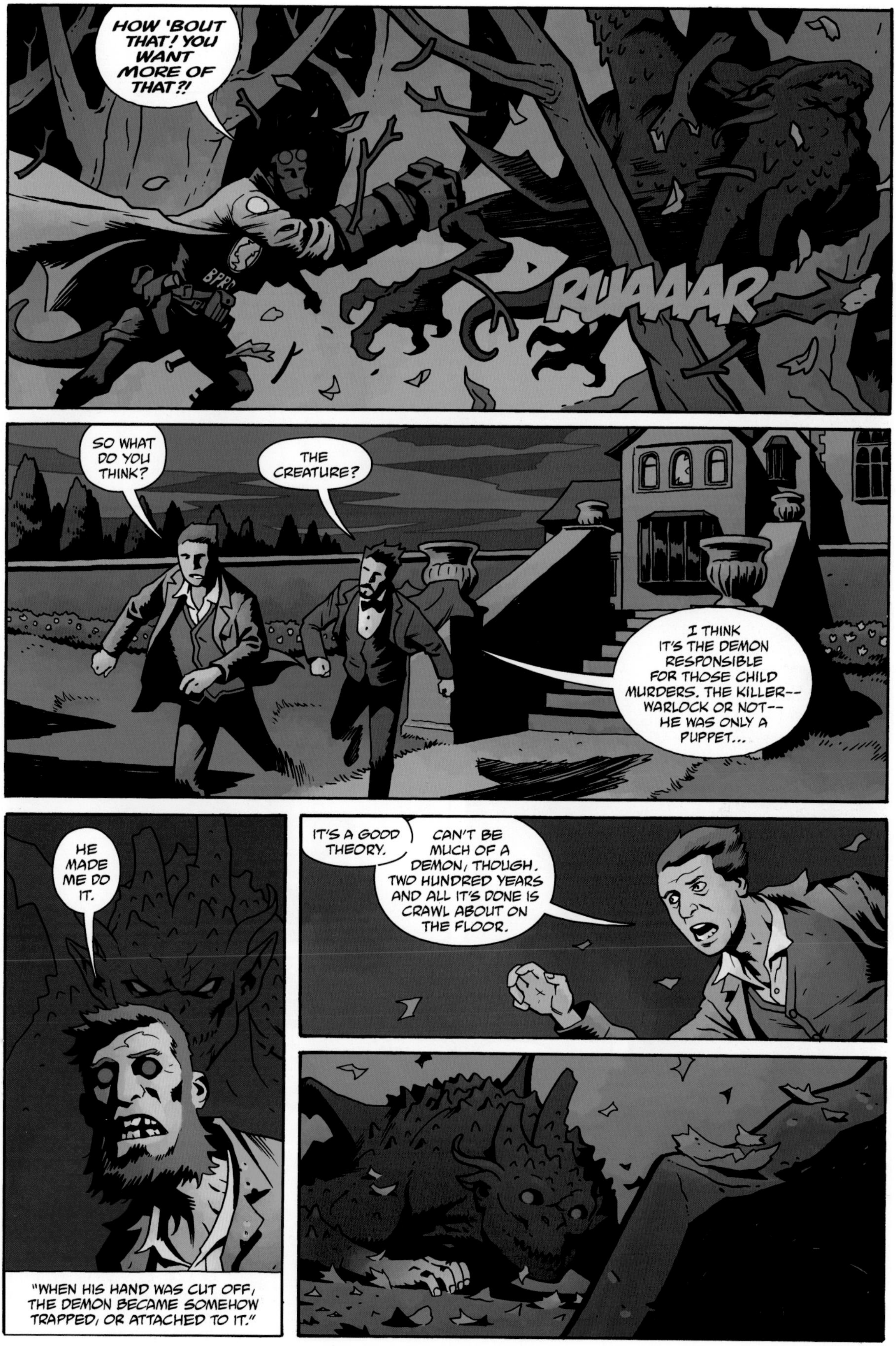
HOW 'BOUT THAT! YOU WANT MORE OF THAT?!
RUAAAR
SO WHAT DO YOU THINK?
THE CREATURE?
I THINK IT'S THE DEMON RESPONSIBLE FOR THOSE CHILD MURDERS. THE KILLER-- WARLOCK OR NOT-- HE WAS ONLY A PUPPET...
HE MADE ME DO IT.
"WHEN HIS HAND WAS CUT OFF, THE DEMON BECAME SOMEHOW TRAPPED, OR ATTACHED TO IT."
IT'S A GOOD THEORY.
CAN'T BE MUCH OF A DEMON, THOUGH. TWO HUNDRED YEARS AND ALL IT'S DONE IS CRAWL ABOUT ON THE FLOOR.

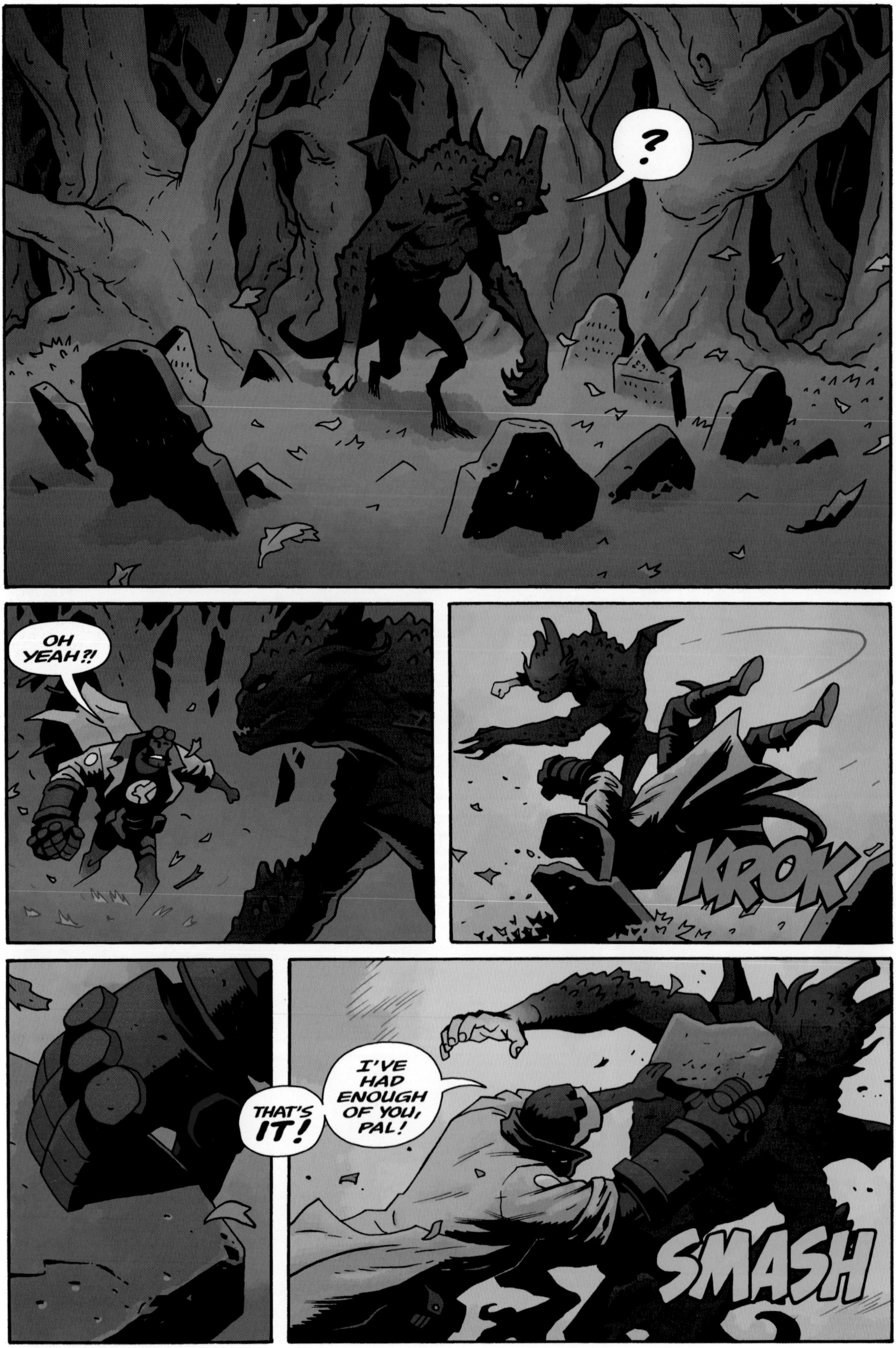
?
OH YEAH?!
KROK
THAT'S IT!
I'VE HAD ENOUGH OF YOU, PAL!
SMASH

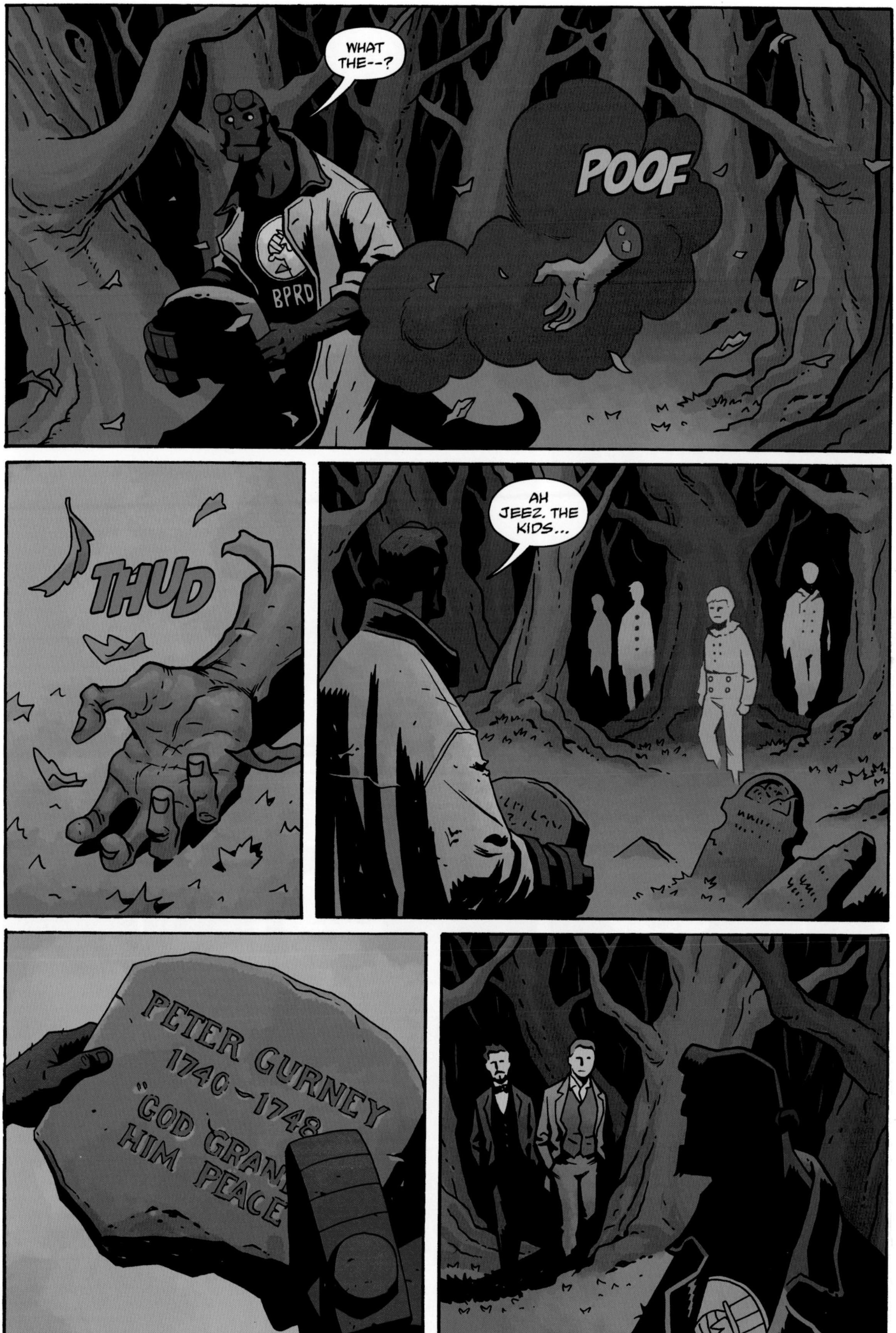
WHAT THE--?
POOF
THUD
AH JEEZ. THE KIDS...
PETER GURNEY 1740-1748 "GOD GRAN HIM PEACE

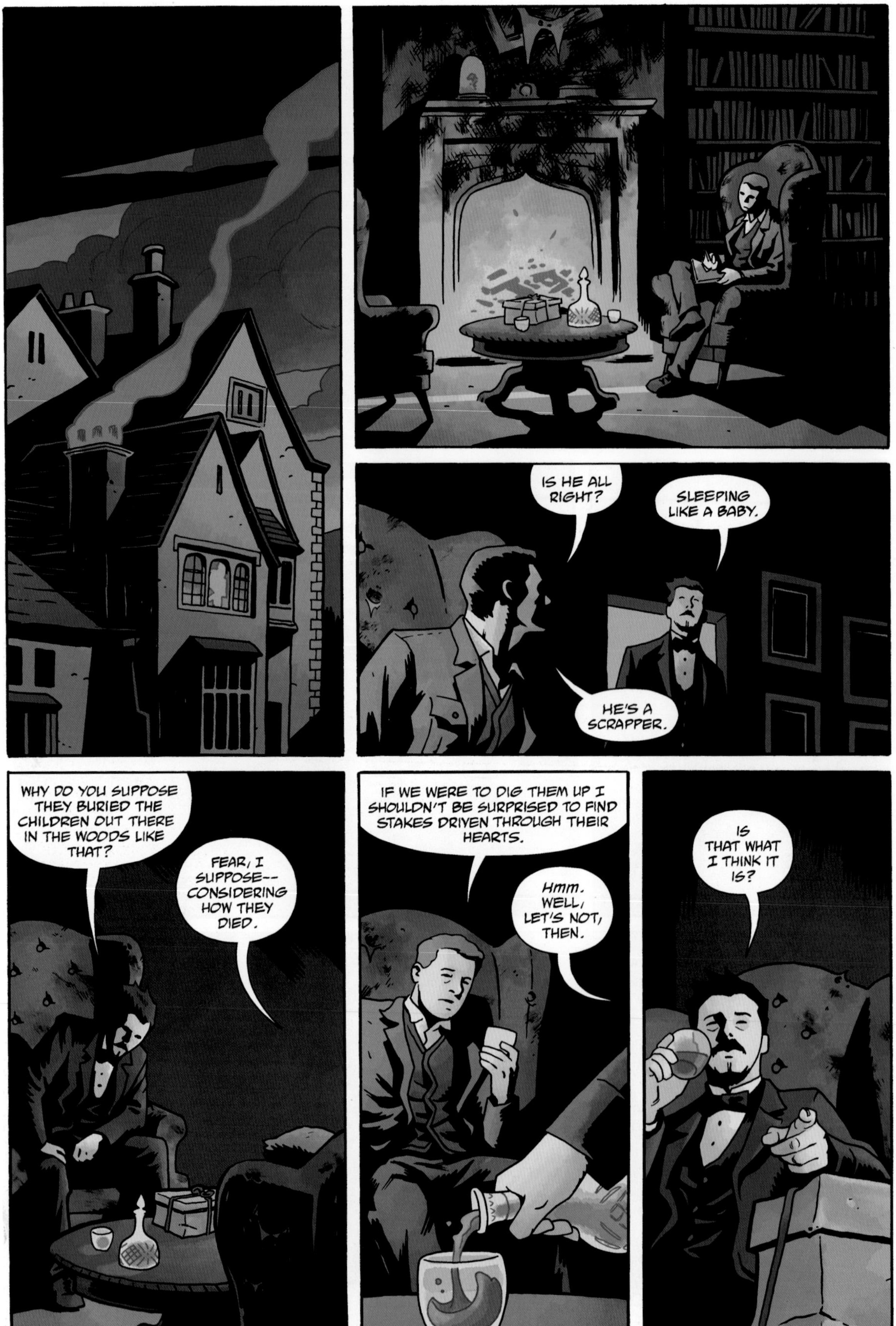
IS HE ALL RIGHT?
SLEEPING LIKE A BABY.
HE'S A SCRAPPER.
WHY DO YOU SUPPOSE THEY BURIED THE CHILDREN OUT THERE IN THE WOODS LIKE THAT?
FEAR, I SUPPOSE-- CONSIDERING HOW THEY DIED.
IF WE WERE TO DIG THEM UP I SHOULDN'T BE SURPRISED TO FIND STAKES DRIVEN THROUGH THEIR HEARTS.
Hmm. WELL, LET'S NOT, THEN.
IS THAT WHAT I THINK IT IS?

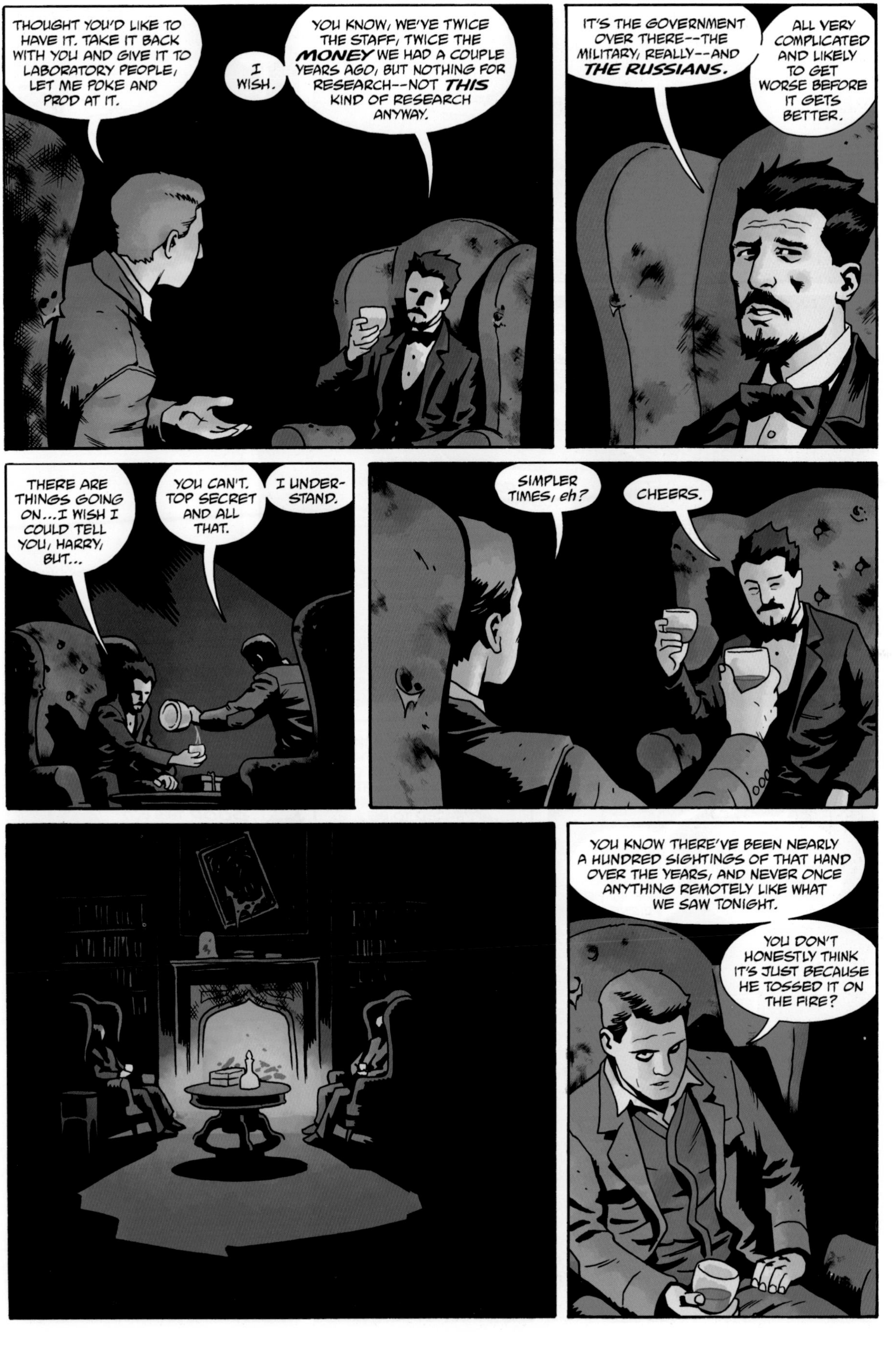
THOUGHT YOU'D LIKE TO HAVE IT. TAKE IT BACK WITH YOU AND GIVE IT TO LABORATORY PEOPLE, LET ME POKE AND PROD AT IT.
I WISH.
YOU KNOW, WE'VE TWICE THE STAFF, TWICE THE MONEY WE HAD A COUPLE YEARS AGO, BUT NOTHING FOR RESEARCH--NOT THIS KIND OF RESEARCH ANYWAY.
IT'S THE GOVERNMENT OVER THERE--THE MILITARY, REALLY--AND THE RUSSIANS.
ALL VERY COMPLICATED AND LIKELY TO GET WORSE BEFORE IT GETS BETTER.
THERE ARE THINGS GOING ON...I WISH I COULD TELL YOU, HARRY, BUT...
YOU CAN'T. TOP SECRET AND ALL THAT.
I UNDERSTAND.
SIMPLER TIMES, eh?
CHEERS.
YOU KNOW THERE'VE BEEN NEARLY A HUNDRED SIGHTINGS OF THAT HAND OVER THE YEARS, AND NEVER ONCE ANYTHING REMOTELY LIKE WHAT WE SAW TONIGHT.
YOU DON'T HONESTLY THINK IT'S JUST BECAUSE HE TOSSED IT ON THE FIRE?

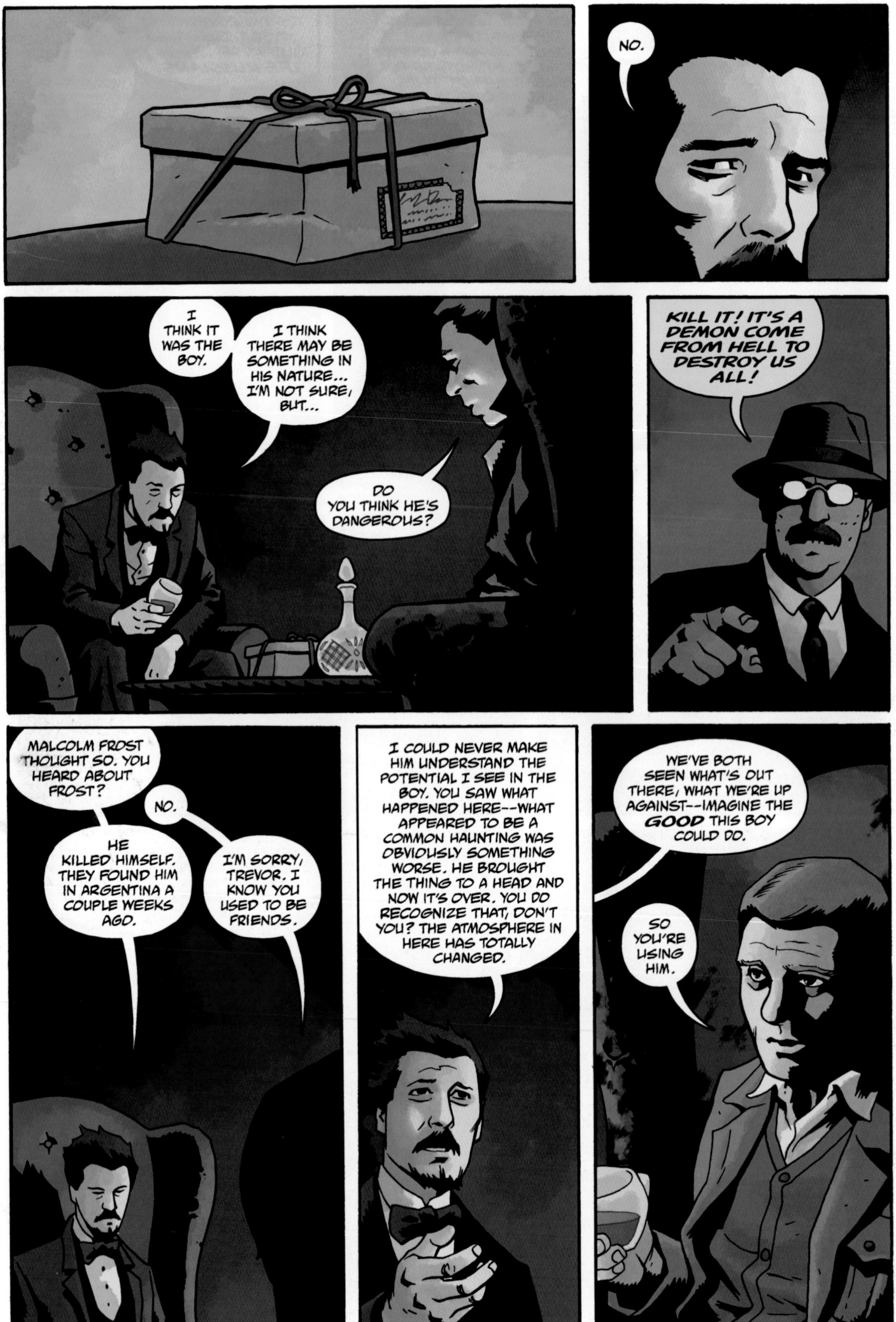
NO.
I THINK IT WAS THE BOY.
I THINK THERE MAY BE SOMETHING IN HIS NATURE... I'M NOT SURE, BUT...
DO YOU THINK HE'S DANGEROUS?
KILL IT! IT'S A DEMON COME FROM HELL TO DESTROY US ALL!
MALCOLM FROST THOUGHT SO. YOU HEARD ABOUT FROST?
NO.
HE KILLED HIMSELF. THEY FOUND HIM IN ARGENTINA A COUPLE WEEKS AGO.
I'M SORRY, TREVOR. I KNOW YOU USED TO BE FRIENDS.
I COULD NEVER MAKE HIM UNDERSTAND THE POTENTIAL I SEE IN THE BOY. YOU SAW WHAT HAPPENED HERE--WHAT APPEARED TO BE A COMMON HAUNTING WAS OBVIOUSLY SOMETHING WORSE. HE BROUGHT THE THING TO A HEAD AND NOW IT'S OVER. YOU DO RECOGNIZE THAT, DON'T YOU? THE ATMOSPHERE IN HERE HAS TOTALLY CHANGED.
WE'VE BOTH SEEN WHAT'S OUT THERE, WHAT WE'RE UP AGAINST--IMAGINE THE GOOD THIS BOY COULD DO.
SO YOU'RE USING HIM.

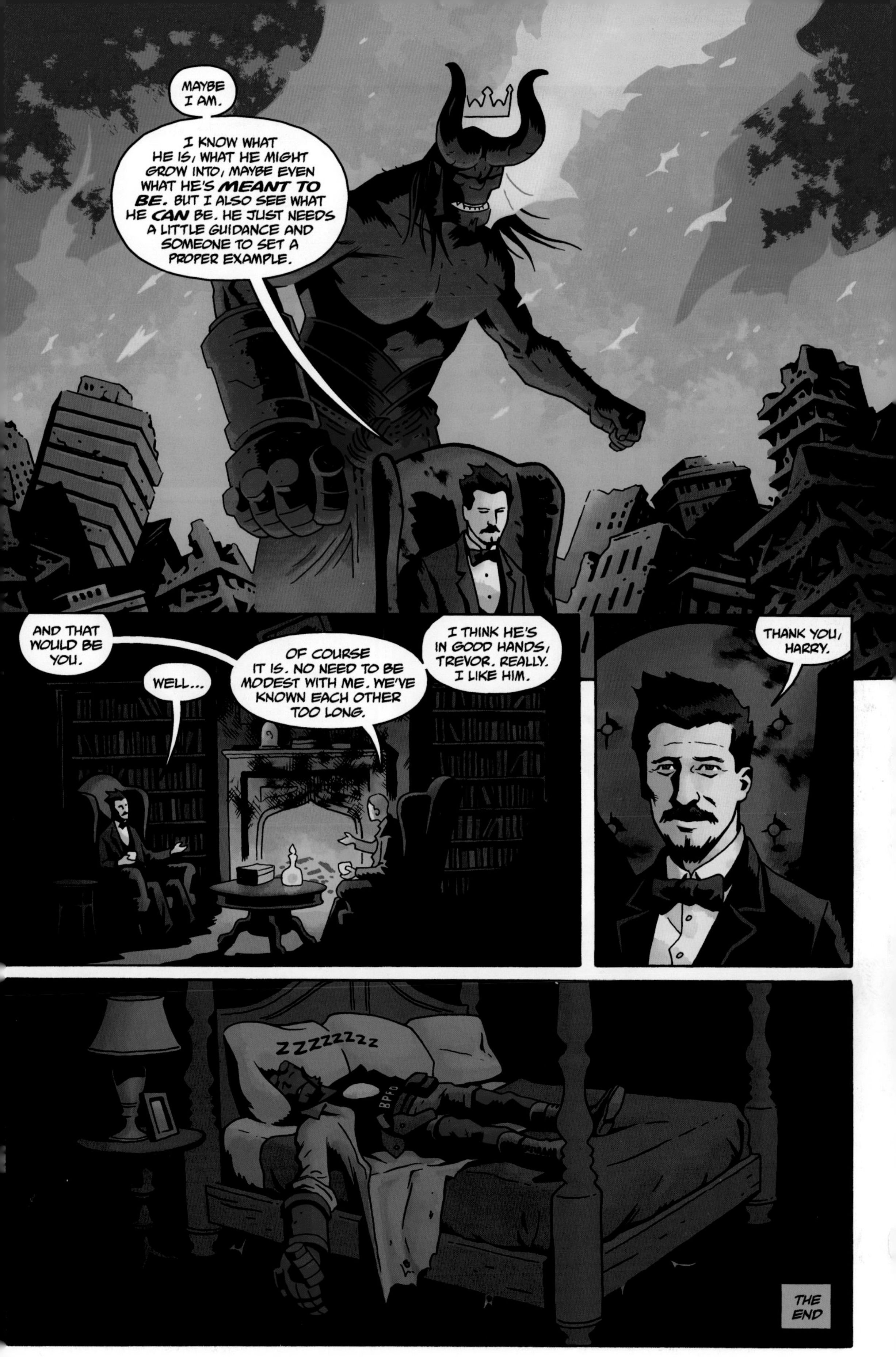
MAYBE I AM.
I KNOW WHAT HE IS, WHAT HE MIGHT GROW INTO, MAYBE EVEN WHAT HE'S MEANT TO BE. BUT I ALSO SEE WHAT HE CAN BE. HE JUST NEEDS A LITTLE GUIDANCE AND SOMEONE TO SET A PROPER EXAMPLE.
AND THAT WOULD BE YOU.
WELL...
OF COURSE IT IS. NO NEED TO BE MODEST WITH ME. WE'VE KNOWN EACH OTHER TOO LONG.
I THINK HE'S IN GOOD HANDS, TREVOR. REALLY. I LIKE HIM.
THANK YOU, HARRY.
ZZZZZZZzz
BPRD
THE END

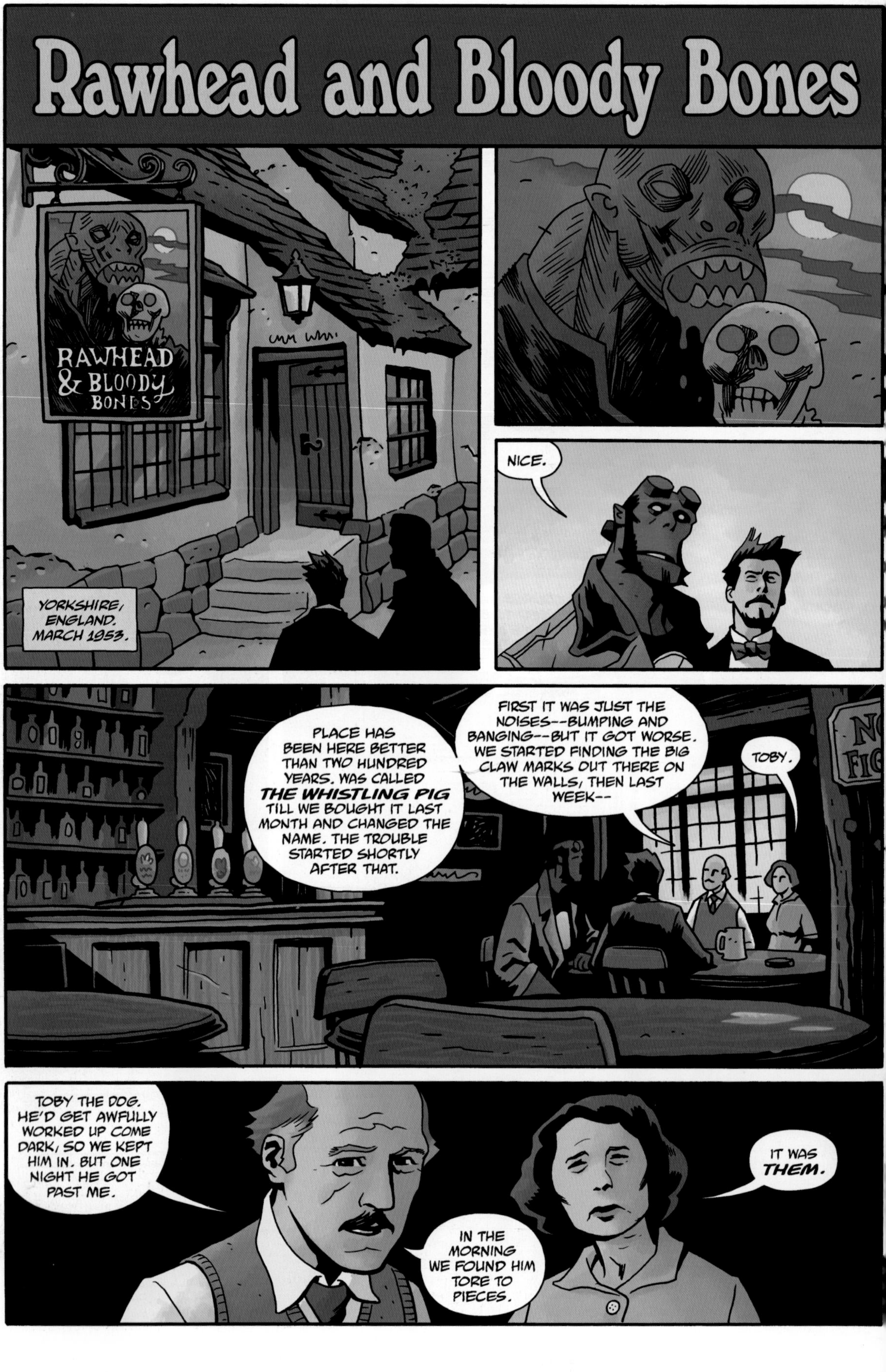

Rawhead and Bloody Boples
RAWHEAD & BLOODY BONES
YORKSHIRE, ENGLAND. MARCH 1953.
NICE.
PLACE HAS BEEN HERE BETTER THAN TWO HUNDRED YEARS. WAS CALLED THE WHISTLING PIG TILL WE BOUGHT IT LAST MONTH AND CHANGED THE NAME. THE TROUBLE STARTED SHORTLY AFTER THAT.
FIRST IT WAS JUST THE NOISES--BUMPING AND BANGING--BUT IT GOT WORSE. WE STARTED FINDING THE BIG CLAW MARKS OUT THERE ON THE WALLS, THEN LAST WEEK--
TOBY.
TOBY THE DOG. HE'D GET AWFULLY WORKED UP COME DARK, SO WE KEPT HIM IN. BUT ONE NIGHT HE GOT PAST ME.
IN THE MORNING WE FOUND HIM TORE TO PIECES.
IT WAS THEM.

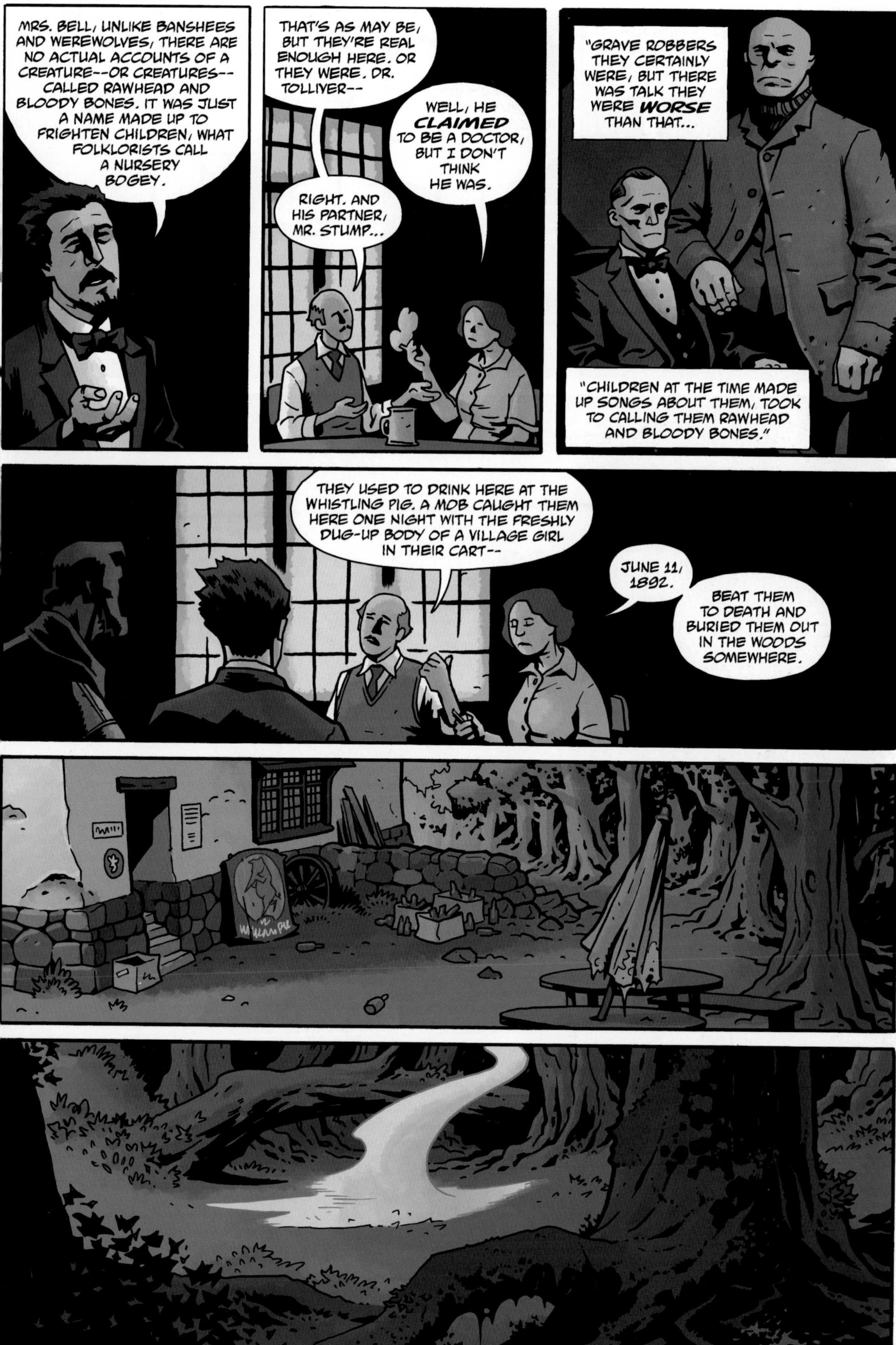
MRS. BELL, UNLIKE BANSHEES AND WEREWOLVES, THERE ARE NO ACTUAL ACCOUNTS OF A CREATURE--OR CREATURES--CALLED RAWHEAD AND BLOODY BONES. IT WAS JUST A NAME MADE UP TO FRIGHTEN CHILDREN, WHAT FOLKLORISTS CALL A NURSERY BOGEY.
THAT'S AS MAY BE, BUT THEY'RE REAL ENOUGH HERE. OR THEY WERE. DR. TOLLIVER--
WELL, HE CLAIMED TO BE A DOCTOR, BUT I DON'T THINK HE WAS.
RIGHT. AND HIS PARTNER, MR. STUMP...
"GRAVE ROBBERS THEY CERTAINLY WERE, BUT THERE WAS TALK THEY WERE WORSE THAN THAT...
"CHILDREN AT THE TIME MADE UP SONGS ABOUT THEM, TOOK TO CALLING THEM RAWHEAD AND BLOODY BONES."
THEY USED TO DRINK HERE AT THE WHISTLING PIG. A MOB CAUGHT THEM HERE ONE NIGHT WITH THE FRESHLY DUG-UP BODY OF A VILLAGE GIRL IN THEIR CART--
JUNE 11, 1892.
BEAT THEM TO DEATH AND BURIED THEM OUT IN THE WOODS SOMEWHERE.

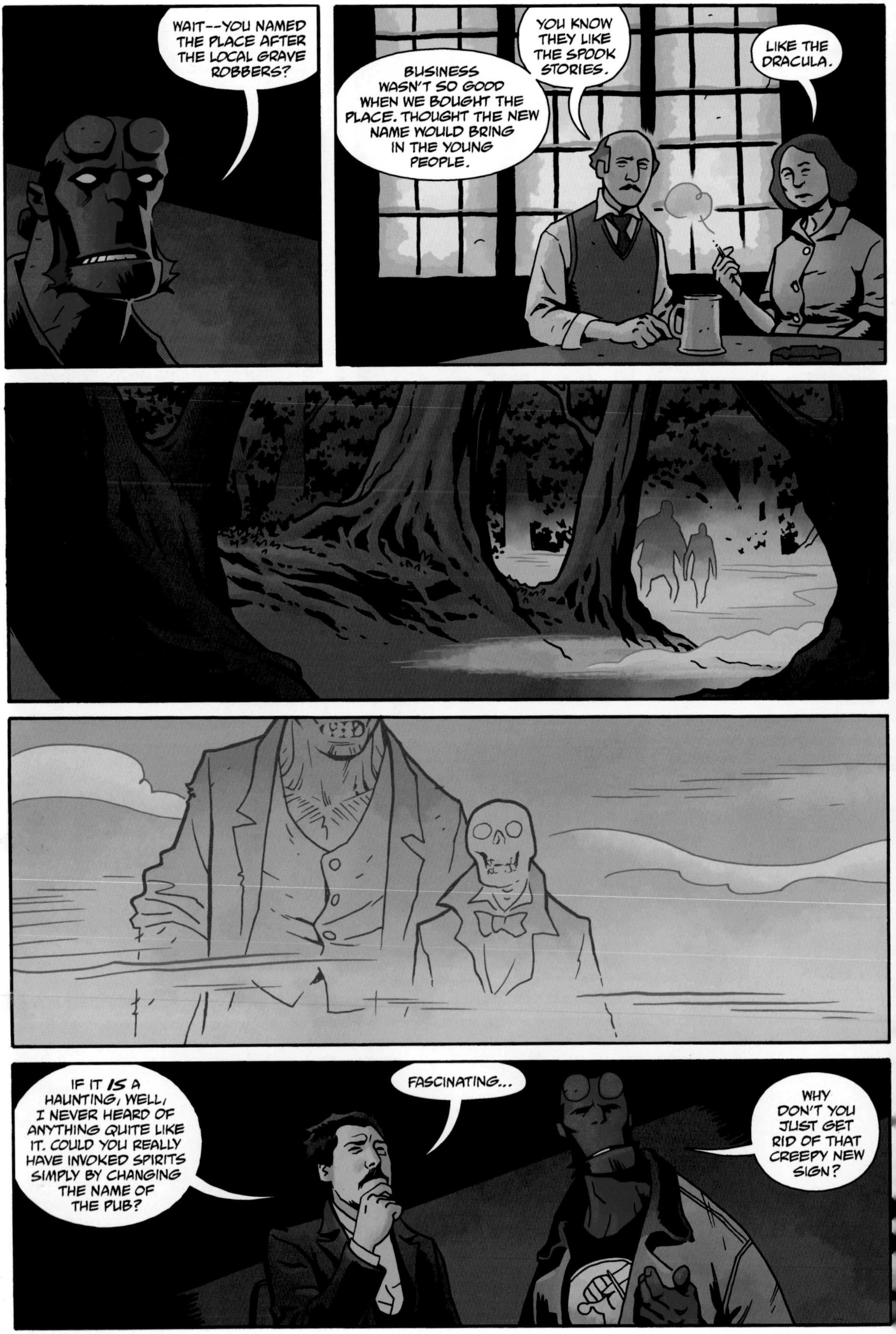
WAIT--YOU NAMED THE PLACE AFTER THE LOCAL GRAVE ROBBERS?
BUSINESS WASN'T SO GOOD WHEN WE BOUGHT THE PLACE. THOUGHT THE NEW NAME WOULD BRING IN THE YOUNG PEOPLE.
YOU KNOW THEY LIKE THE SPOOK STORIES.
LIKE THE DRACULA.
IF IT *IS* A HAUNTING, WELL, I NEVER HEARD OF ANYTHING QUITE LIKE IT. COULD YOU REALLY HAVE INVOKED SPIRITS SIMPLY BY CHANGING THE NAME OF THE PUB?
FASCINATING...
WHY DON'T YOU JUST GET RID OF THAT CREEPY NEW SIGN?

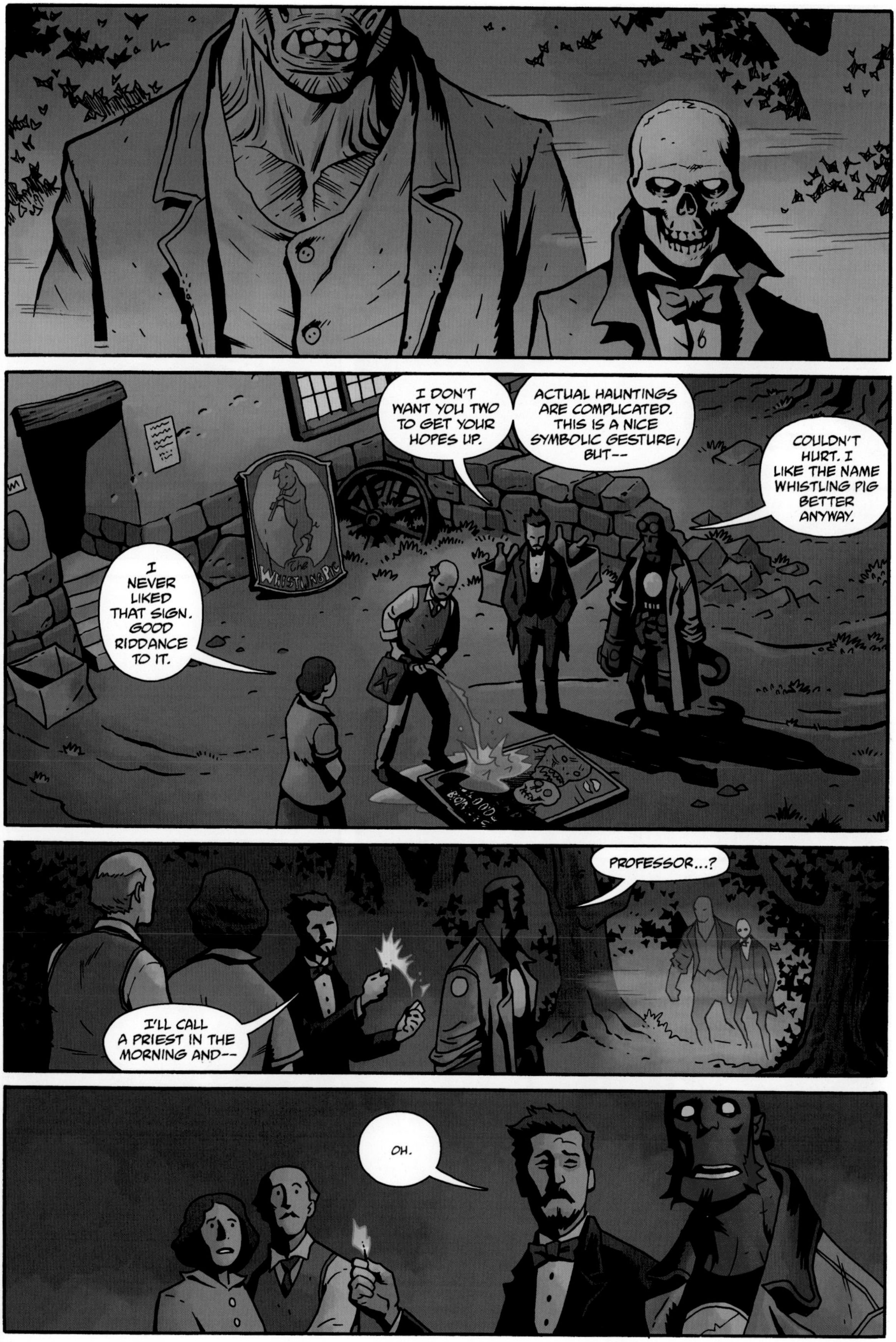
I DON'T WANT YOU TWO TO GET YOUR HOPES UP.
ACTUAL HAUNTINGS ARE COMPLICATED. THIS IS A NICE SYMBOLIC GESTURE, BUT--
COULDN'T HURT. I LIKE THE NAME WHISTLING PIG BETTER ANYWAY.
I NEVER LIKED THAT SIGN. GOOD RIDDANCE TO IT.
The WHISTLING PIG
PROFESSOR...?
I'LL CALL A PRIEST IN THE MORNING AND--
OH.

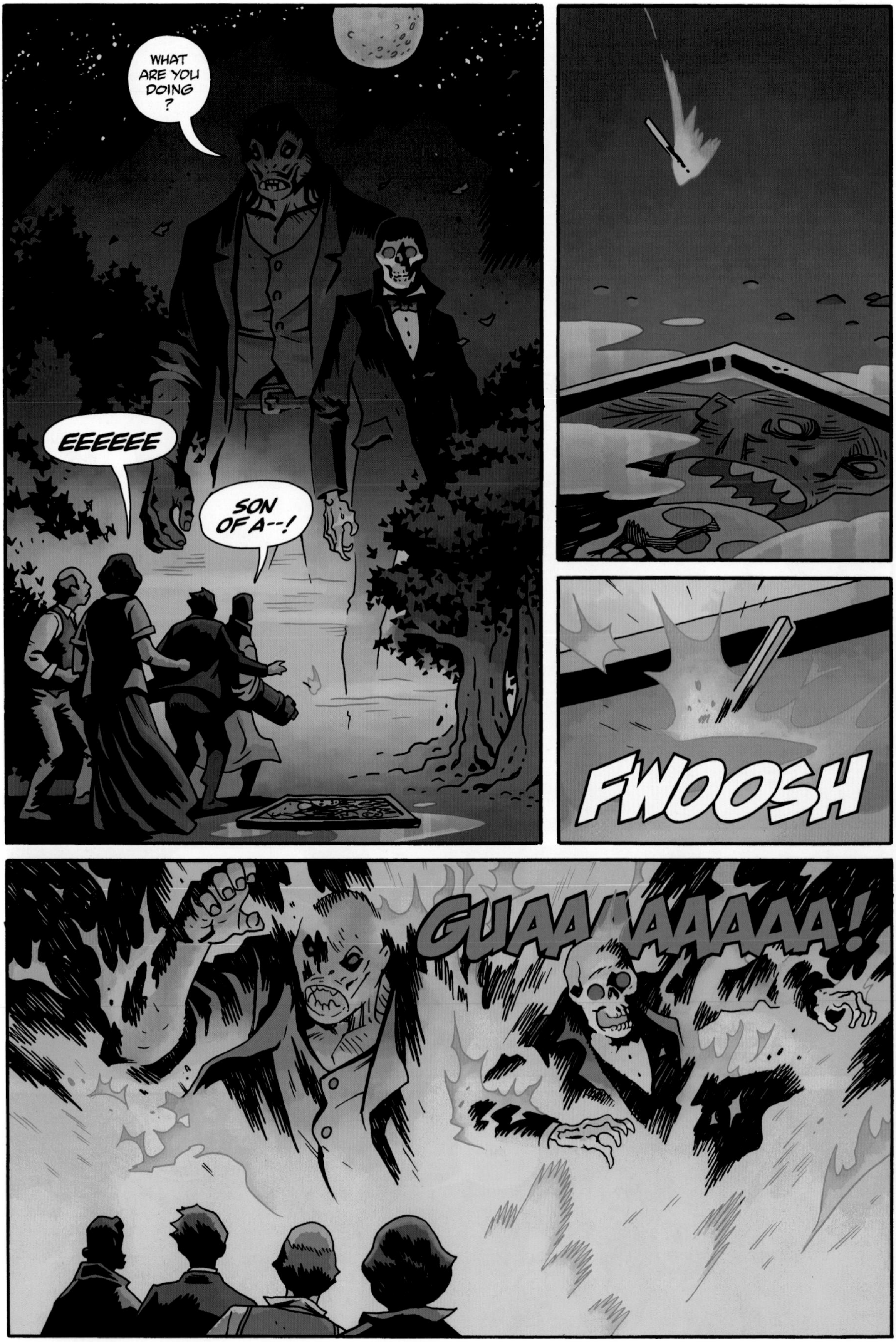
WHAT ARE YOU DOING ?
EEEEEE
SON OF A--!
FWOOSH
GUAAAAAAAAA!

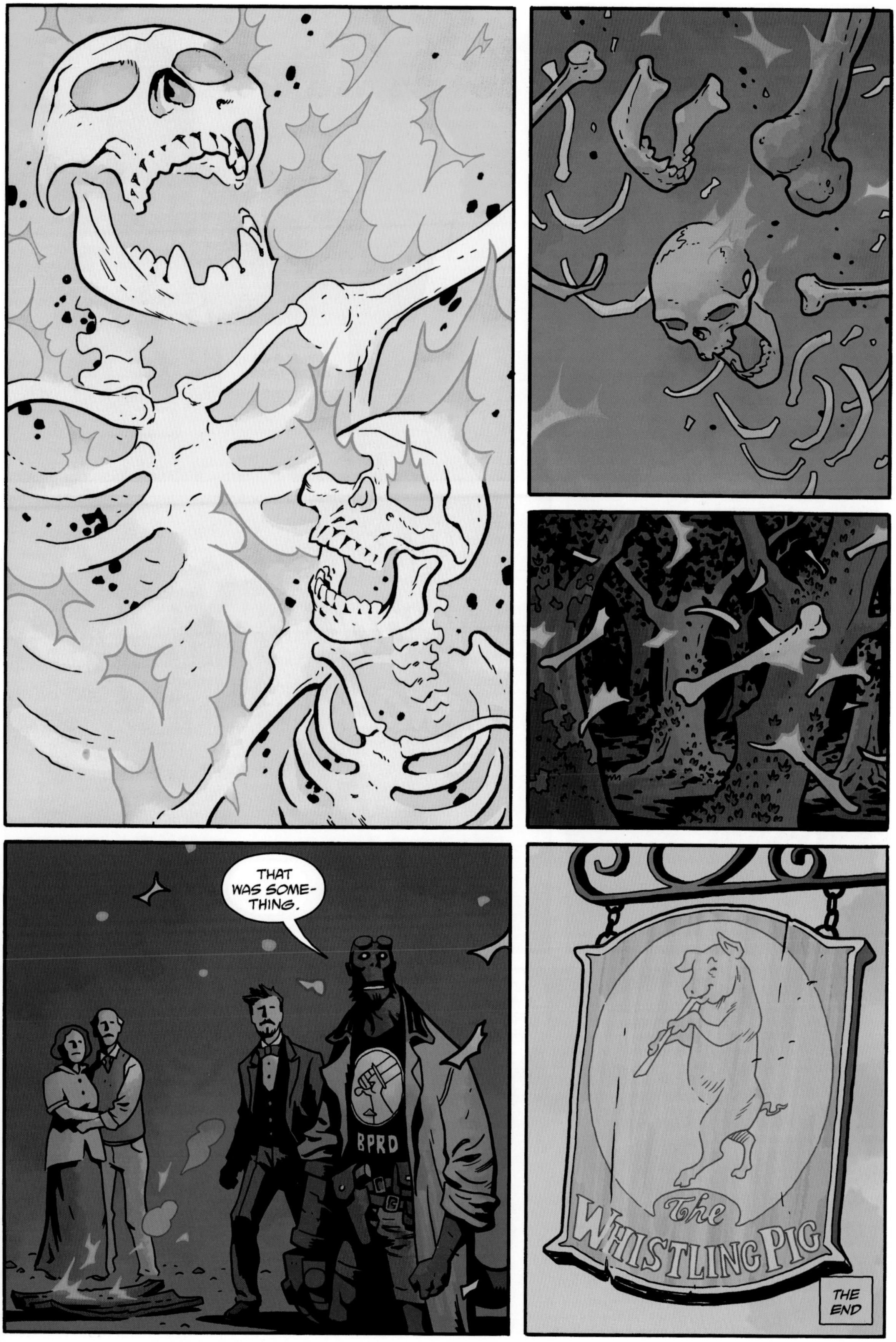
THAT WAS SOME-THING.
BPRD
The WHISTLING PIG
THE END

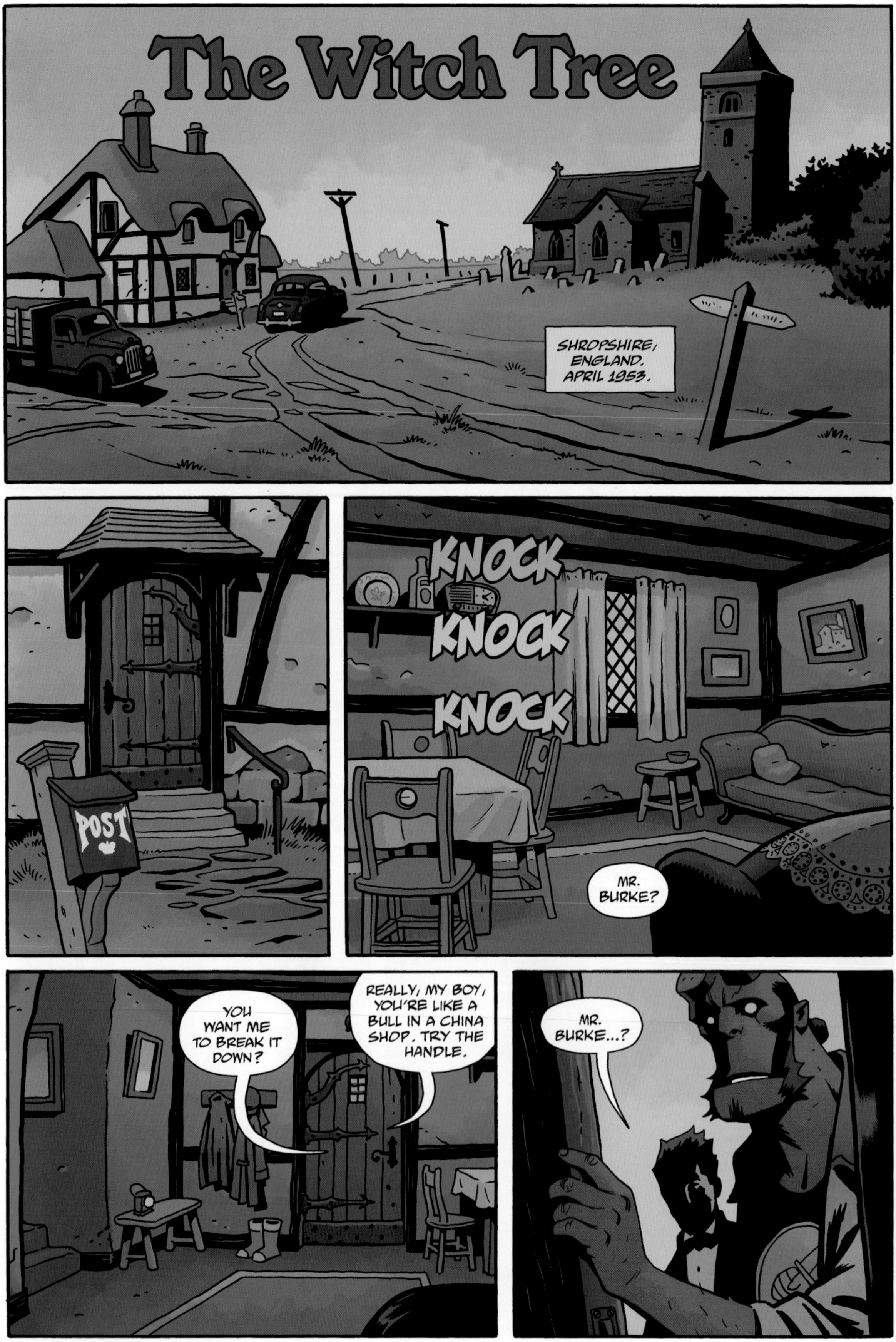
The Witch Tree
SHROPSHIRE, ENGLAND. APRIL 1953.
KNOCK
KNOCK
KNOCK
MR. BURKE?
YOU WANT ME TO BREAK IT DOWN?
REALLY, MY BOY, YOU'RE LIKE A BULL IN A CHINA SHOP. TRY THE HANDLE.
MR. BURKE...?

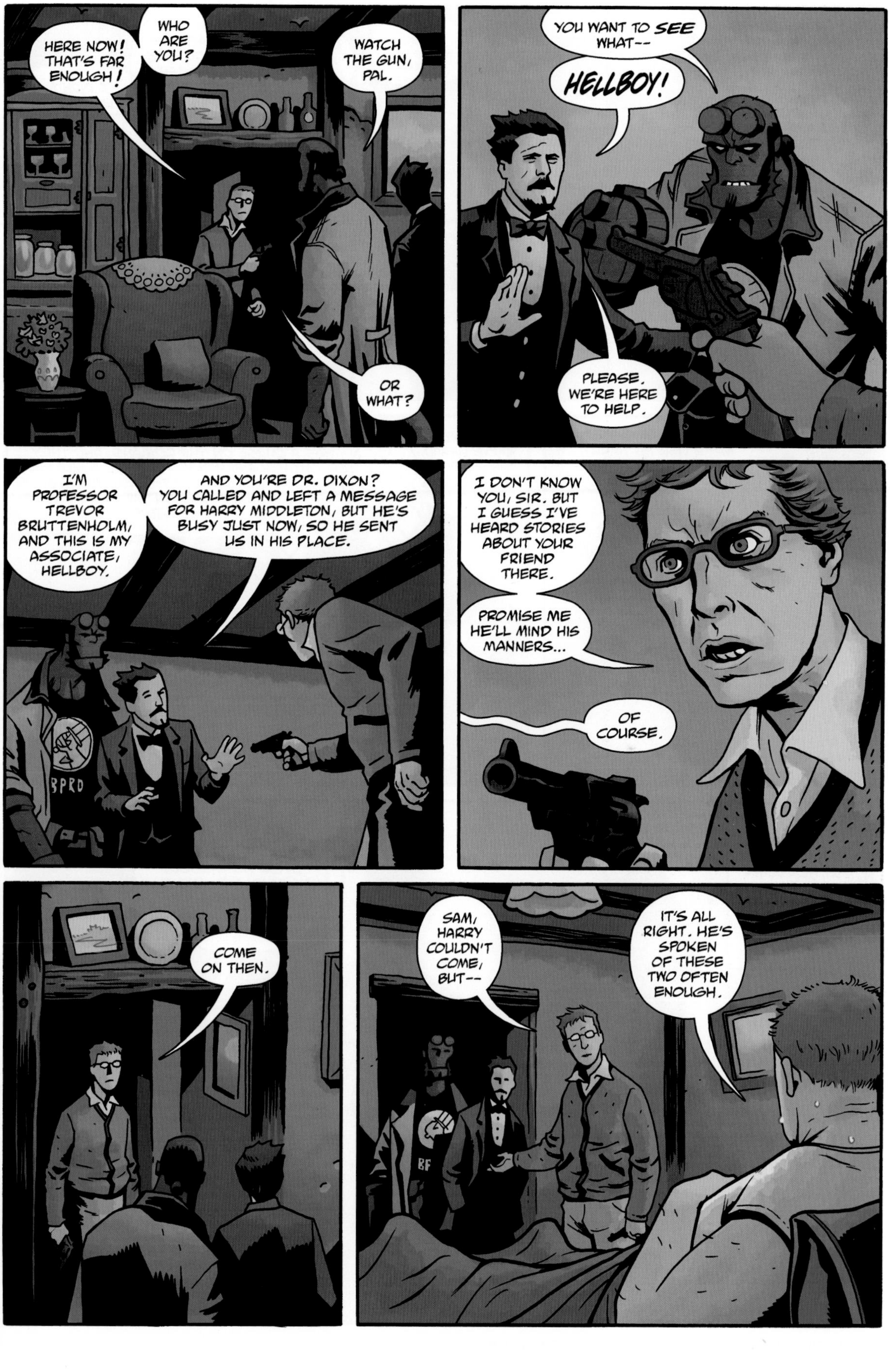
HERE NOW! THAT'S FAR ENOUGH!
WHO ARE YOU?
WATCH THE GUN, PAL.
OR WHAT?
YOU WANT TO SEE WHAT--
HELLBOY!
PLEASE. WE'RE HERE TO HELP.
I'M PROFESSOR TREVOR BRUTTENHOLM, AND THIS IS MY ASSOCIATE, HELLBOY.
AND YOU'RE DR. DIXON? YOU CALLED AND LEFT A MESSAGE FOR HARRY MIDDLETON, BUT HE'S BUSY JUST NOW, SO HE SENT US IN HIS PLACE.
BPRD
I DON'T KNOW YOU, SIR. BUT I GUESS I'VE HEARD STORIES ABOUT YOUR FRIEND THERE.
PROMISE ME HE'LL MIND HIS MANNERS...
OF COURSE.
COME ON THEN.
SAM, HARRY COULDN'T COME, BUT--
IT'S ALL RIGHT. HE'S SPOKEN OF THESE TWO OFTEN ENOUGH.

COME CLOSER SO I CAN SEE YOU BETTER. I WON'T BITE.

EVEN IF I WAS INCLINED TO, I DON'T KNOW AS I COULD MANAGE IT NOW.

WHAT'S WRONG WITH HIM?

STROKE, I THINK.

MR. BURKE, I'M AFRAID THE DOCTOR'S MESSAGE WAS RATHER VAGUE.

I DIDN'T TELL HIM WHAT HAPPENED. I WAS SAVING IT FOR HARRY...

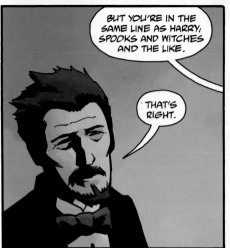

BUT YOU'RE IN THE SAME LINE AS HARRY, SPOOKS AND WITCHES AND THE LIKE.

THAT'S RIGHT.

SO I GUESS YOU'VE HEARD THE STORY OF BOUDICCA'S HAG.

I HAVE.

WELL, IT'S TRUE. MOST OF IT, ANYWAY. THAT WITCH WAS A CURSE ON THE ROMANS, AND THEY CAUGHT HER AND HANGED HER NOT A MILE FROM HERE. AND THE LAST SIXTY-SEVEN YEARS SHE'S BEEN GATHERING DUST IN THE BASEMENT OF OLD ST. AGNES NEXT DOOR...

"IT WAS ED GREY* HIMSELF PUT HER DOWN THERE, I GUESS FIGURING ALL THAT RELIGION WOULD KEEP HER QUIET."

AND IT WAS GREY HIRED MY FATHER TO MIND THE PLACE, AND SINCE HE PASSED, IT'S BEEN ME. AND ALL THOSE YEARS, NO TROUBLE TILL LAST NIGHT...

*SIR EDWARD GREY WAS, FROM 1879 TO 1889, QUEEN VICTORIA'S SPECIAL AGENT FOR THE INVESTIGATION OF OCCULT MATTERS.

"I MADE MY USUAL ROUNDS AND SAW SOMEBODY HAD FORCED THE LOCK, AND THE WITCH WAS GONE. SO I WENT TO CHECK THE TREE WHERE SHE WAS HANGED--I'D HEARD THAT IN THE OLD DAYS, BEFORE GREY HAD GOT AHOLD OF HER, OTHER WITCHES USED TO HANG HER BACK UP THERE WHEN THEY'D HOLD THEIR SABBATH..."

"AND SURE ENOUGH SHE WAS THERE."

CHRIST.

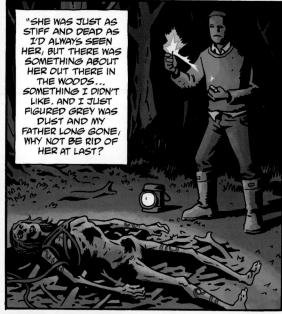

"SHE WAS JUST AS STIFF AND DEAD AS I'D ALWAYS SEEN HER, BUT THERE WAS SOMETHING ABOUT HER OUT THERE IN THE WOODS... SOMETHING I DIDN'T LIKE. AND I JUST FIGURED GREY WAS DUST AND MY FATHER LONG GONE, WHY NOT BE RID OF HER AT LAST?"

"BUT THERE WAS SOMETHING...EVEN NOW I CAN'T TELL YOU WHAT, BUT I LOST MY NERVE..."

HUNTS
1608
est

"I LEFT HER OUT THERE, BUT TOLD MYSELF I'D GO BACK AND FINISH THE JOB JUST AS SOON AS I'D--"

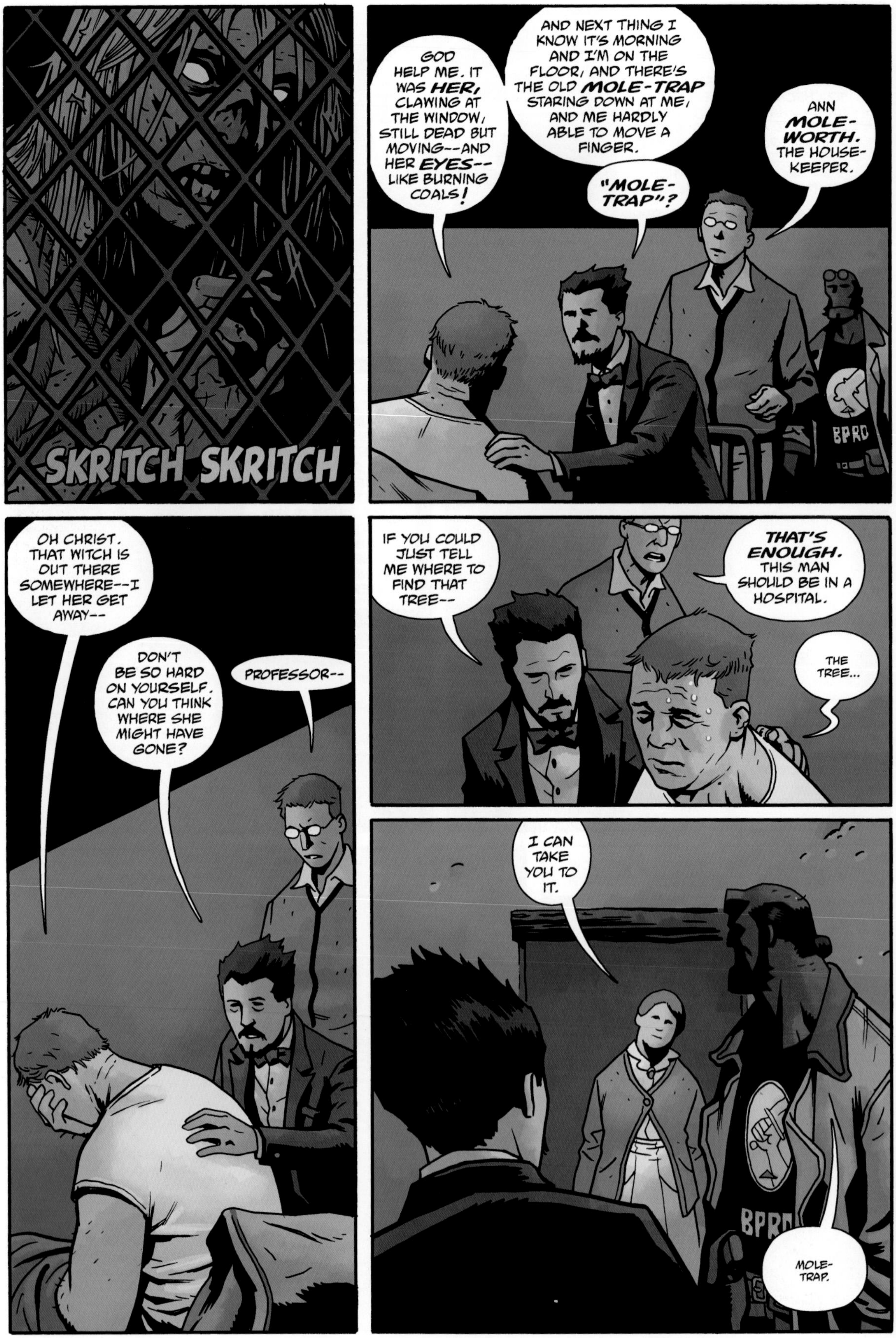
SKRITCH SKRITCH
GOD HELP ME. IT WAS HER, CLAWING AT THE WINDOW, STILL DEAD BUT MOVING--AND HER EYES--LIKE BURNING COALS!
AND NEXT THING I KNOW IT'S MORNING AND I'M ON THE FLOOR, AND THERE'S THE OLD MOLE-TRAP STARING DOWN AT ME, AND ME HARDLY ABLE TO MOVE A FINGER.
"MOLE-TRAP"?
ANN MOLE-WORTH. THE HOUSE-KEEPER.
OH CHRIST. THAT WITCH IS OUT THERE SOMEWHERE--I LET HER GET AWAY--
DON'T BE SO HARD ON YOURSELF. CAN YOU THINK WHERE SHE MIGHT HAVE GONE?
PROFESSOR--
IF YOU COULD JUST TELL ME WHERE TO FIND THAT TREE--
THAT'S ENOUGH. THIS MAN SHOULD BE IN A HOSPITAL.
THE TREE...
I CAN TAKE YOU TO IT.
MOLE-TRAP.

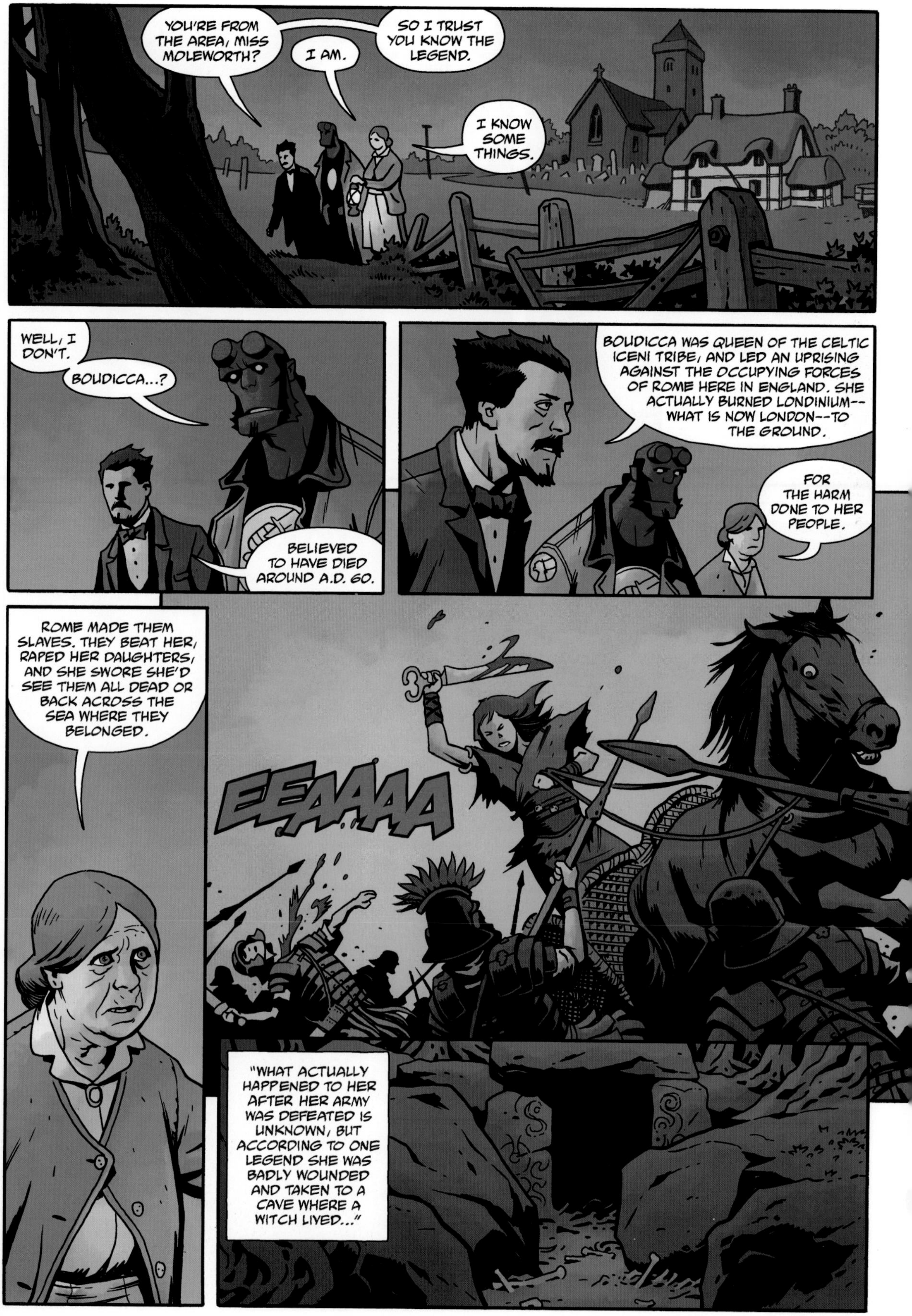

YOU'RE FROM THE AREA, MISS MOLEWORTH?
I AM.
SO I TRUST YOU KNOW THE LEGEND.
I KNOW SOME THINGS.
WELL, I DON'T.
BOUDICCA...?
BELIEVED TO HAVE DIED AROUND A.D. 60.
BOUDICCA WAS QUEEN OF THE CELTIC ICENI TRIBE, AND LED AN UPRISING AGAINST THE OCCUPYING FORCES OF ROME HERE IN ENGLAND. SHE ACTUALLY BURNED LONDINIUM-- WHAT IS NOW LONDON--TO THE GROUND.
FOR THE HARM DONE TO HER PEOPLE.
ROME MADE THEM SLAVES. THEY BEAT HER, RAPED HER DAUGHTERS, AND SHE SWORE SHE'D SEE THEM ALL DEAD OR BACK ACROSS THE SEA WHERE THEY BELONGED.
EEAAAA
"WHAT ACTUALLY HAPPENED TO HER AFTER HER ARMY WAS DEFEATED IS UNKNOWN, BUT ACCORDING TO ONE LEGEND SHE WAS BADLY WOUNDED AND TAKEN TO A CAVE WHERE A WITCH LIVED..."

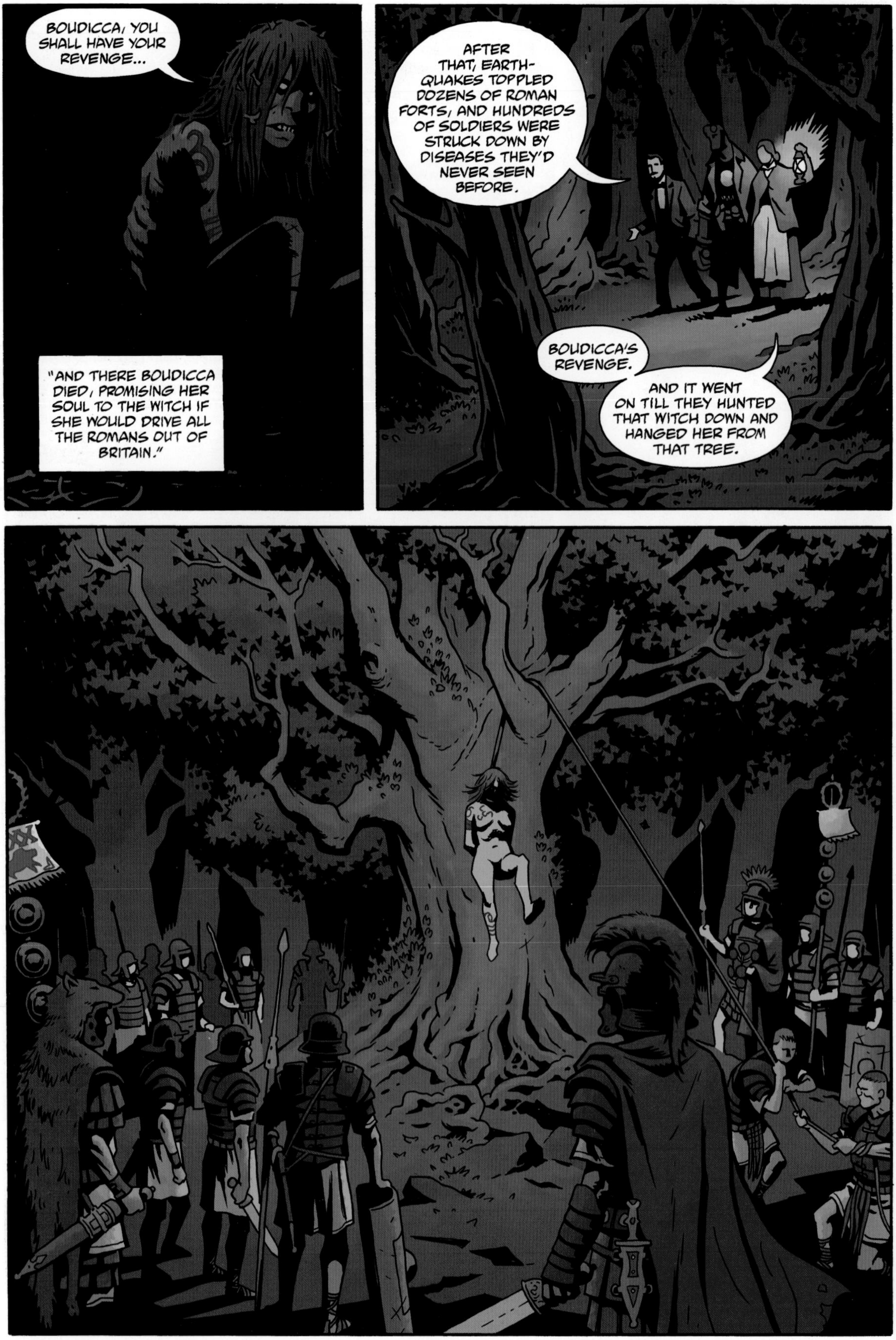
BOUDICCA, YOU SHALL HAVE YOUR REVENGE...
"AND THERE BOUDICCA DIED, PROMISING HER SOUL TO THE WITCH IF SHE WOULD DRIVE ALL THE ROMANS OUT OF BRITAIN."
AFTER THAT, EARTH-QUAKES TOPPLED DOZENS OF ROMAN FORTS, AND HUNDREDS OF SOLDIERS WERE STRUCK DOWN BY DISEASES THEY'D NEVER SEEN BEFORE.
BOUDICCA'S REVENGE.
AND IT WENT ON TILL THEY HUNTED THAT WITCH DOWN AND HANGED HER FROM THAT TREE.

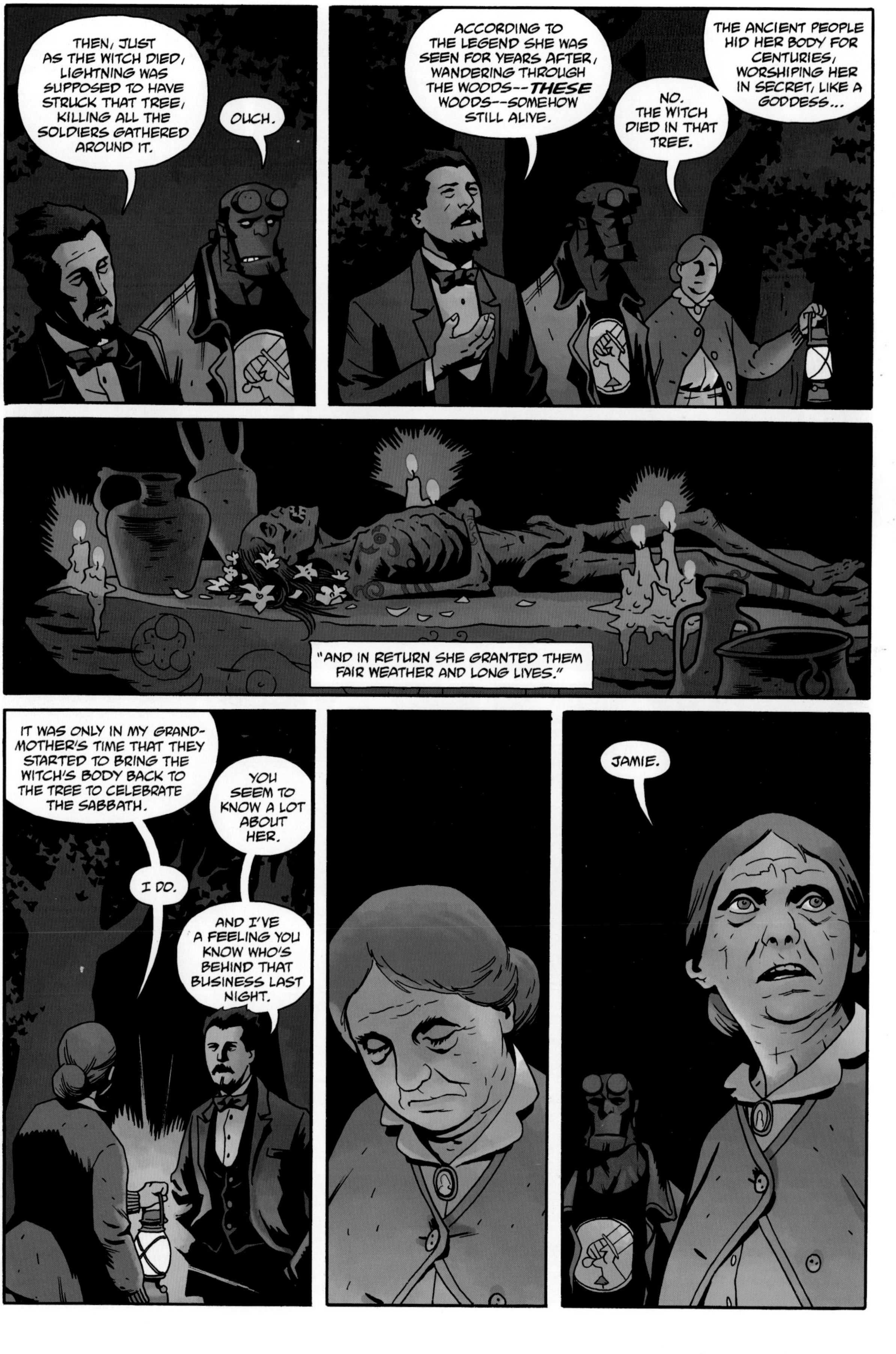

THEN, JUST AS THE WITCH DIED, LIGHTNING WAS SUPPOSED TO HAVE STRUCK THAT TREE, KILLING ALL THE SOLDIERS GATHERED AROUND IT.
OUCH.
ACCORDING TO THE LEGEND SHE WAS SEEN FOR YEARS AFTER, WANDERING THROUGH THE WOODS--*THESE* WOODS--SOMEHOW STILL ALIVE.
NO. THE WITCH DIED IN THAT TREE.
THE ANCIENT PEOPLE HID HER BODY FOR CENTURIES, WORSHIPING HER IN SECRET, LIKE A GODDESS...
"AND IN RETURN SHE GRANTED THEM FAIR WEATHER AND LONG LIVES."
IT WAS ONLY IN MY GRAND-MOTHER'S TIME THAT THEY STARTED TO BRING THE WITCH'S BODY BACK TO THE TREE TO CELEBRATE THE SABBATH.
YOU SEEM TO KNOW A LOT ABOUT HER.
I DO.
AND I'VE A FEELING YOU KNOW WHO'S BEHIND THAT BUSINESS LAST NIGHT.
JAMIE.

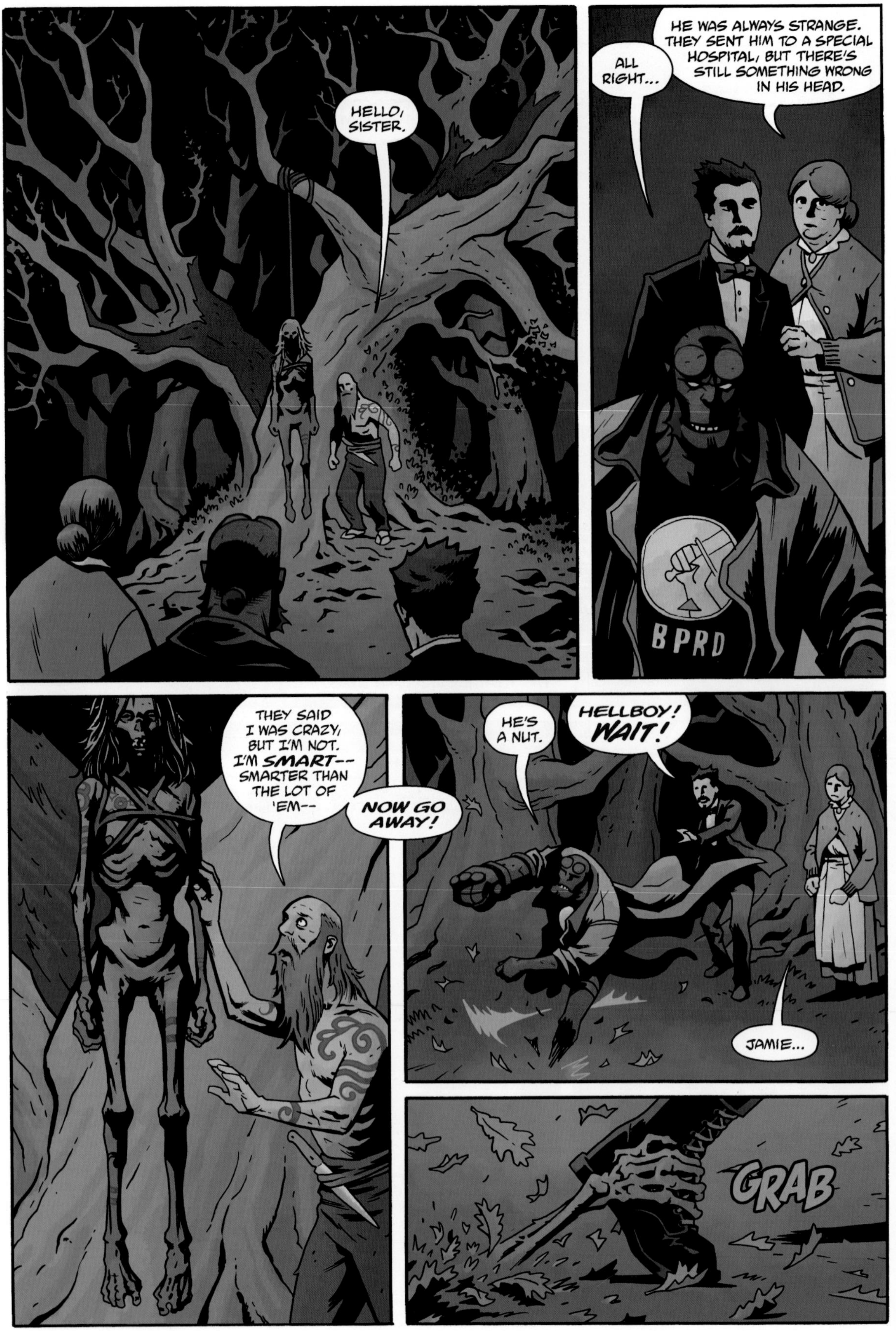
HELLO, SISTER.
ALL RIGHT...
HE WAS ALWAYS STRANGE. THEY SENT HIM TO A SPECIAL HOSPITAL, BUT THERE'S STILL SOMETHING WRONG IN HIS HEAD.
BPRD
THEY SAID I WAS CRAZY, BUT I'M NOT. I'M SMART-- SMARTER THAN THE LOT OF 'EM--
NOW GO AWAY!
HE'S A NUT.
HELLBOY! WAIT!
JAMIE...
GRAB

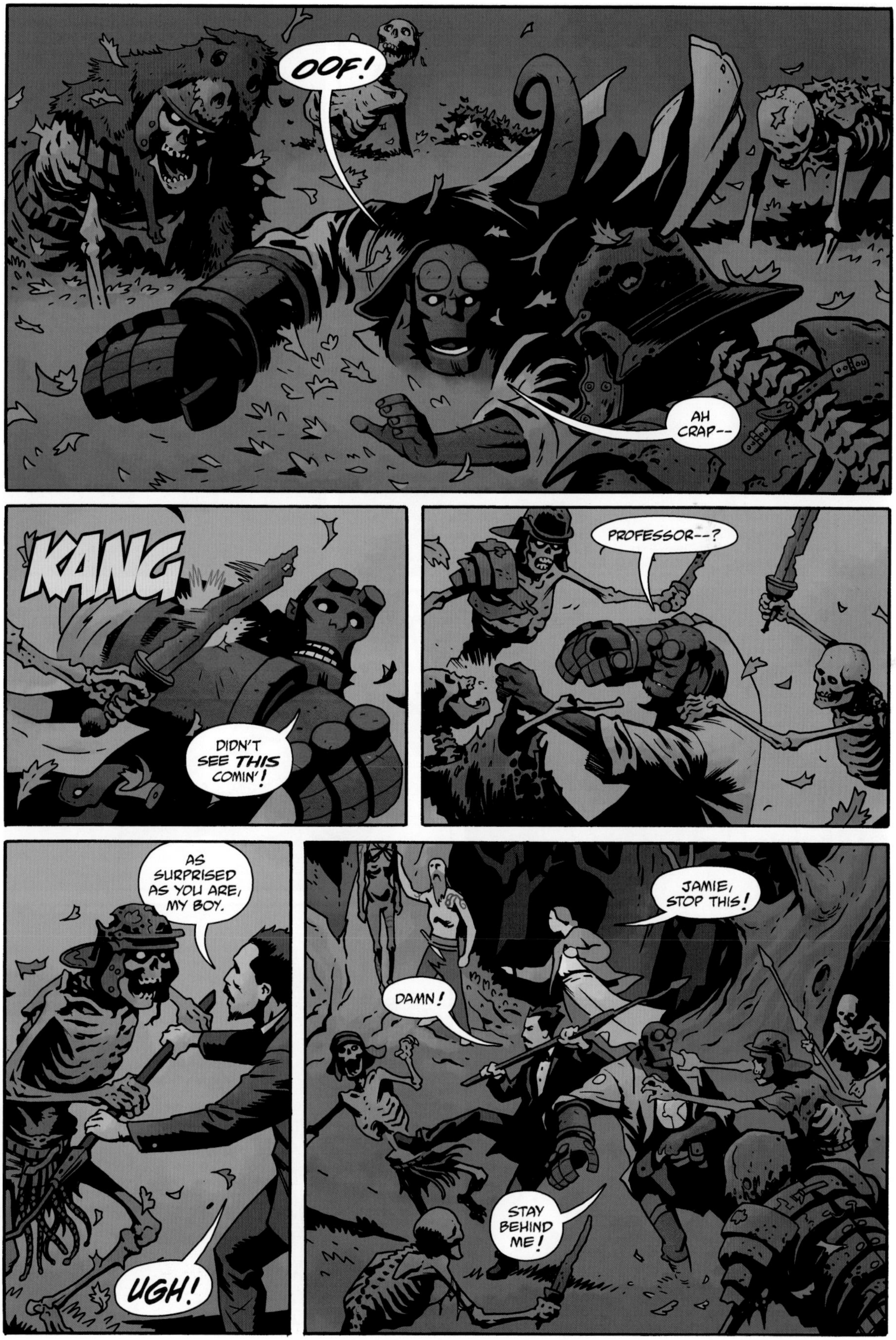
OOF!
AH CRAP--
KANG
DIDN'T SEE THIS COMIN'!
PROFESSOR--?
AS SURPRISED AS YOU ARE, MY BOY.
UGH!
JAMIE, STOP THIS!
DAMN!
STAY BEHIND ME!

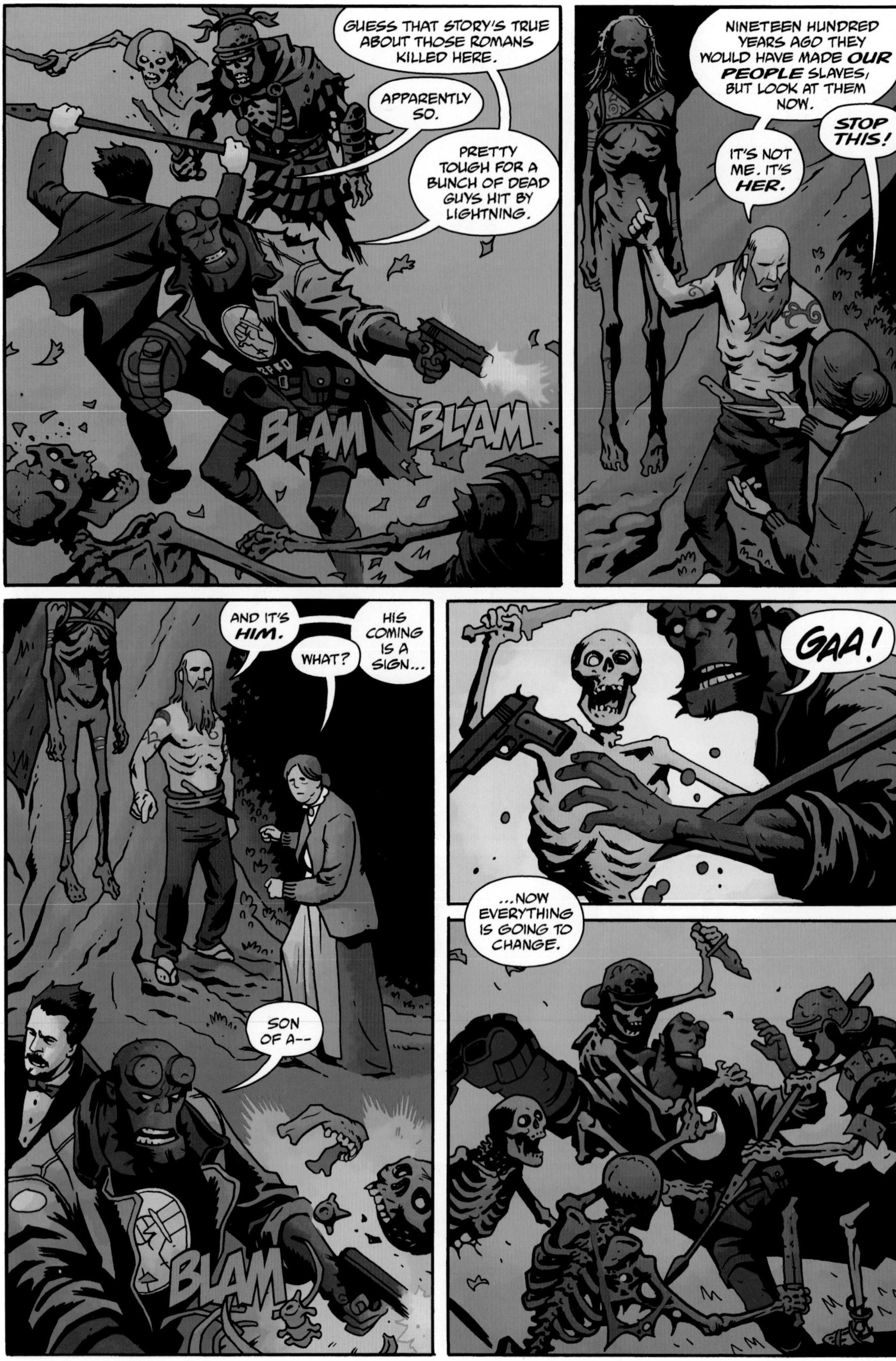
GUESS THAT STORY'S TRUE ABOUT THOSE ROMANS KILLED HERE.
APPARENTLY SO.
PRETTY TOUGH FOR A BUNCH OF DEAD GUYS HIT BY LIGHTNING.
BLAM
BLAM
NINETEEN HUNDRED YEARS AGO THEY WOULD HAVE MADE **OUR PEOPLE** SLAVES, BUT LOOK AT THEM NOW.
IT'S NOT ME. IT'S **HER.**
STOP THIS!
AND IT'S **HIM.**
WHAT?
HIS COMING IS A SIGN...
SON OF A--
BLAM
GAA!
...NOW EVERYTHING IS GOING TO CHANGE.

THAT'S WHY SHE CALLED ME. SHE SENSED THAT *HE* WAS NEAR.

SHE KNOWS WHAT HE IS, WHAT HE MEANS; AND NOW HE'S HERE--NOW *SHE KNOWS* IT'S TIME TO LOOSE *THE POWERS THAT WILL CHANGE THE WORLD!*

OH, JAMIE, NO...

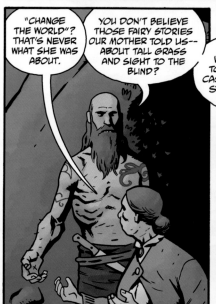

"CHANGE THE WORLD"? THAT'S NEVER WHAT SHE WAS ABOUT.

YOU DON'T BELIEVE THOSE FAIRY STORIES OUR MOTHER TOLD US-- ABOUT TALL GRASS AND SIGHT TO THE BLIND?

SISTER, THERE WERE GODS MEANT TO RULE THIS WORLD, CAST DOWN OUT OF THE STARS AND BURIED IN THE EARTH...

NO.

"SHE WAS DOWN THERE ALL THOSE YEARS, IN THAT CAVE WITH ONE OF THEM...

"TILL IT BECAME A PART OF HER."

NOW IT'S TIME FOR THAT GOD TO WAKE UP AND CHANGE THINGS.

SHE *WANTS* TO DO IT, BUT SHE'S STILL TOO WEAK.

NO!

BLOOD'S WANTED!

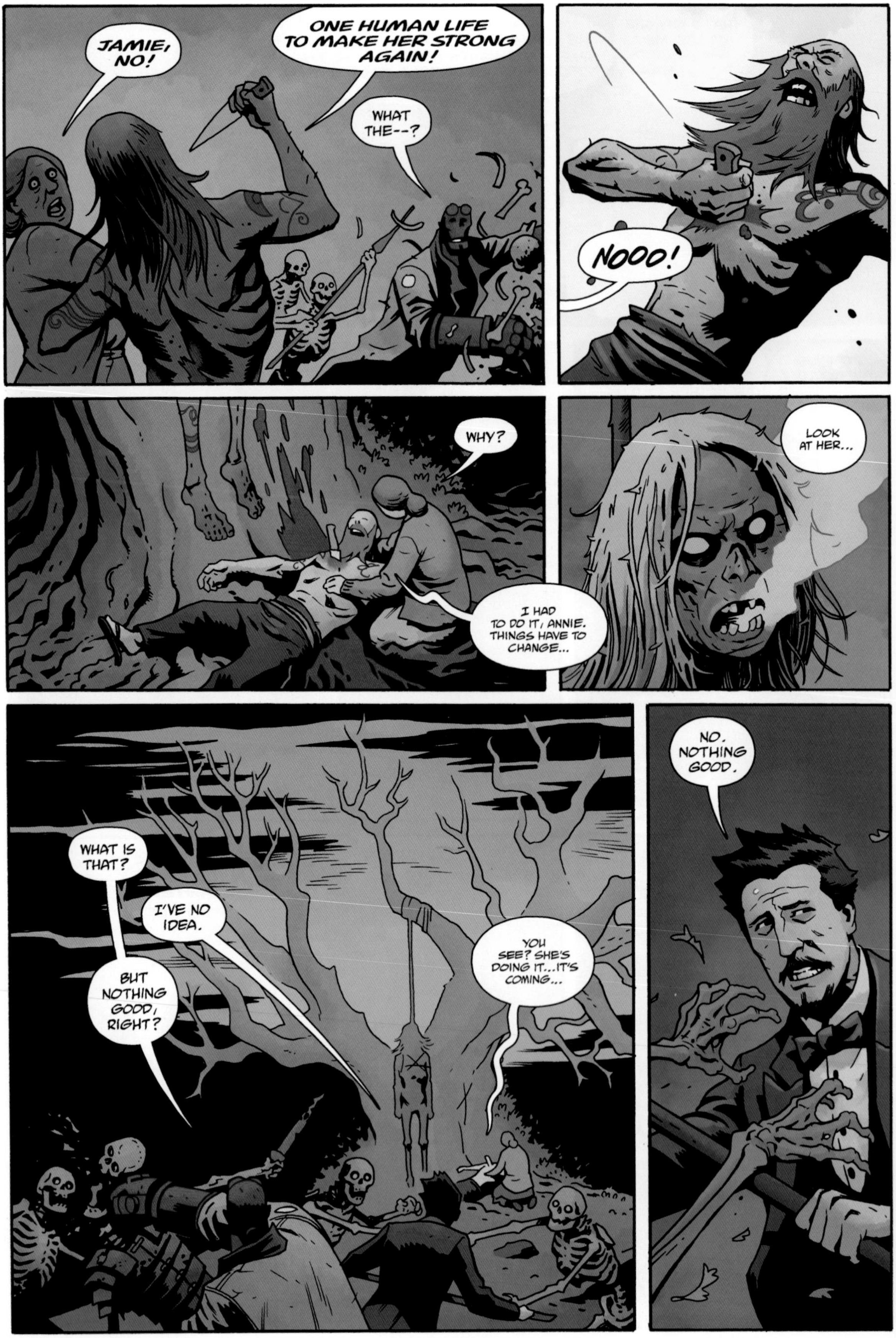
JAMIE, NO!
ONE HUMAN LIFE TO MAKE HER STRONG AGAIN!
WHAT THE--?
NOOO!
WHY?
I HAD TO DO IT, ANNIE. THINGS HAVE TO CHANGE...
LOOK AT HER...
WHAT IS THAT?
I'VE NO IDEA.
BUT NOTHING GOOD, RIGHT?
YOU SEE? SHE'S DOING IT...IT'S COMING...
NO. NOTHING GOOD.

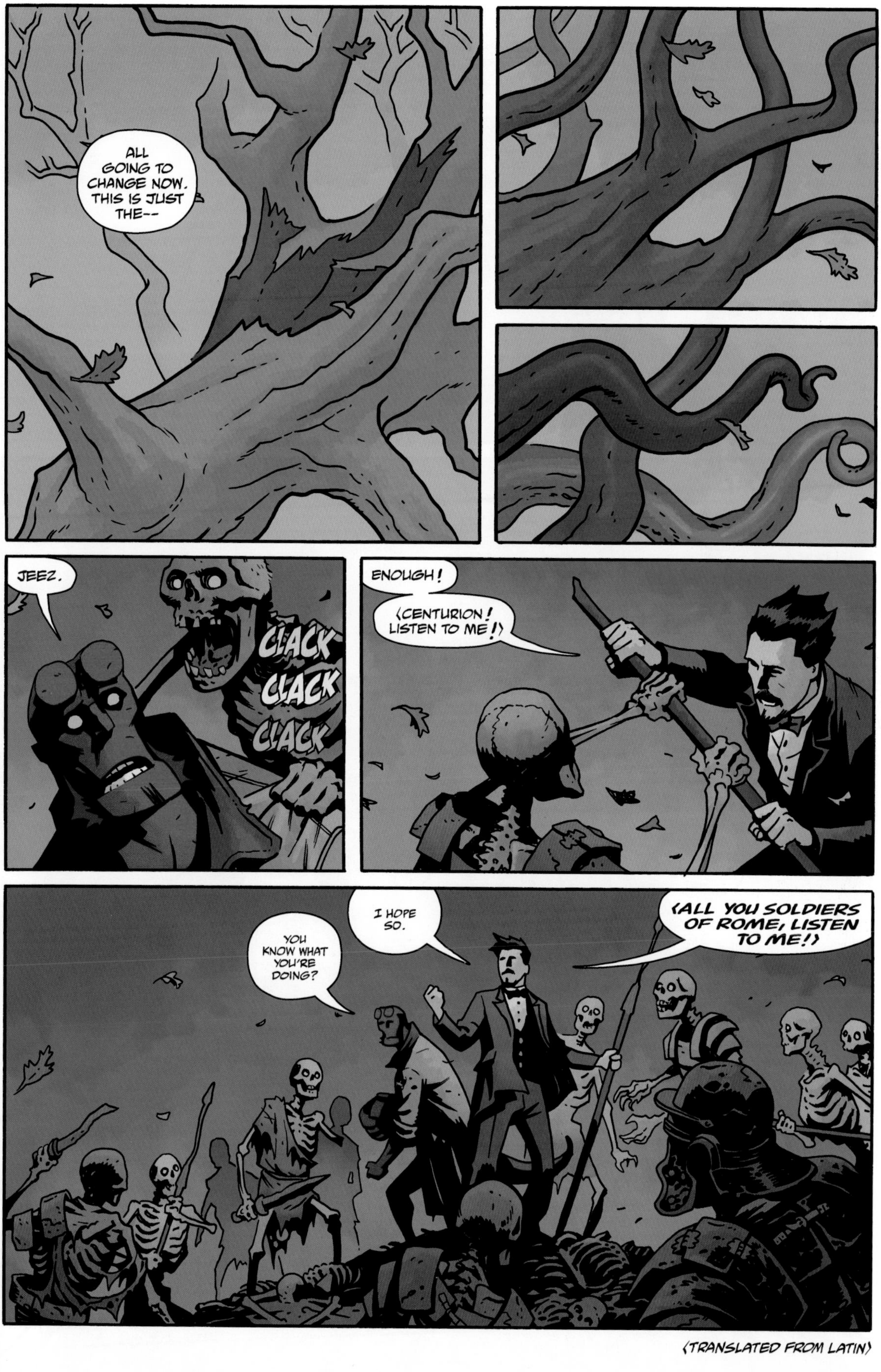
ALL GOING TO CHANGE NOW. THIS IS JUST THE--
JEEZ.
CLACK
CLACK
CLACK
ENOUGH!
⟨CENTURION! LISTEN TO ME!⟩
YOU KNOW WHAT YOU'RE DOING?
I HOPE SO.
⟨ALL YOU SOLDIERS OF ROME, LISTEN TO ME!⟩

⟨TRANSLATED FROM LATIN⟩

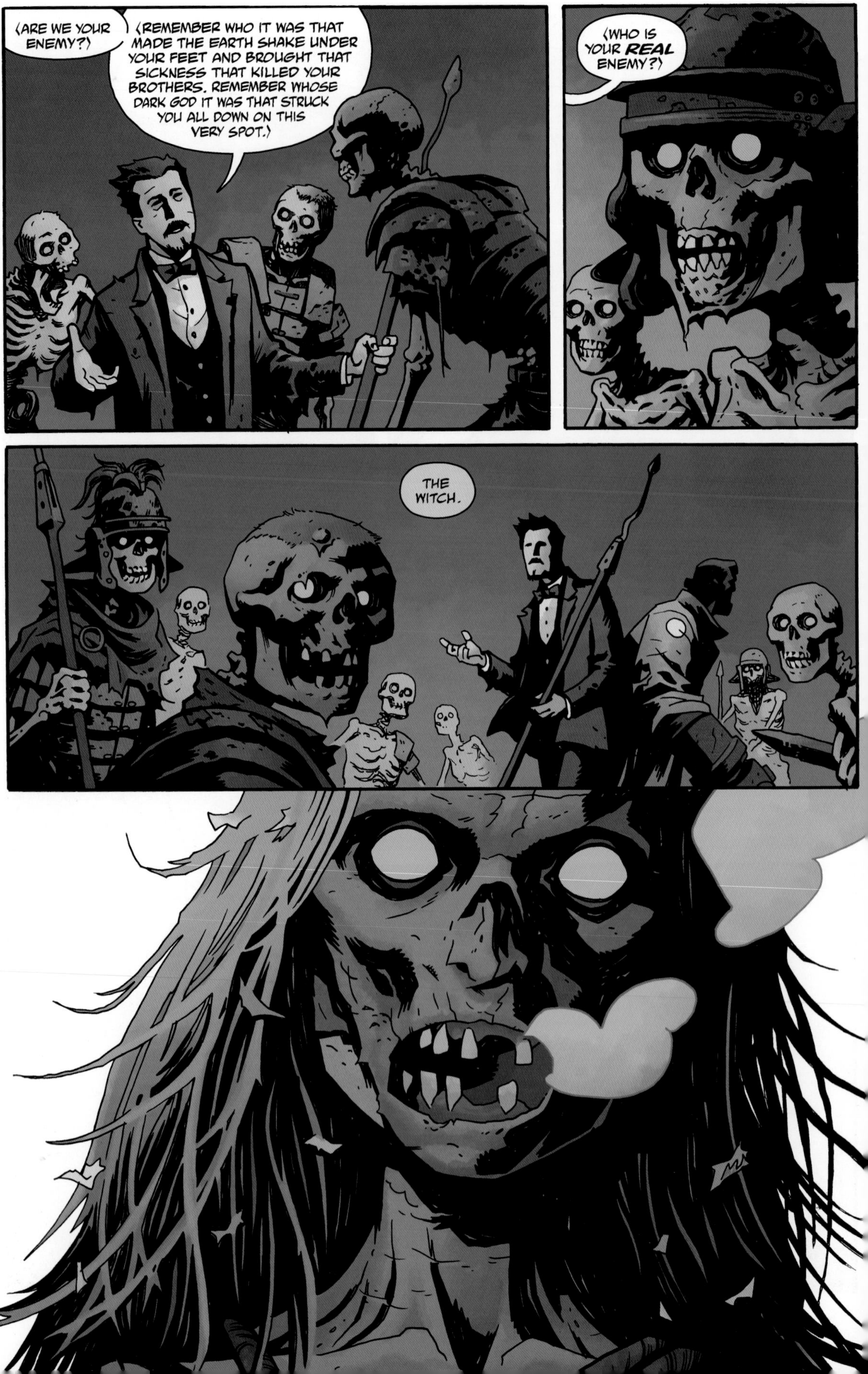
⟨ARE WE YOUR ENEMY?⟩
⟨REMEMBER WHO IT WAS THAT MADE THE EARTH SHAKE UNDER YOUR FEET AND BROUGHT THAT SICKNESS THAT KILLED YOUR BROTHERS. REMEMBER WHOSE DARK GOD IT WAS THAT STRUCK YOU ALL DOWN ON THIS VERY SPOT.⟩
⟨WHO IS YOUR REAL ENEMY?⟩
THE WITCH.

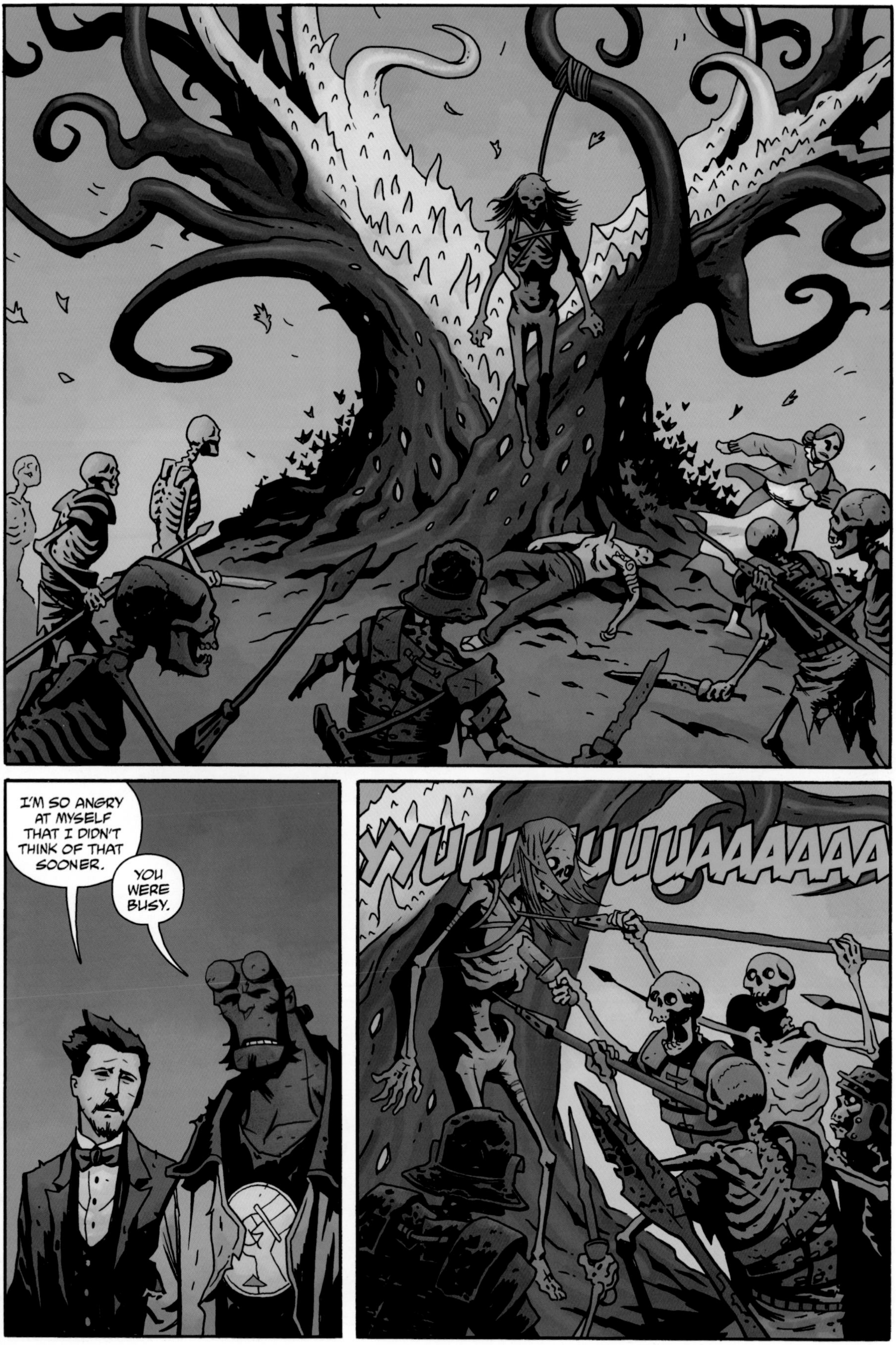
I'M SO ANGRY AT MYSELF THAT I DIDN'T THINK OF THAT SOONER.
YOU WERE BUSY.
YYUU UUUAAAAAA

AAAAAAAAAAAAAAAAAAAAAAA

I'M SO SORRY, MISS MOLEWORTH.

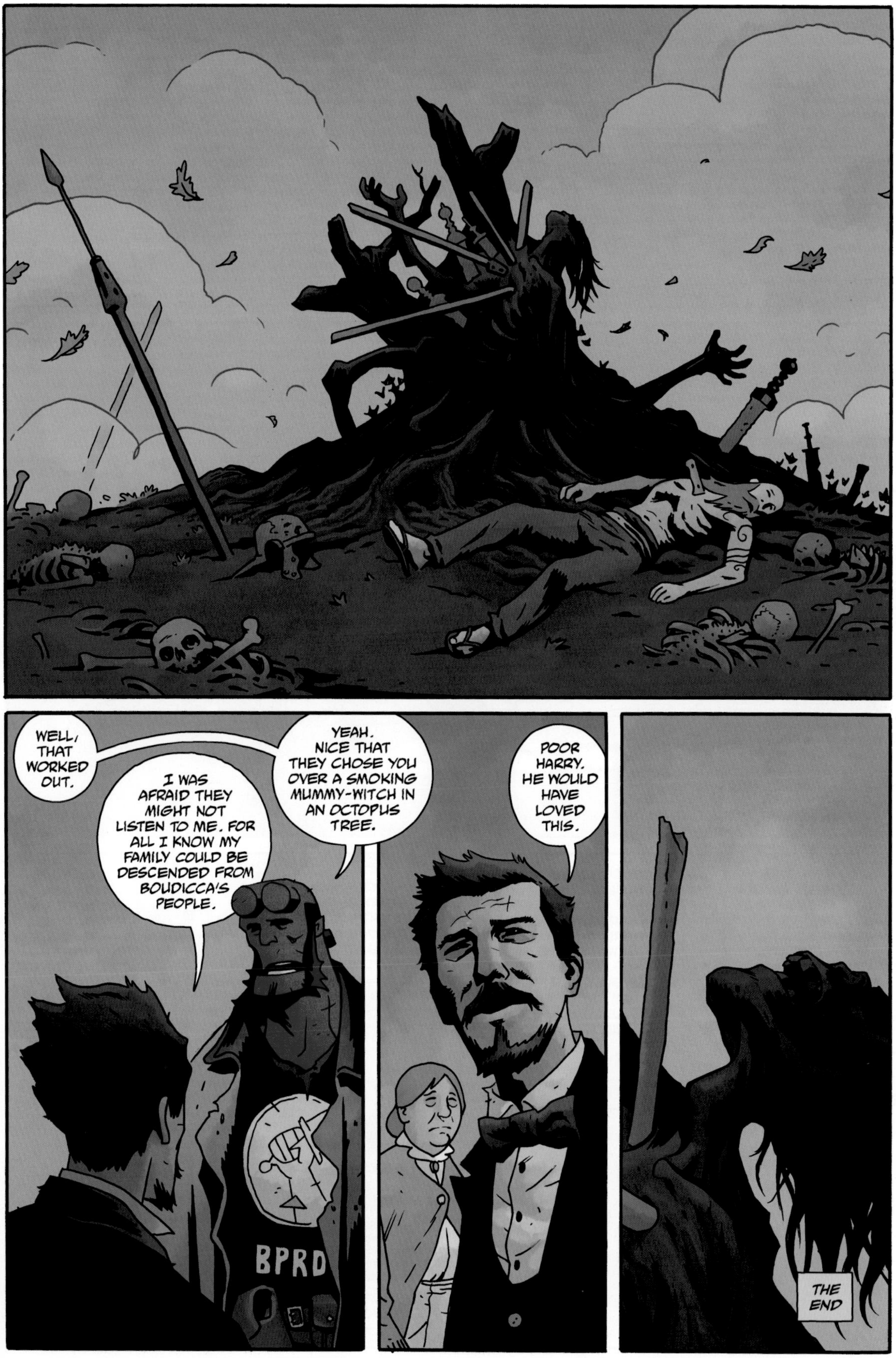
WELL, THAT WORKED OUT.
YEAH. NICE THAT THEY CHOSE YOU OVER A SMOKING MUMMY-WITCH IN AN OCTOPUS TREE.
I WAS AFRAID THEY MIGHT NOT LISTEN TO ME. FOR ALL I KNOW MY FAMILY COULD BE DESCENDED FROM BOUDICCA'S PEOPLE.
BPRD
POOR HARRY. HE WOULD HAVE LOVED THIS.
THE END

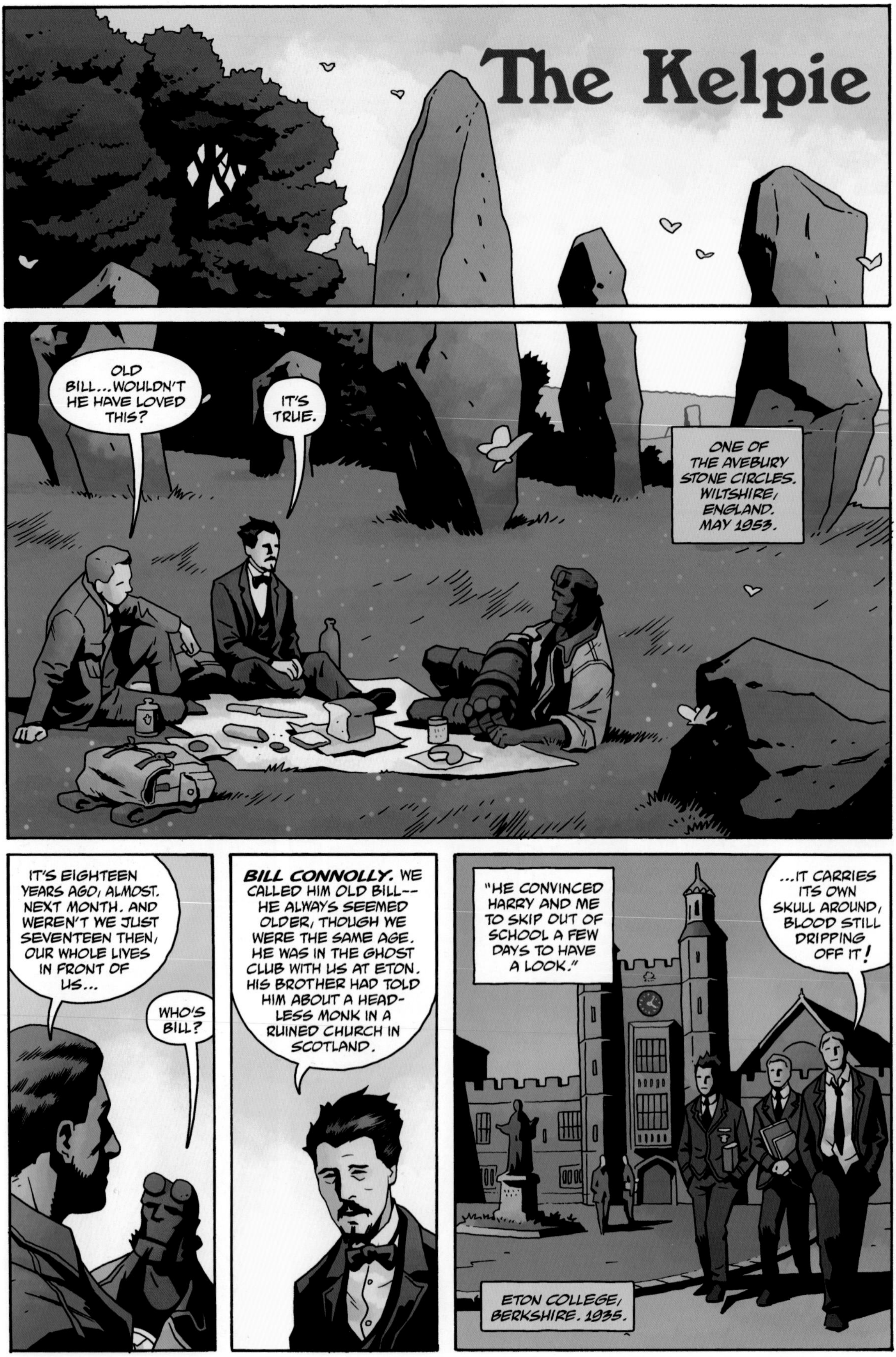
The Kelpie
OLD BILL...WOULDN'T HE HAVE LOVED THIS?
IT'S TRUE.
ONE OF THE AVEBURY STONE CIRCLES. WILTSHIRE, ENGLAND. MAY 1953.
IT'S EIGHTEEN YEARS AGO, ALMOST. NEXT MONTH. AND WEREN'T WE JUST SEVENTEEN THEN, OUR WHOLE LIVES IN FRONT OF US...
WHO'S BILL?
BILL CONNOLLY. WE CALLED HIM OLD BILL-- HE ALWAYS SEEMED OLDER, THOUGH WE WERE THE SAME AGE. HE WAS IN THE GHOST CLUB WITH US AT ETON. HIS BROTHER HAD TOLD HIM ABOUT A HEADLESS MONK IN A RUINED CHURCH IN SCOTLAND.
"HE CONVINCED HARRY AND ME TO SKIP OUT OF SCHOOL A FEW DAYS TO HAVE A LOOK."
...IT CARRIES ITS OWN SKULL AROUND, BLOOD STILL DRIPPING OFF IT!
ETON COLLEGE, BERKSHIRE. 1935.

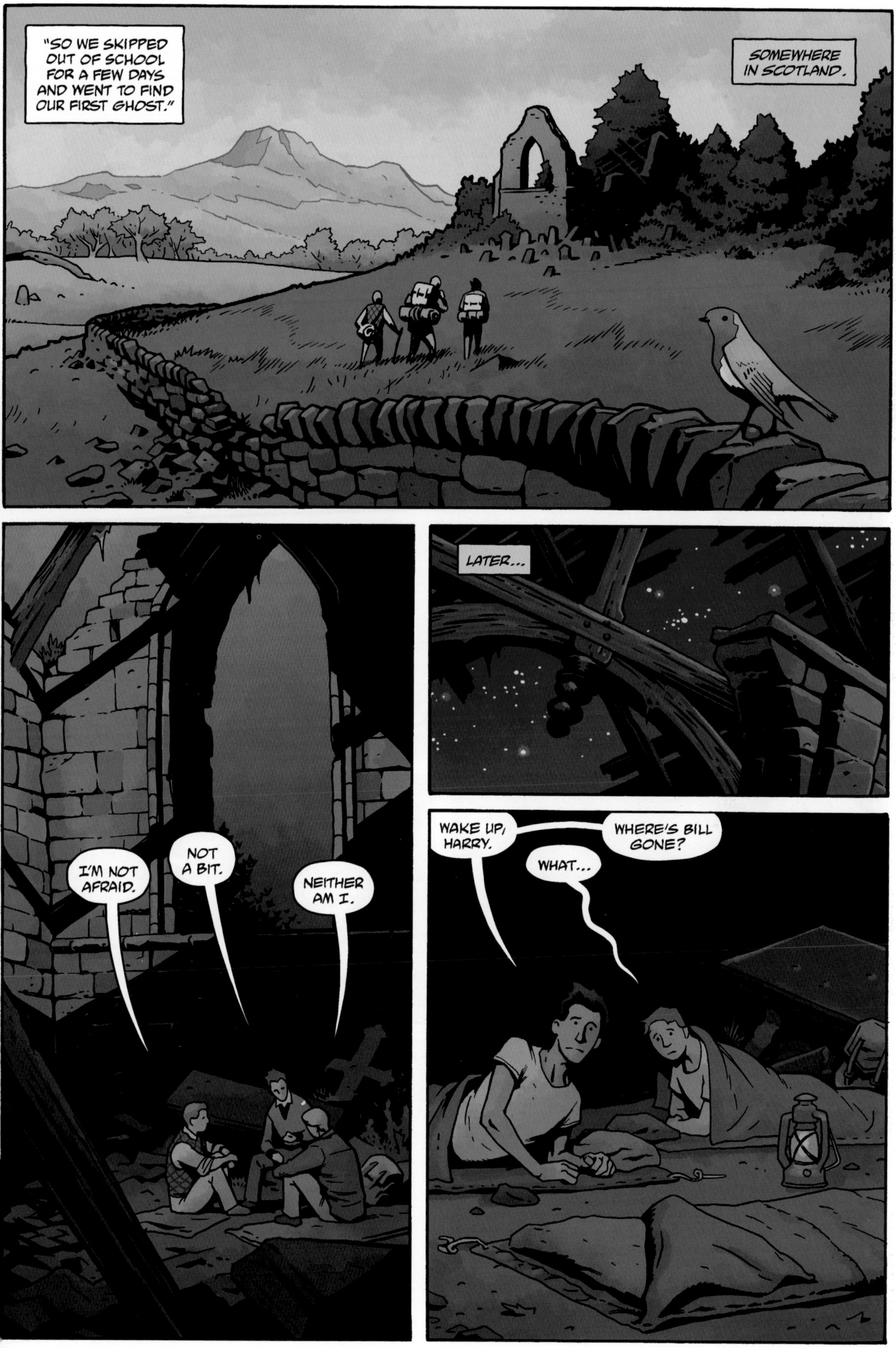
"SO WE SKIPPED OUT OF SCHOOL FOR A FEW DAYS AND WENT TO FIND OUR FIRST GHOST."
SOMEWHERE IN SCOTLAND.
I'M NOT AFRAID.
NOT A BIT.
NEITHER AM I.
LATER...
WAKE UP, HARRY.
WHERE'S BILL GONE?
WHAT...

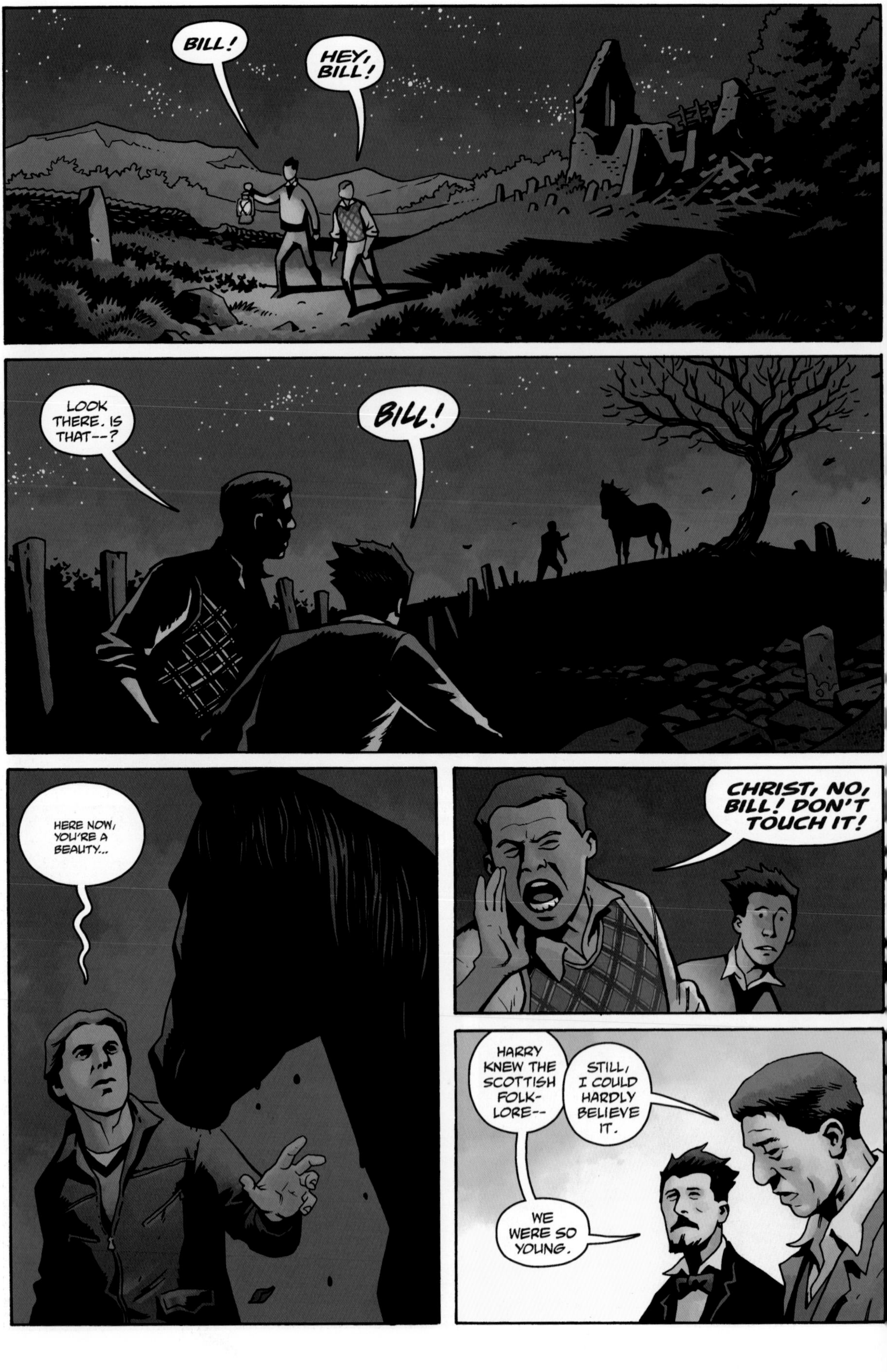
BILL!
HEY, BILL!
LOOK THERE. IS THAT--?
BILL!
HERE NOW, YOU'RE A BEAUTY...
CHRIST, NO, BILL! DON'T TOUCH IT!
HARRY KNEW THE SCOTTISH FOLK-LORE--
STILL, I COULD HARDLY BELIEVE IT.
WE WERE SO YOUNG.

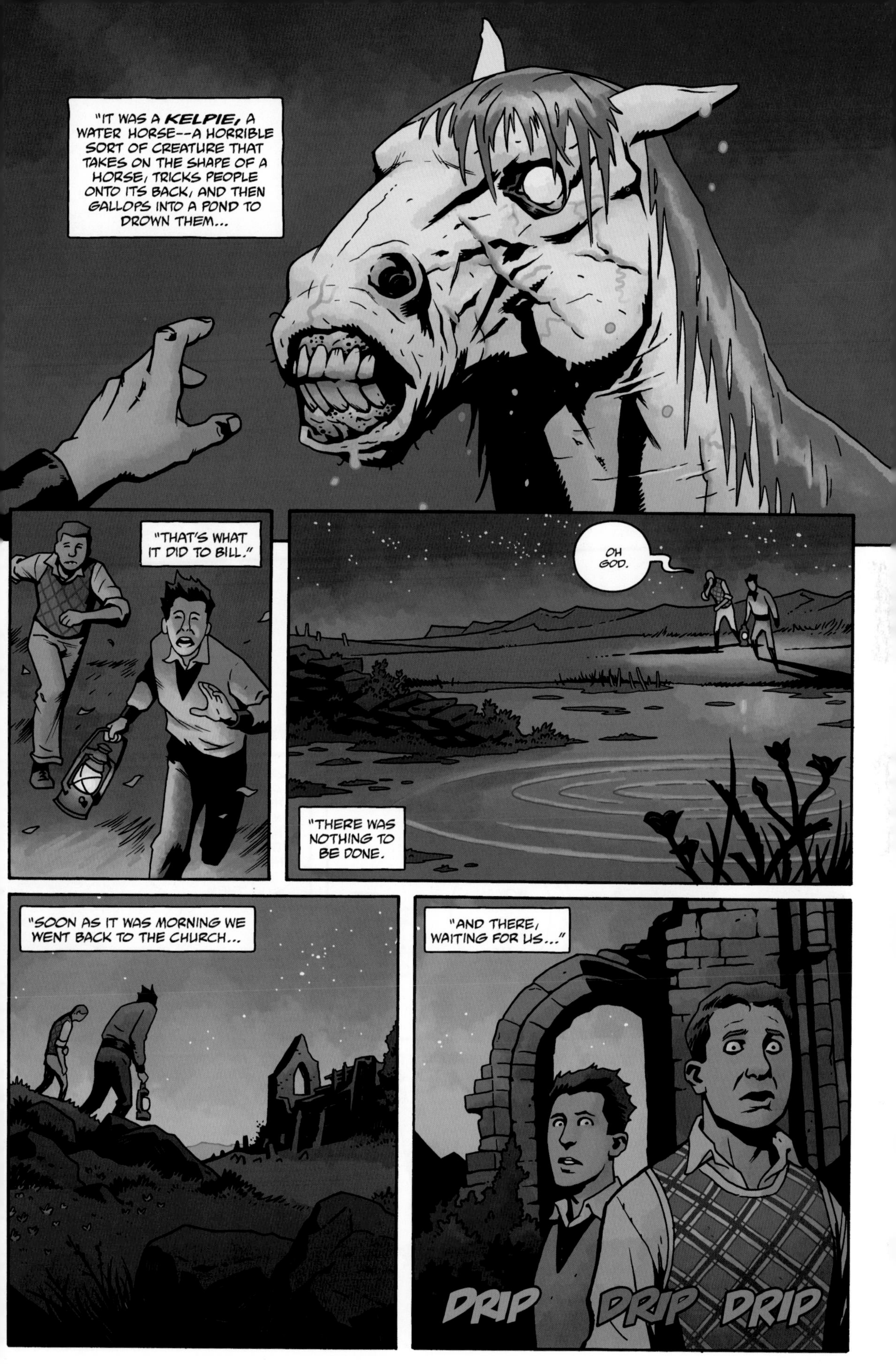
"IT WAS A **KELPIE,** A WATER HORSE--A HORRIBLE SORT OF CREATURE THAT TAKES ON THE SHAPE OF A HORSE, TRICKS PEOPLE ONTO ITS BACK, AND THEN GALLOPS INTO A POND TO DROWN THEM...
"THAT'S WHAT IT DID TO BILL."
OH GOD.
"THERE WAS NOTHING TO BE DONE.
"SOON AS IT WAS MORNING WE WENT BACK TO THE CHURCH...
"AND THERE, WAITING FOR US..."
DRIP
DRIP
DRIP

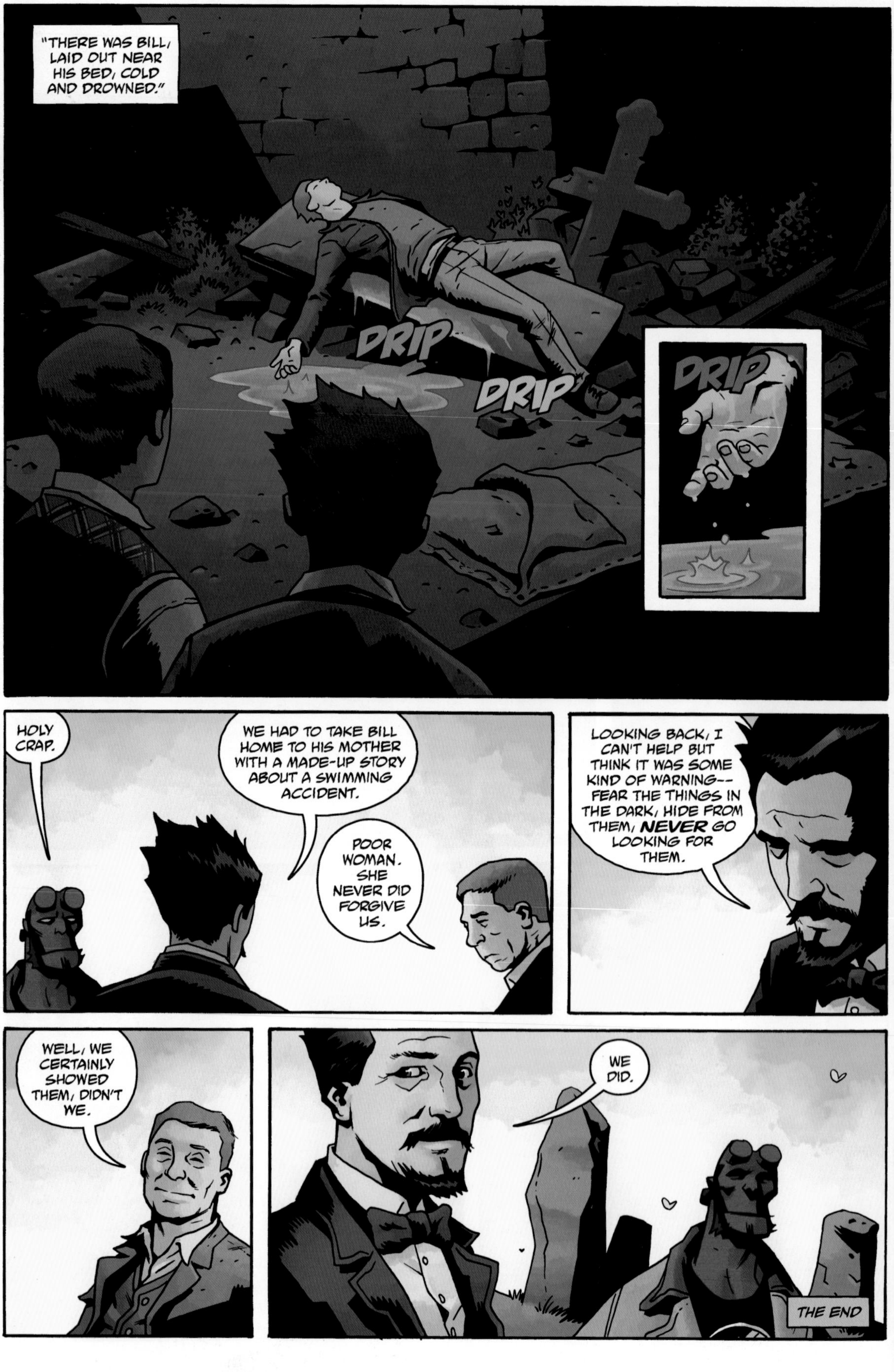
"THERE WAS BILL, LAID OUT NEAR HIS BED, COLD AND DROWNED."
DRIP
DRIP
DRIP
HOLY CRAP.
WE HAD TO TAKE BILL HOME TO HIS MOTHER WITH A MADE-UP STORY ABOUT A SWIMMING ACCIDENT.
POOR WOMAN. SHE NEVER DID FORGIVE US.
LOOKING BACK, I CAN'T HELP BUT THINK IT WAS SOME KIND OF WARNING-- FEAR THE THINGS IN THE DARK, HIDE FROM THEM, NEVER GO LOOKING FOR THEM.
WELL, WE CERTAINLY SHOWED THEM, DIDN'T WE.
WE DID.
THE END

WANDERING SOULS

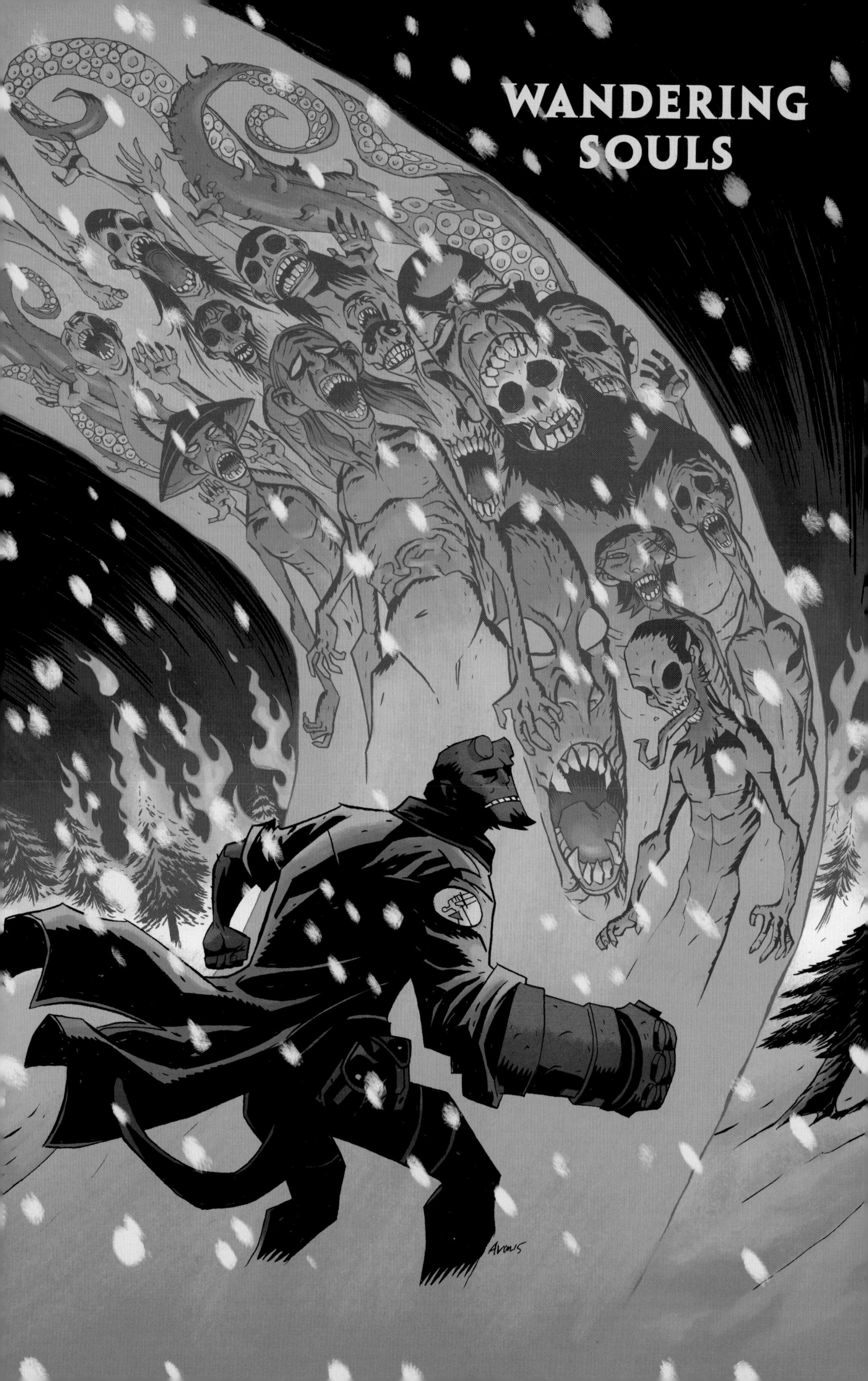

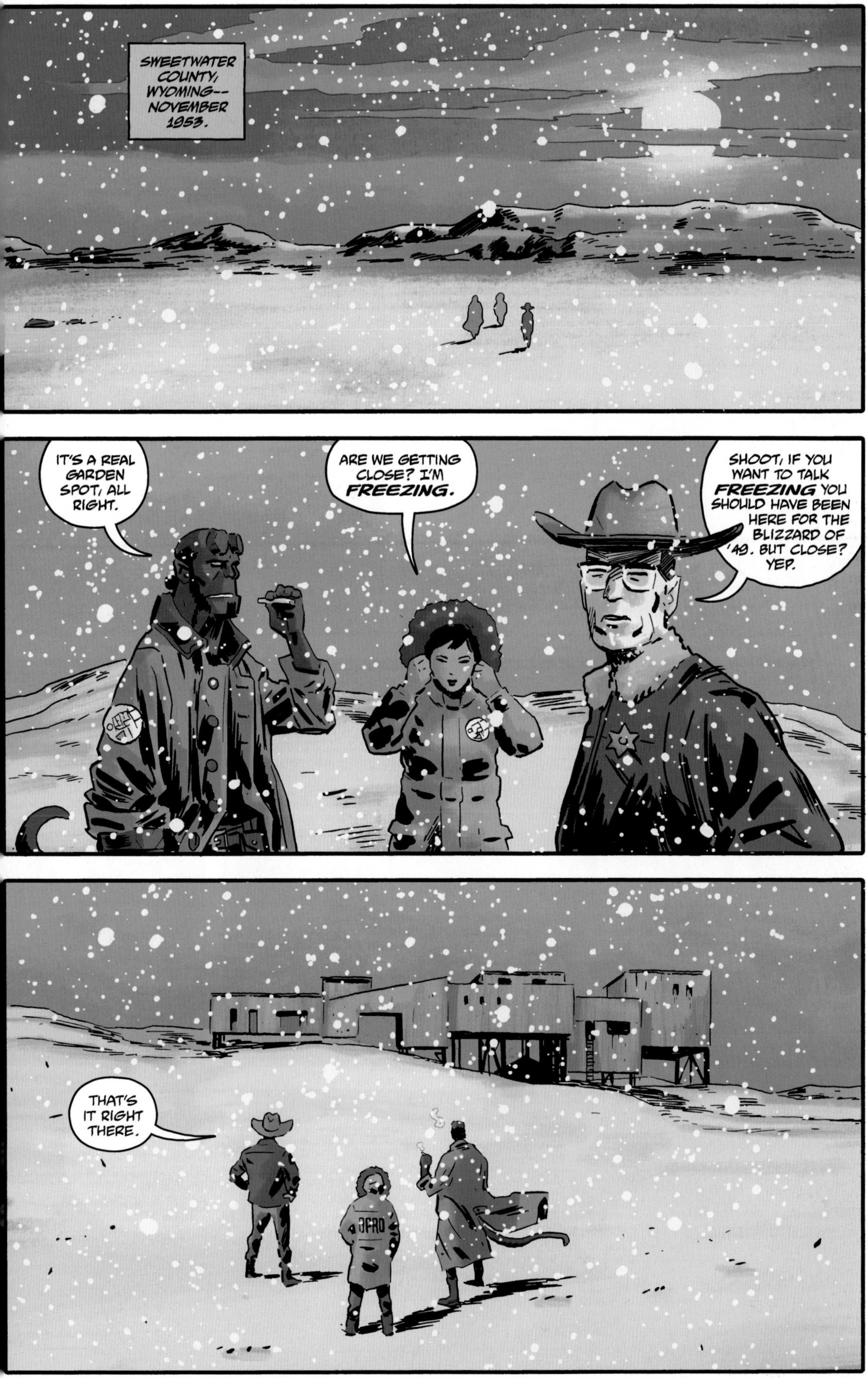
SWEETWATER COUNTY, WYOMING-- NOVEMBER 1953.
IT'S A REAL GARDEN SPOT, ALL RIGHT.
ARE WE GETTING CLOSE? I'M FREEZING.
SHOOT, IF YOU WANT TO TALK FREEZING YOU SHOULD HAVE BEEN HERE FOR THE BLIZZARD OF '49. BUT CLOSE? YEP.
THAT'S IT RIGHT THERE.

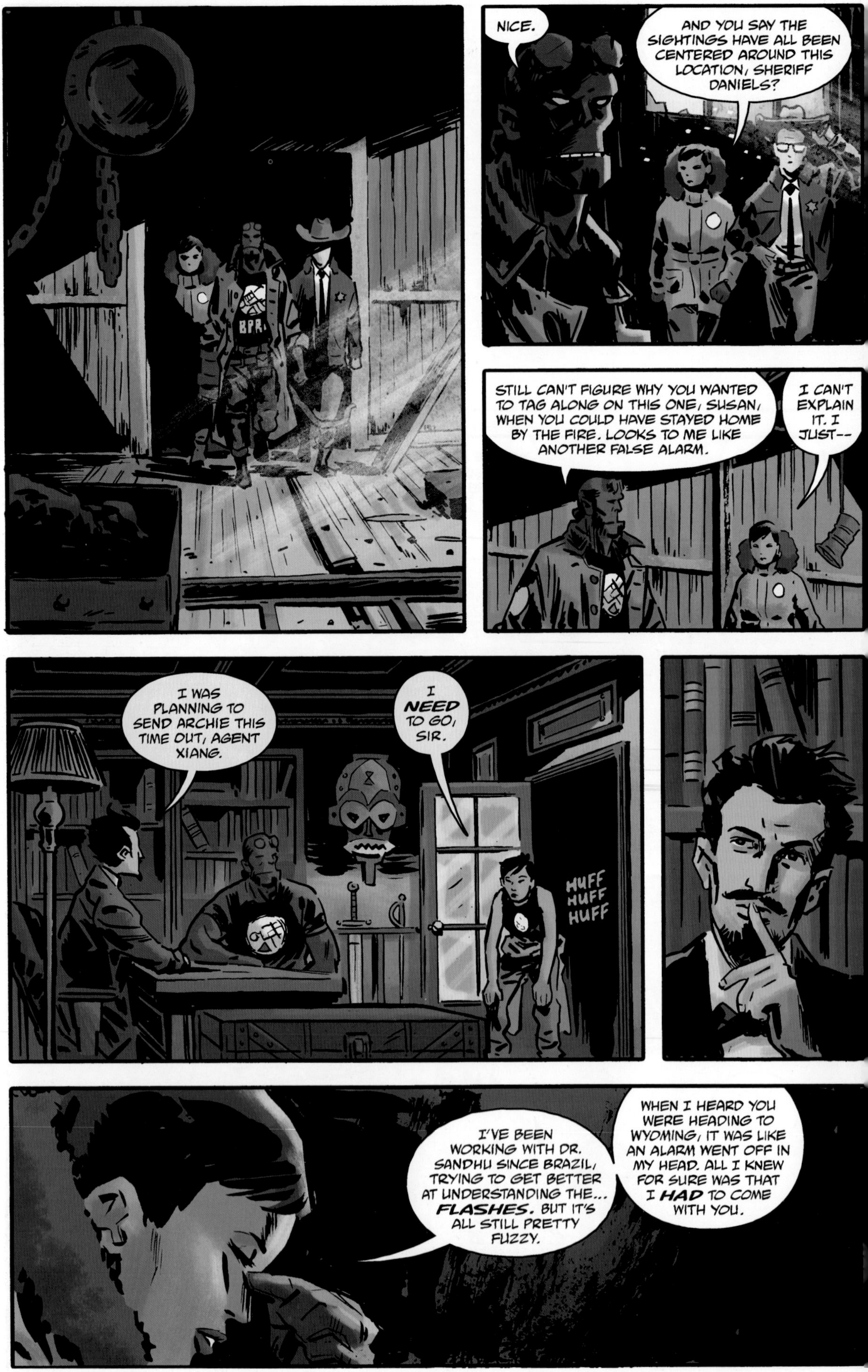
NICE.
AND YOU SAY THE SIGHTINGS HAVE ALL BEEN CENTERED AROUND THIS LOCATION, SHERIFF DANIELS?
STILL CAN'T FIGURE WHY YOU WANTED TO TAG ALONG ON THIS ONE, SUSAN, WHEN YOU COULD HAVE STAYED HOME BY THE FIRE. LOOKS TO ME LIKE ANOTHER FALSE ALARM.
I CAN'T EXPLAIN IT. I JUST--
I WAS PLANNING TO SEND ARCHIE THIS TIME OUT, AGENT XIANG.
I NEED TO GO, SIR.
HUFF HUFF HUFF
I'VE BEEN WORKING WITH DR. SANDHU SINCE BRAZIL, TRYING TO GET BETTER AT UNDERSTANDING THE... FLASHES. BUT IT'S ALL STILL PRETTY FUZZY.
WHEN I HEARD YOU WERE HEADING TO WYOMING, IT WAS LIKE AN ALARM WENT OFF IN MY HEAD. ALL I KNEW FOR SURE WAS THAT I HAD TO COME WITH YOU.

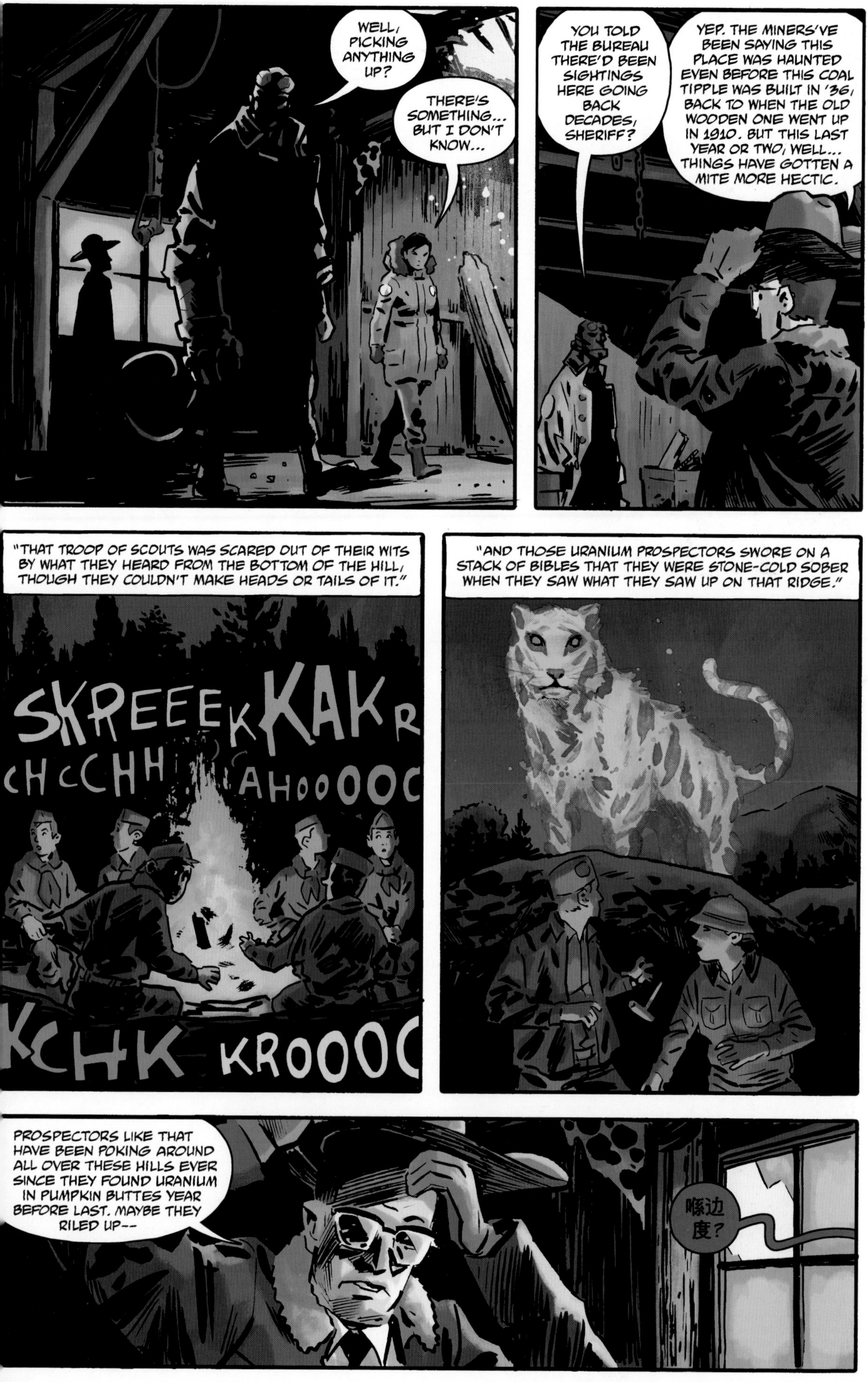
WELL, PICKING ANYTHING UP?
THERE'S SOMETHING... BUT I DON'T KNOW...
YOU TOLD THE BUREAU THERE'D BEEN SIGHTINGS HERE GOING BACK DECADES, SHERIFF?
YEP. THE MINERS'VE BEEN SAYING THIS PLACE WAS HAUNTED EVEN BEFORE THIS COAL TIPPLE WAS BUILT IN '36, BACK TO WHEN THE OLD WOODEN ONE WENT UP IN 1910. BUT THIS LAST YEAR OR TWO, WELL... THINGS HAVE GOTTEN A MITE MORE HECTIC.
"THAT TROOP OF SCOUTS WAS SCARED OUT OF THEIR WITS BY WHAT THEY HEARD FROM THE BOTTOM OF THE HILL, THOUGH THEY COULDN'T MAKE HEADS OR TAILS OF IT."
SKREEEKKAKR
CHCCHH
AHOOOOC
KCHK
KROOOC
"AND THOSE URANIUM PROSPECTORS SWORE ON A STACK OF BIBLES THAT THEY WERE STONE-COLD SOBER WHEN THEY SAW WHAT THEY SAW UP ON THAT RIDGE."
PROSPECTORS LIKE THAT HAVE BEEN POKING AROUND ALL OVER THESE HILLS EVER SINCE THEY FOUND URANIUM IN PUMPKIN BUTTES YEAR BEFORE LAST. MAYBE THEY RILED UP--
喺边度?

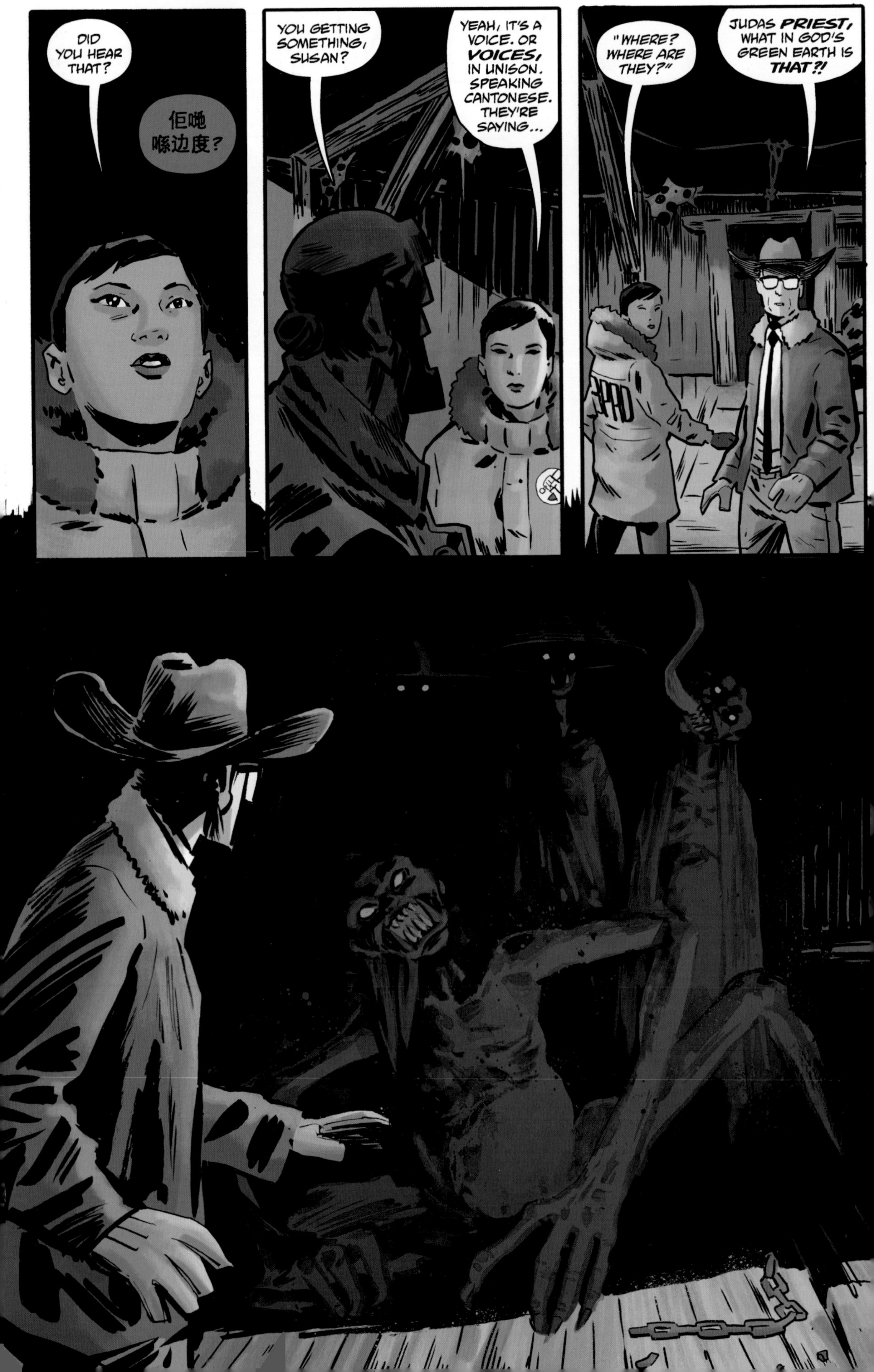

DID YOU HEAR THAT?
佢哋喺边度?
YOU GETTING SOMETHING, SUSAN?
YEAH, IT'S A VOICE. OR VOICES, IN UNISON. SPEAKING CANTONESE. THEY'RE SAYING...
"WHERE? WHERE ARE THEY?"
JUDAS PRIEST, WHAT IN GOD'S GREEN EARTH IS THAT?!

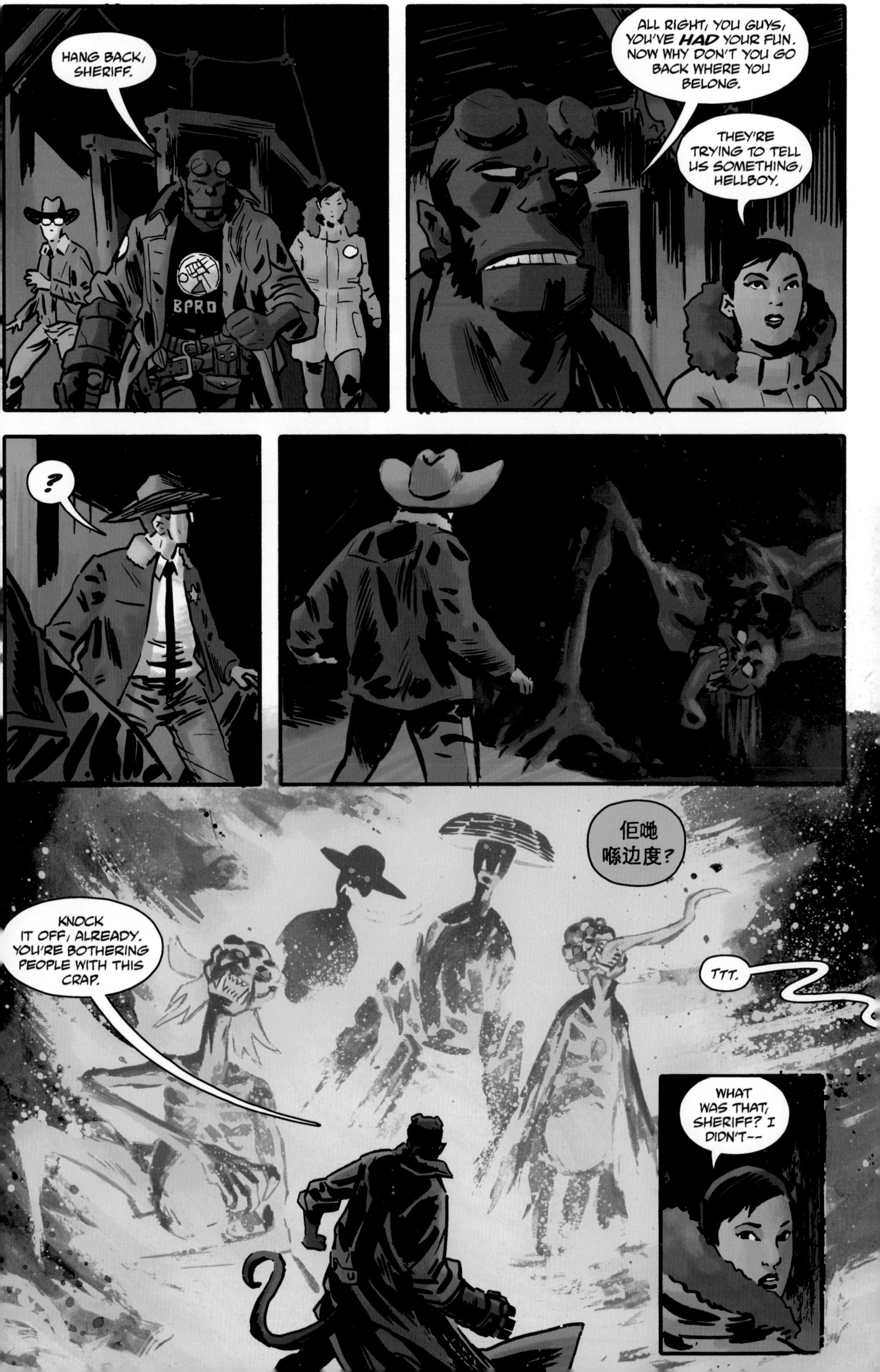
HANG BACK, SHERIFF.
ALL RIGHT, YOU GUYS, YOU'VE **HAD** YOUR FUN. NOW WHY DON'T YOU GO BACK WHERE YOU BELONG.
THEY'RE TRYING TO TELL US SOMETHING, HELLBOY.
?
佢哋喺边度?
KNOCK IT OFF, ALREADY. YOU'RE BOTHERING PEOPLE WITH THIS CRAP.
TTT.
WHAT WAS THAT, SHERIFF? I DIDN'T--

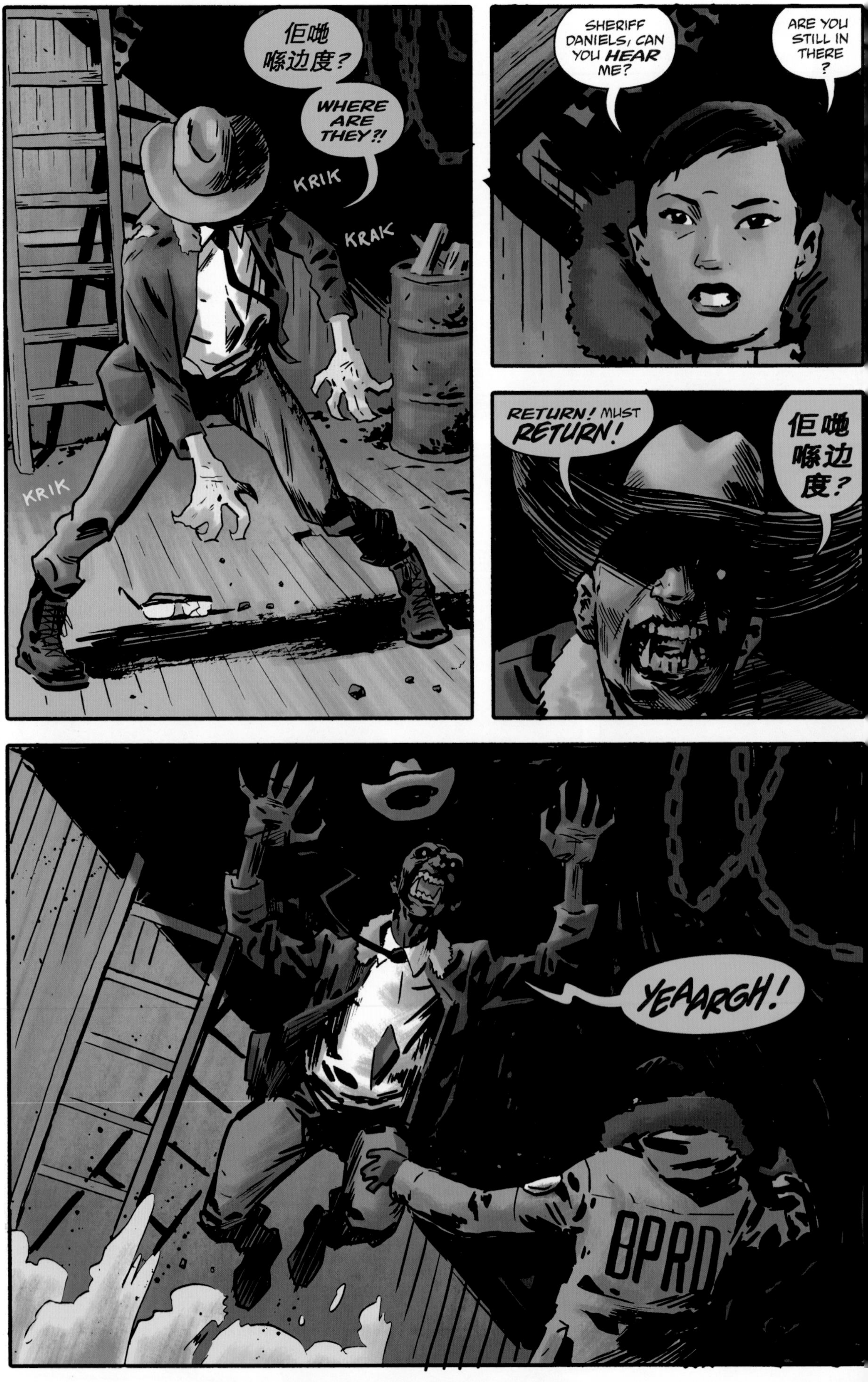

佢哋喺边度?
WHERE ARE THEY?!
KRIK
KRAK
KRIK
SHERIFF DANIELS, CAN YOU HEAR ME?
ARE YOU STILL IN THERE?
RETURN! MUST RETURN!
佢哋喺边度?
YEAARGH!
BPRD

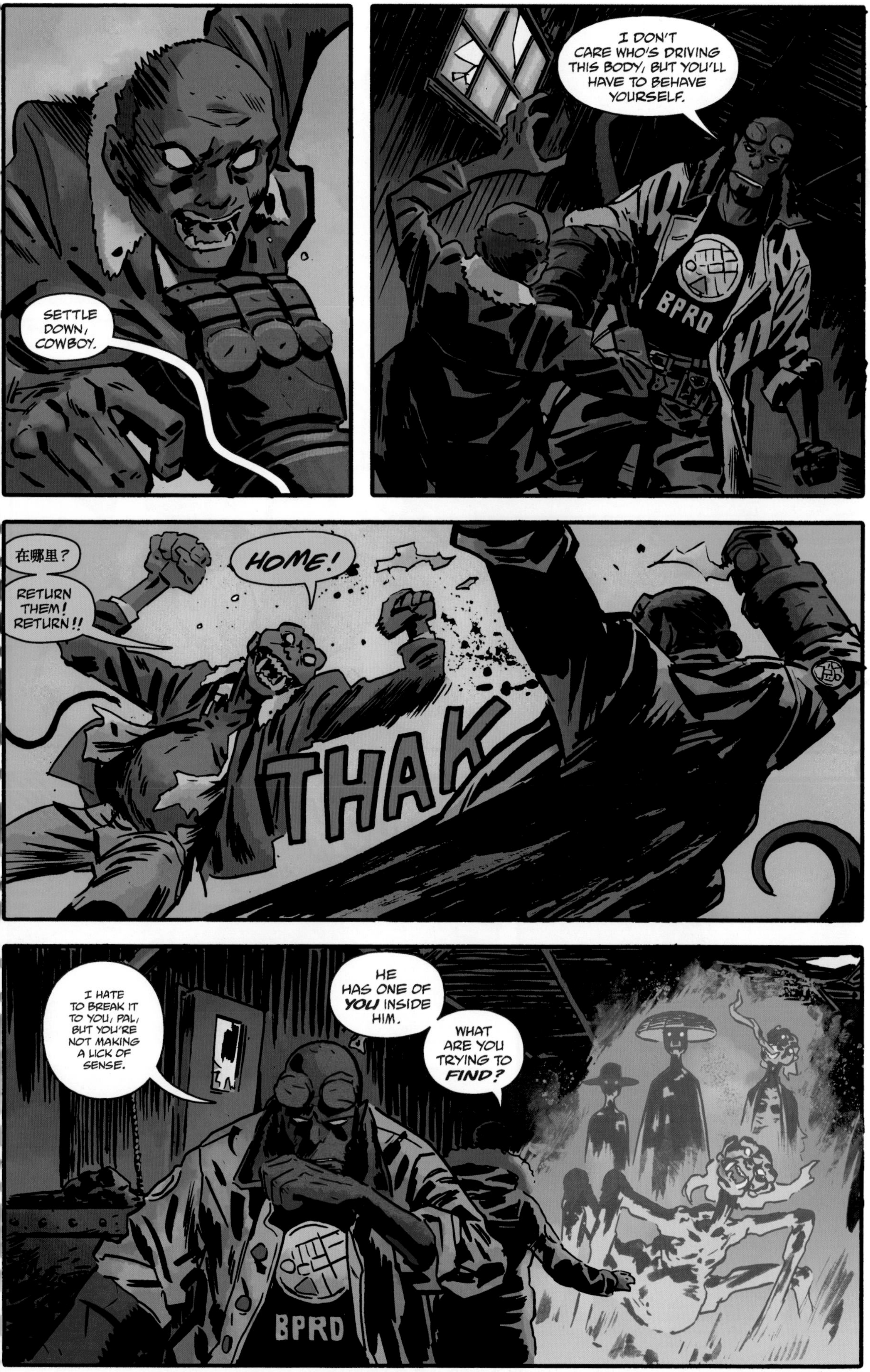
SETTLE DOWN, COWBOY.
I DON'T CARE WHO'S DRIVING THIS BODY, BUT YOU'LL HAVE TO BEHAVE YOURSELF.
在哪里？
RETURN THEM! RETURN!!
HOME!
THAK
I HATE TO BREAK IT TO YOU, PAL, BUT YOU'RE NOT MAKING A LICK OF SENSE.
HE HAS ONE OF YOU INSIDE HIM.
WHAT ARE YOU TRYING TO FIND?
BPRD

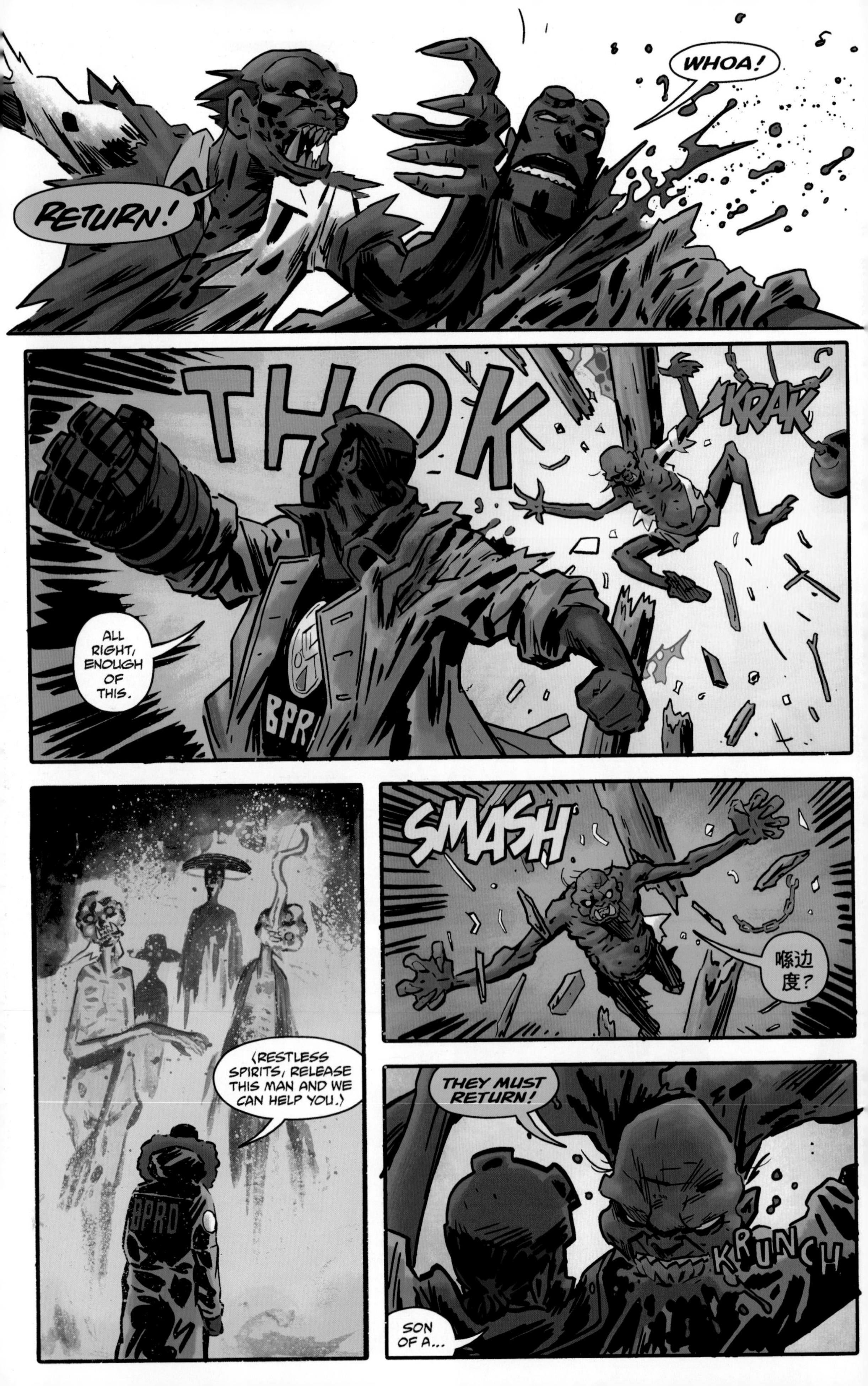
RETURN!
WHOA!
THOK
KRAK
ALL RIGHT, ENOUGH OF THIS.
SMASH
喺边度?
⟨RESTLESS SPIRITS, RELEASE THIS MAN AND WE CAN HELP YOU.⟩
THEY MUST RETURN!
KRUNCH
SON OF A...

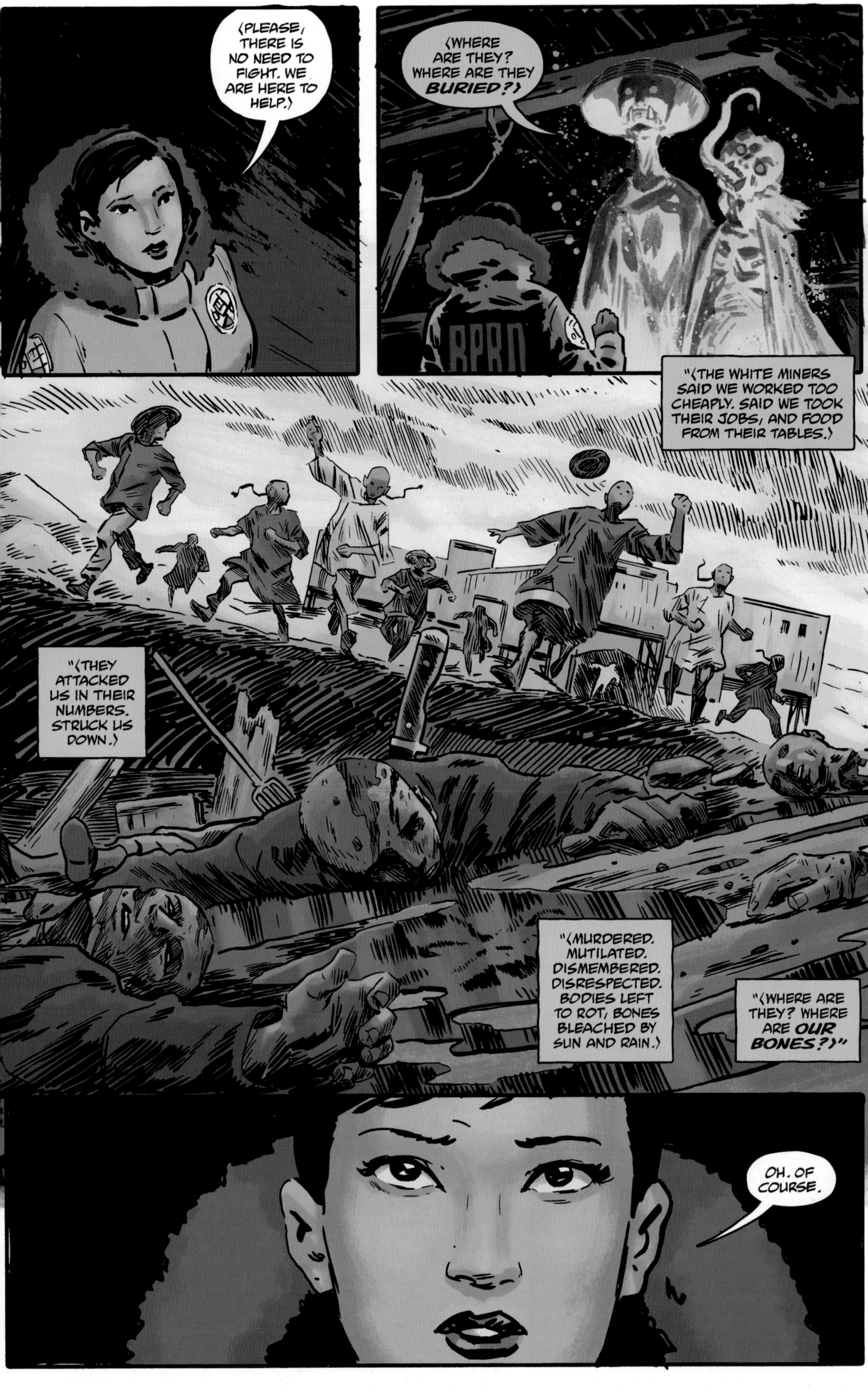
<PLEASE, THERE IS NO NEED TO FIGHT. WE ARE HERE TO HELP.>
<WHERE ARE THEY? WHERE ARE THEY **BURIED?**>
BPRD
"<THE WHITE MINERS SAID WE WORKED TOO CHEAPLY. SAID WE TOOK THEIR JOBS, AND FOOD FROM THEIR TABLES.>
"<THEY ATTACKED US IN THEIR NUMBERS. STRUCK US DOWN.>
"<MURDERED. MUTILATED. DISMEMBERED. DISRESPECTED. BODIES LEFT TO ROT, BONES BLEACHED BY SUN AND RAIN.>
"<WHERE ARE THEY? WHERE ARE **OUR BONES?**>"
OH. OF COURSE.

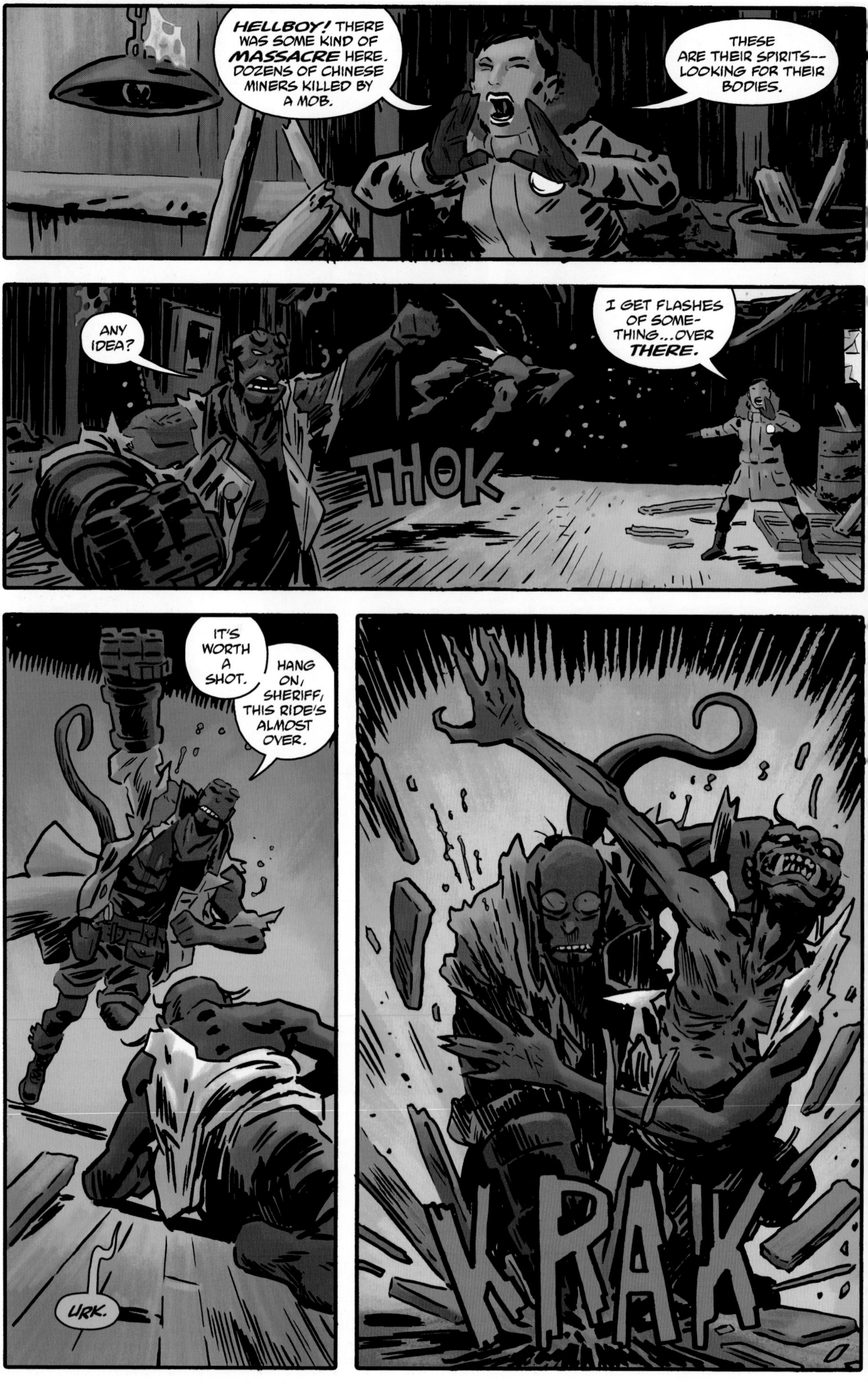
HELLBOY! THERE WAS SOME KIND OF MASSACRE HERE. DOZENS OF CHINESE MINERS KILLED BY A MOB.
THESE ARE THEIR SPIRITS-- LOOKING FOR THEIR BODIES.
ANY IDEA?
I GET FLASHES OF SOME-THING...OVER THERE.
THOK
IT'S WORTH A SHOT.
HANG ON, SHERIFF, THIS RIDE'S ALMOST OVER.
URK.
KRAK

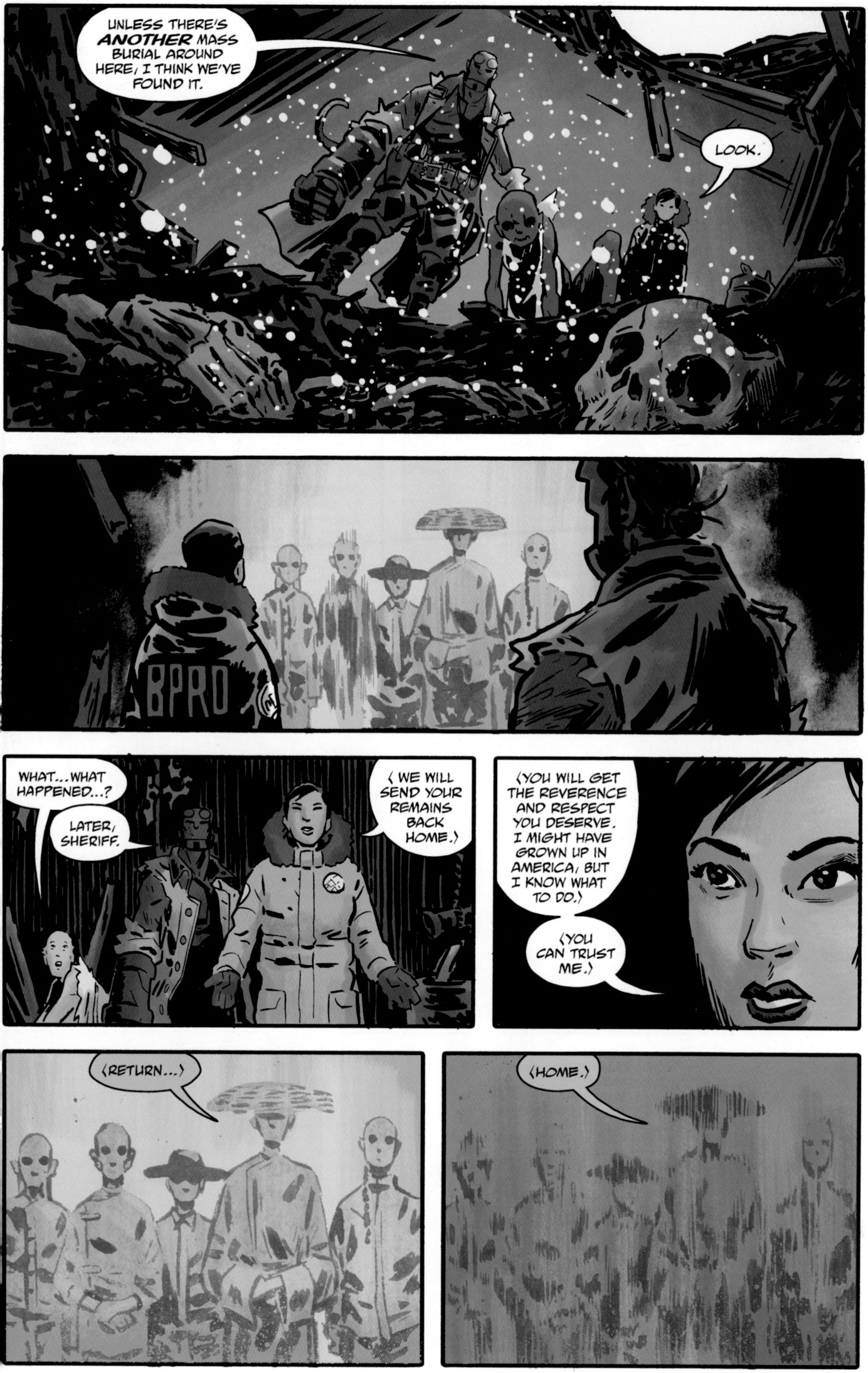
UNLESS THERE'S ANOTHER MASS BURIAL AROUND HERE, I THINK WE'VE FOUND IT.
LOOK.
BPRD
WHAT...WHAT HAPPENED...?
LATER, SHERIFF.
‹ WE WILL SEND YOUR REMAINS BACK HOME.›
‹YOU WILL GET THE REVERENCE AND RESPECT YOU DESERVE. I MIGHT HAVE GROWN UP IN AMERICA, BUT I KNOW WHAT TO DO.›
‹YOU CAN TRUST ME.›
‹RETURN...›
‹HOME.›

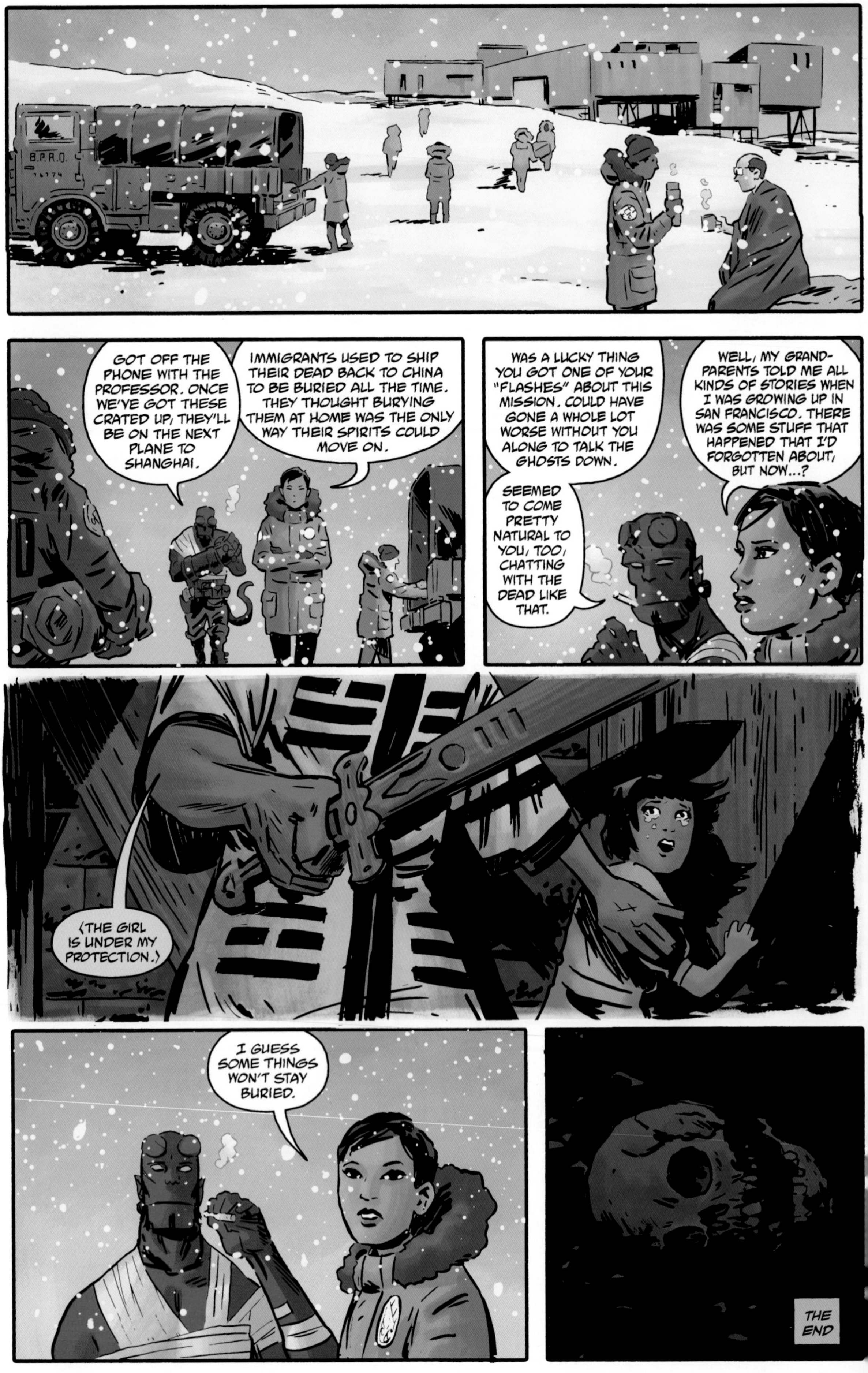
B.P.R.O.
GOT OFF THE PHONE WITH THE PROFESSOR. ONCE WE'VE GOT THESE CRATED UP, THEY'LL BE ON THE NEXT PLANE TO SHANGHAI.
IMMIGRANTS USED TO SHIP THEIR DEAD BACK TO CHINA TO BE BURIED ALL THE TIME. THEY THOUGHT BURYING THEM AT HOME WAS THE ONLY WAY THEIR SPIRITS COULD MOVE ON.
WAS A LUCKY THING YOU GOT ONE OF YOUR "FLASHES" ABOUT THIS MISSION. COULD HAVE GONE A WHOLE LOT WORSE WITHOUT YOU ALONG TO TALK THE GHOSTS DOWN.
SEEMED TO COME PRETTY NATURAL TO YOU, TOO, CHATTING WITH THE DEAD LIKE THAT.
WELL, MY GRAND-PARENTS TOLD ME ALL KINDS OF STORIES WHEN I WAS GROWING UP IN SAN FRANCISCO. THERE WAS SOME STUFF THAT HAPPENED THAT I'D FORGOTTEN ABOUT, BUT NOW...?
⟨THE GIRL IS UNDER MY PROTECTION.⟩
I GUESS SOME THINGS WON'T STAY BURIED.
THE END

BEYOND THE FENCES

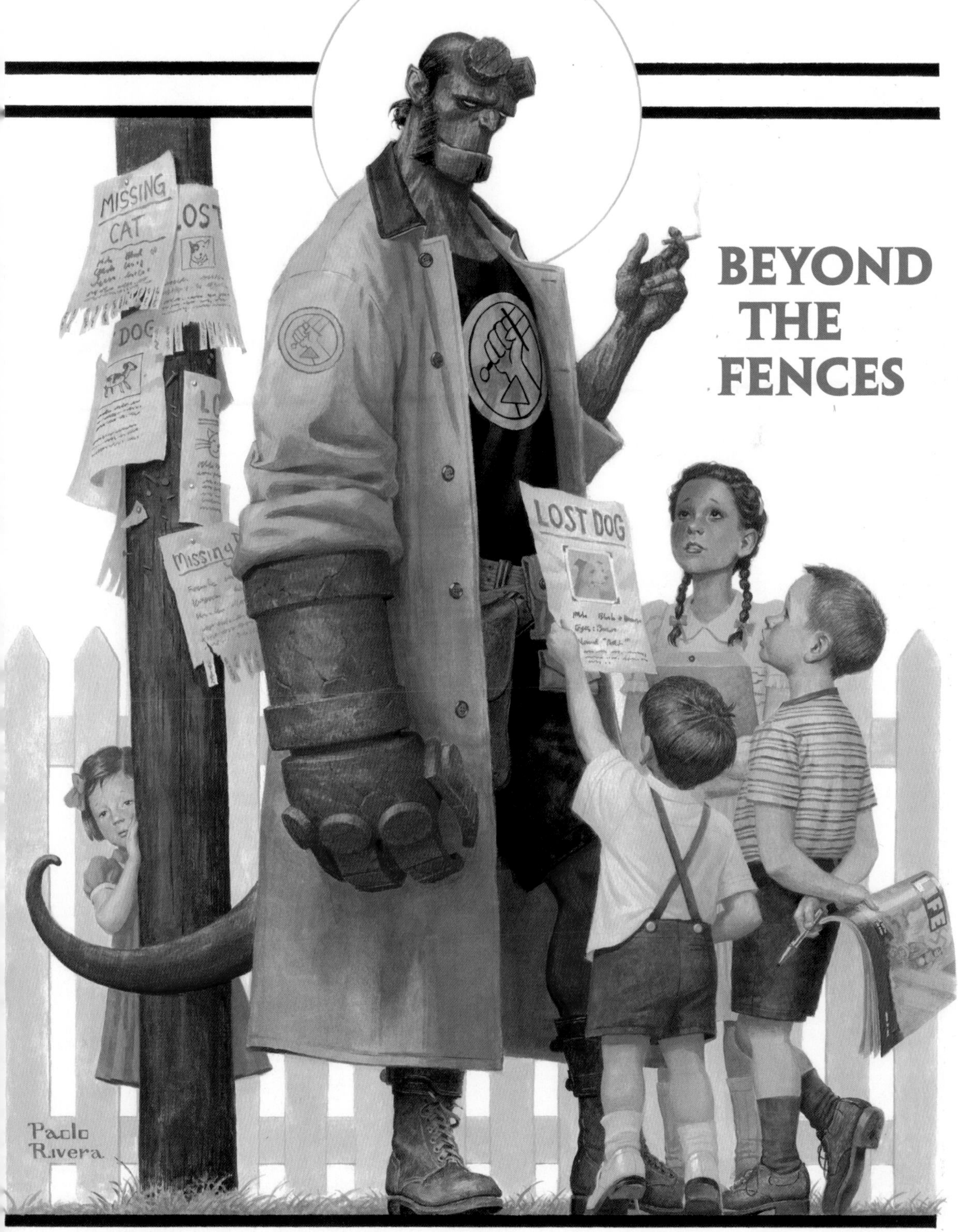
MISSING CAT
LOST
DOG
LOST DOG
Missing
Paolo Rivera
LIFE

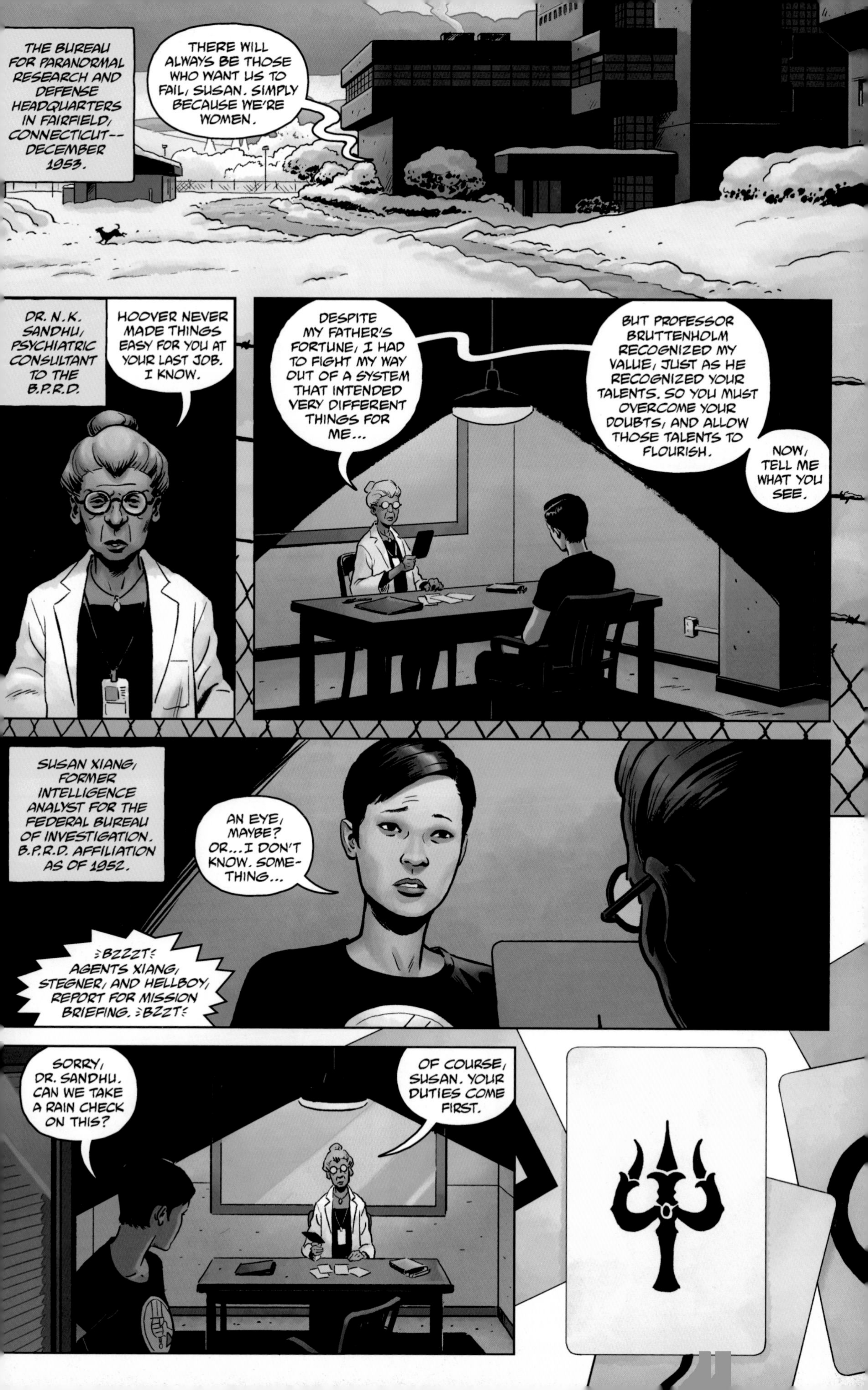
THE BUREAU FOR PARANORMAL RESEARCH AND DEFENSE HEADQUARTERS IN FAIRFIELD, CONNECTICUT--DECEMBER 1953.
THERE WILL ALWAYS BE THOSE WHO WANT US TO FAIL, SUSAN. SIMPLY BECAUSE WE'RE WOMEN.
DR. N. K. SANDHU, PSYCHIATRIC CONSULTANT TO THE B.P.R.D.
HOOVER NEVER MADE THINGS EASY FOR YOU AT YOUR LAST JOB. I KNOW.
DESPITE MY FATHER'S FORTUNE, I HAD TO FIGHT MY WAY OUT OF A SYSTEM THAT INTENDED VERY DIFFERENT THINGS FOR ME...
BUT PROFESSOR BRUTTENHOLM RECOGNIZED MY VALUE, JUST AS HE RECOGNIZED YOUR TALENTS. SO YOU MUST OVERCOME YOUR DOUBTS, AND ALLOW THOSE TALENTS TO FLOURISH.
NOW, TELL ME WHAT YOU SEE.
SUSAN XIANG, FORMER INTELLIGENCE ANALYST FOR THE FEDERAL BUREAU OF INVESTIGATION. B.P.R.D. AFFILIATION AS OF 1952.
AN EYE, MAYBE? OR...I DON'T KNOW. SOME-THING...
BZZZT AGENTS XIANG, STEGNER, AND HELLBOY, REPORT FOR MISSION BRIEFING. BZZT
SORRY, DR. SANDHU. CAN WE TAKE A RAIN CHECK ON THIS?
OF COURSE, SUSAN. YOUR DUTIES COME FIRST.

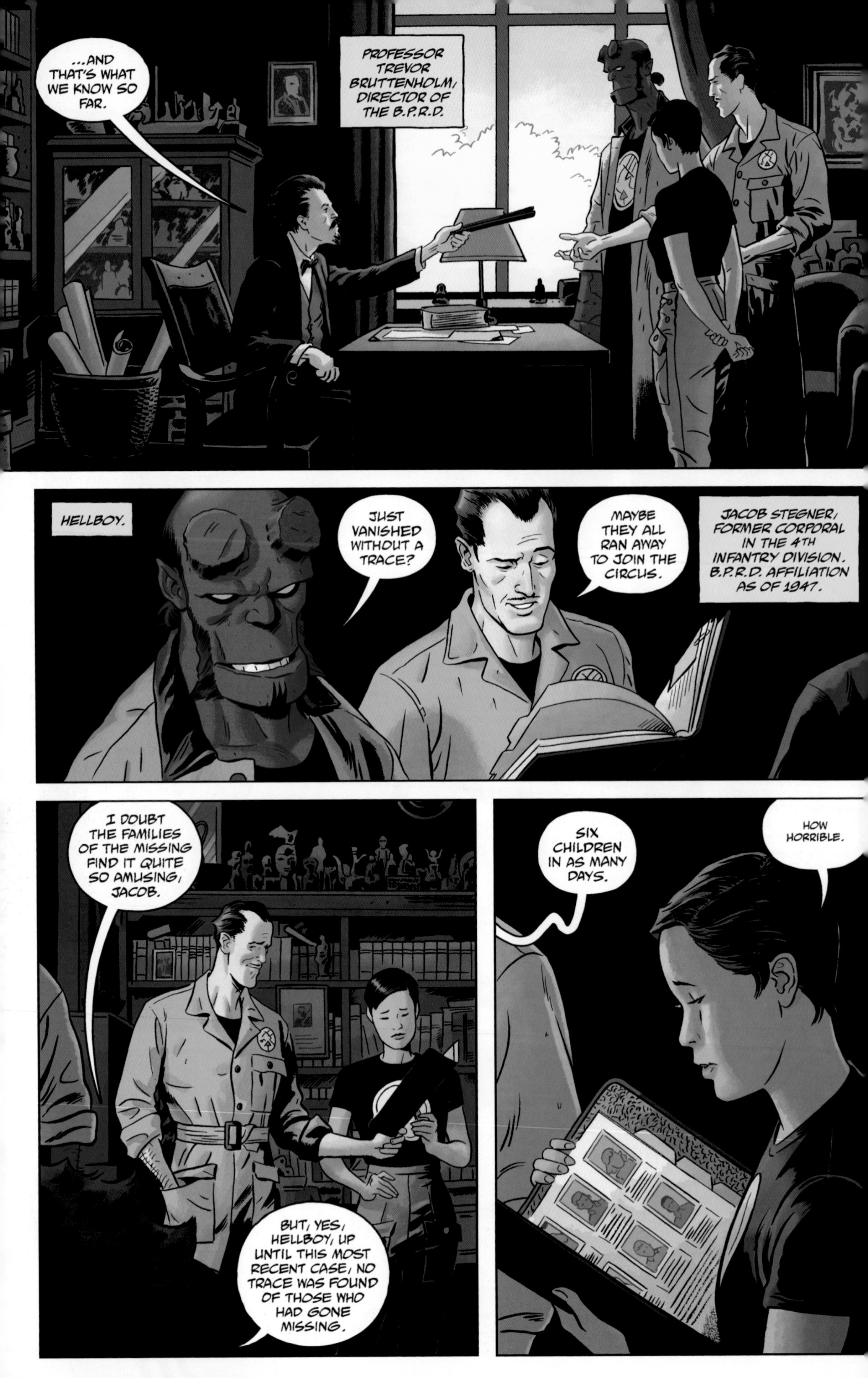
...AND THAT'S WHAT WE KNOW SO FAR.
PROFESSOR TREVOR BRUTTENHOLM, DIRECTOR OF THE B.P.R.D.
HELLBOY.
JUST VANISHED WITHOUT A TRACE?
MAYBE THEY ALL RAN AWAY TO JOIN THE CIRCUS.
JACOB STEGNER, FORMER CORPORAL IN THE 4TH INFANTRY DIVISION. B.P.R.D. AFFILIATION AS OF 1947.
I DOUBT THE FAMILIES OF THE MISSING FIND IT QUITE SO AMUSING, JACOB.
BUT, YES, HELLBOY, UP UNTIL THIS MOST RECENT CASE, NO TRACE WAS FOUND OF THOSE WHO HAD GONE MISSING.
SIX CHILDREN IN AS MANY DAYS.
HOW HORRIBLE.

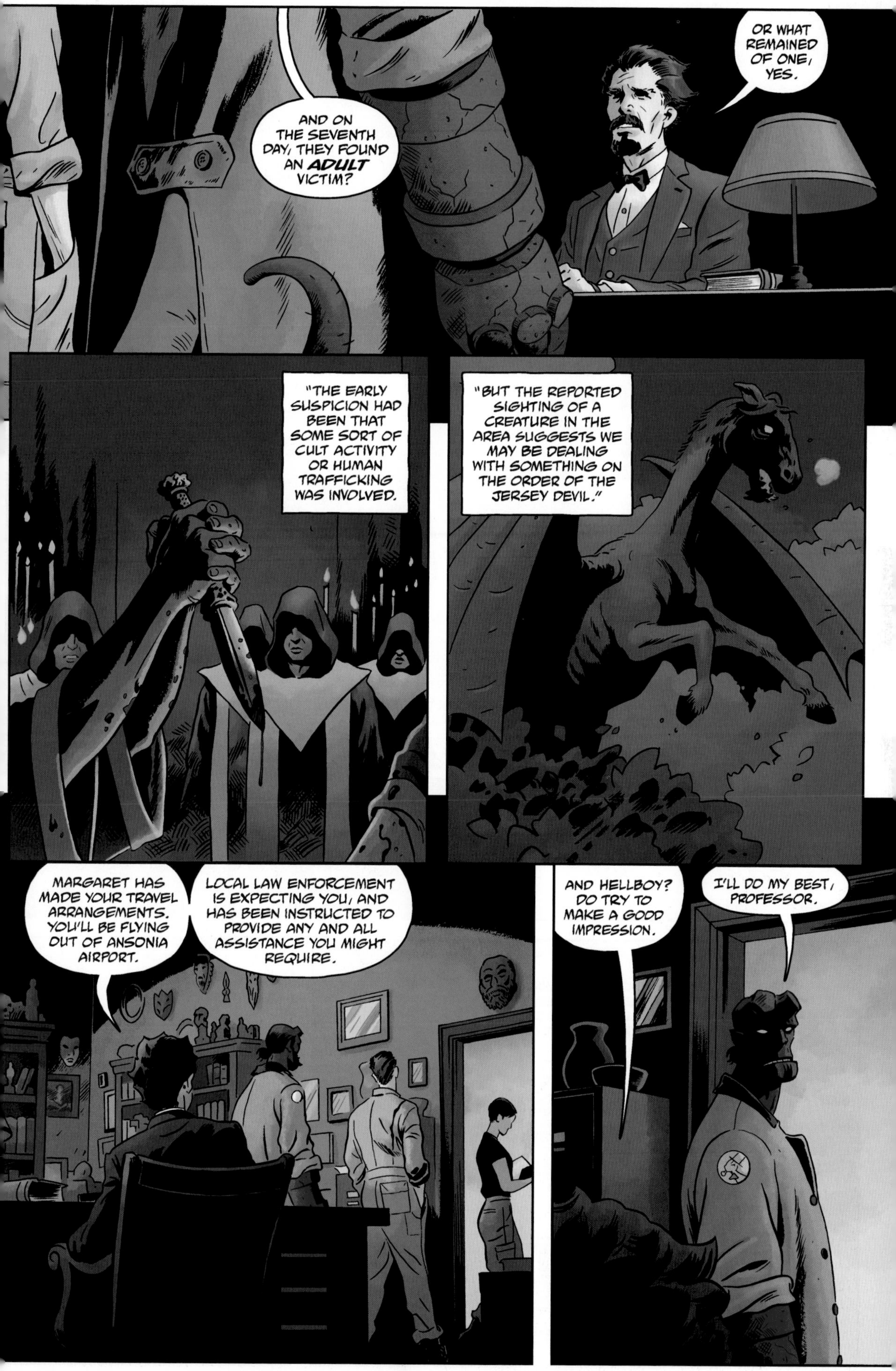
AND ON THE SEVENTH DAY, THEY FOUND AN ADULT VICTIM?
OR WHAT REMAINED OF ONE, YES.
"THE EARLY SUSPICION HAD BEEN THAT SOME SORT OF CULT ACTIVITY OR HUMAN TRAFFICKING WAS INVOLVED.
"BUT THE REPORTED SIGHTING OF A CREATURE IN THE AREA SUGGESTS WE MAY BE DEALING WITH SOMETHING ON THE ORDER OF THE JERSEY DEVIL."
MARGARET HAS MADE YOUR TRAVEL ARRANGEMENTS. YOU'LL BE FLYING OUT OF ANSONIA AIRPORT.
LOCAL LAW ENFORCEMENT IS EXPECTING YOU, AND HAS BEEN INSTRUCTED TO PROVIDE ANY AND ALL ASSISTANCE YOU MIGHT REQUIRE.
AND HELLBOY? DO TRY TO MAKE A GOOD IMPRESSION.
I'LL DO MY BEST, PROFESSOR.

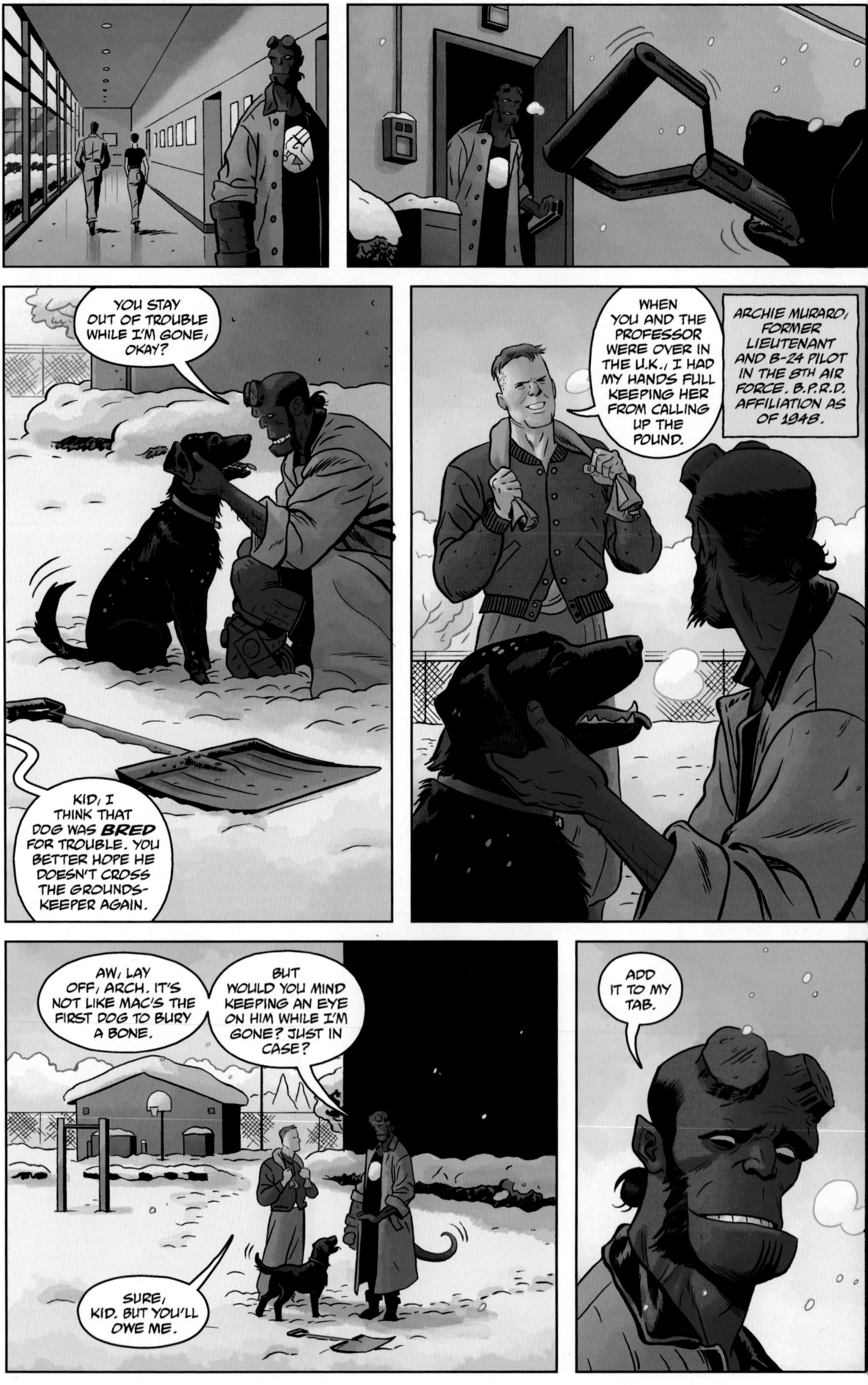
YOU STAY OUT OF TROUBLE WHILE I'M GONE, OKAY?
WHEN YOU AND THE PROFESSOR WERE OVER IN THE U.K., I HAD MY HANDS FULL KEEPING HER FROM CALLING UP THE POUND.
ARCHIE MURARO, FORMER LIEUTENANT AND B-24 PILOT IN THE 8TH AIR FORCE. B.P.R.D. AFFILIATION AS OF 1948.
KID, I THINK THAT DOG WAS BRED FOR TROUBLE. YOU BETTER HOPE HE DOESN'T CROSS THE GROUNDS-KEEPER AGAIN.
AW, LAY OFF, ARCH. IT'S NOT LIKE MAC'S THE FIRST DOG TO BURY A BONE.
BUT WOULD YOU MIND KEEPING AN EYE ON HIM WHILE I'M GONE? JUST IN CASE?
SURE, KID. BUT YOU'LL OWE ME.
ADD IT TO MY TAB.

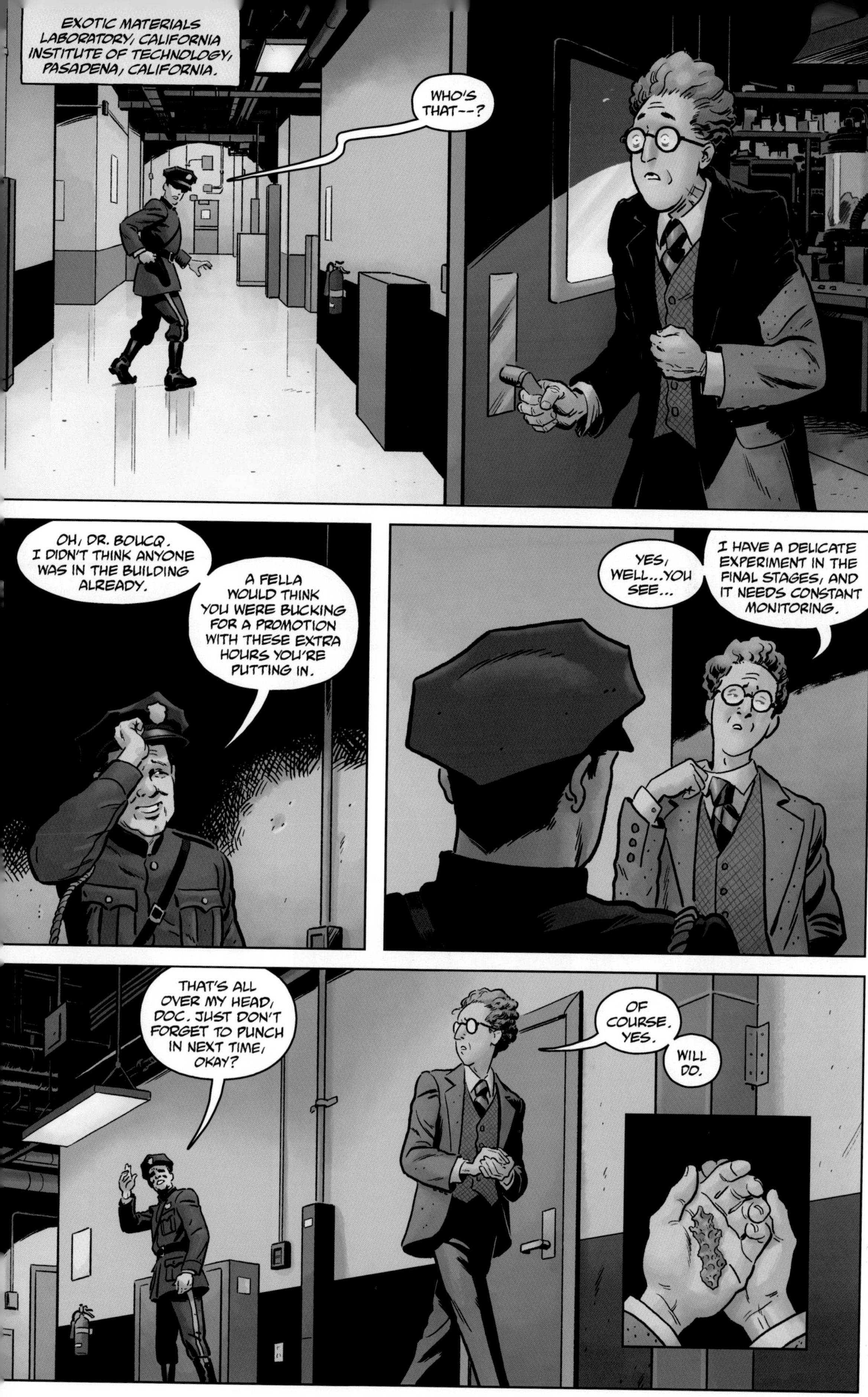
EXOTIC MATERIALS LABORATORY, CALIFORNIA INSTITUTE OF TECHNOLOGY, PASADENA, CALIFORNIA.
WHO'S THAT--?
OH, DR. BOUCQ. I DIDN'T THINK ANYONE WAS IN THE BUILDING ALREADY.
A FELLA WOULD THINK YOU WERE BUCKING FOR A PROMOTION WITH THESE EXTRA HOURS YOU'RE PUTTING IN.
YES, WELL...YOU SEE...
I HAVE A DELICATE EXPERIMENT IN THE FINAL STAGES, AND IT NEEDS CONSTANT MONITORING.
THAT'S ALL OVER MY HEAD, DOC. JUST DON'T FORGET TO PUNCH IN NEXT TIME, OKAY?
OF COURSE. YES.
WILL DO.

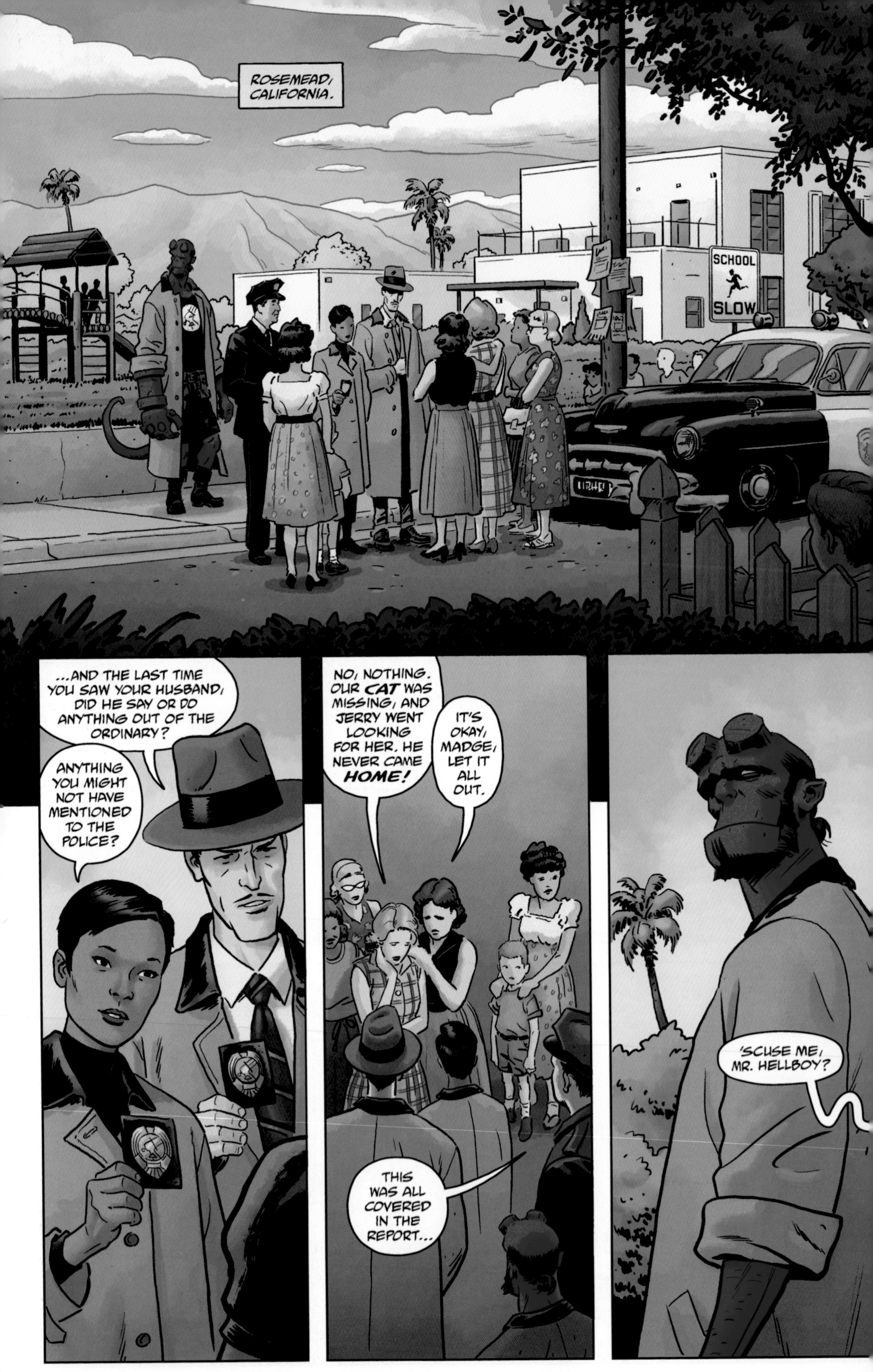
ROSEMEAD, CALIFORNIA.
SCHOOL SLOW
...AND THE LAST TIME YOU SAW YOUR HUSBAND, DID HE SAY OR DO ANYTHING OUT OF THE ORDINARY?
ANYTHING YOU MIGHT NOT HAVE MENTIONED TO THE POLICE?
NO, NOTHING. OUR CAT WAS MISSING, AND JERRY WENT LOOKING FOR HER. HE NEVER CAME HOME!
IT'S OKAY, MADGE, LET IT ALL OUT.
THIS WAS ALL COVERED IN THE REPORT...
'SCUSE ME, MR. HELLBOY?

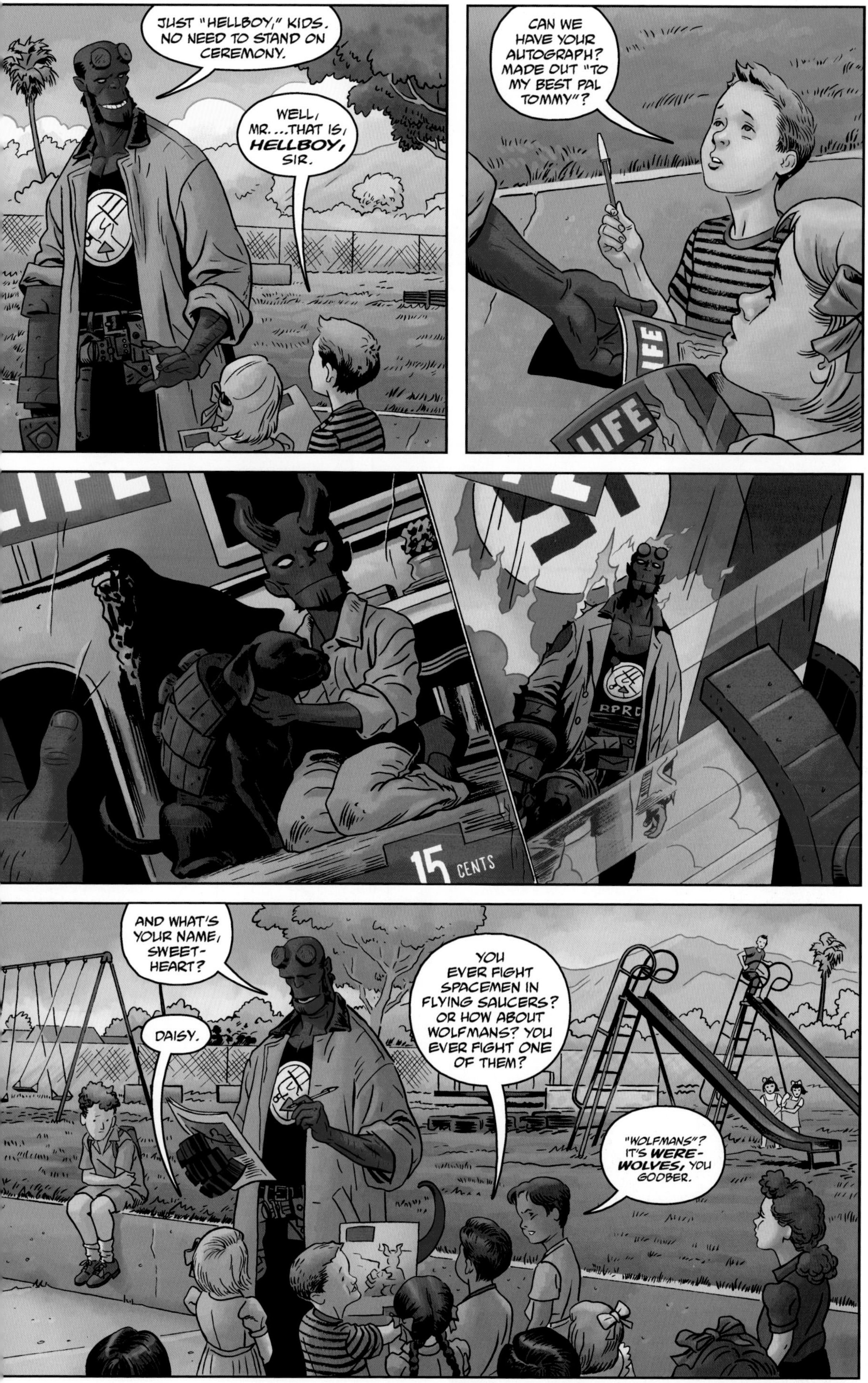
JUST "HELLBOY," KIDS. NO NEED TO STAND ON CEREMONY.
WELL, MR. ...THAT IS, HELLBOY, SIR.
CAN WE HAVE YOUR AUTOGRAPH? MADE OUT "TO MY BEST PAL TOMMY"?
LIFE
LIFE
LIFE
15 CENTS
BPRD
AND WHAT'S YOUR NAME, SWEET-HEART?
DAISY.
YOU EVER FIGHT SPACEMEN IN FLYING SAUCERS? OR HOW ABOUT WOLFMANS? YOU EVER FIGHT ONE OF THEM?
"WOLFMANS"? IT'S WERE-WOLVES, YOU GOOBER.

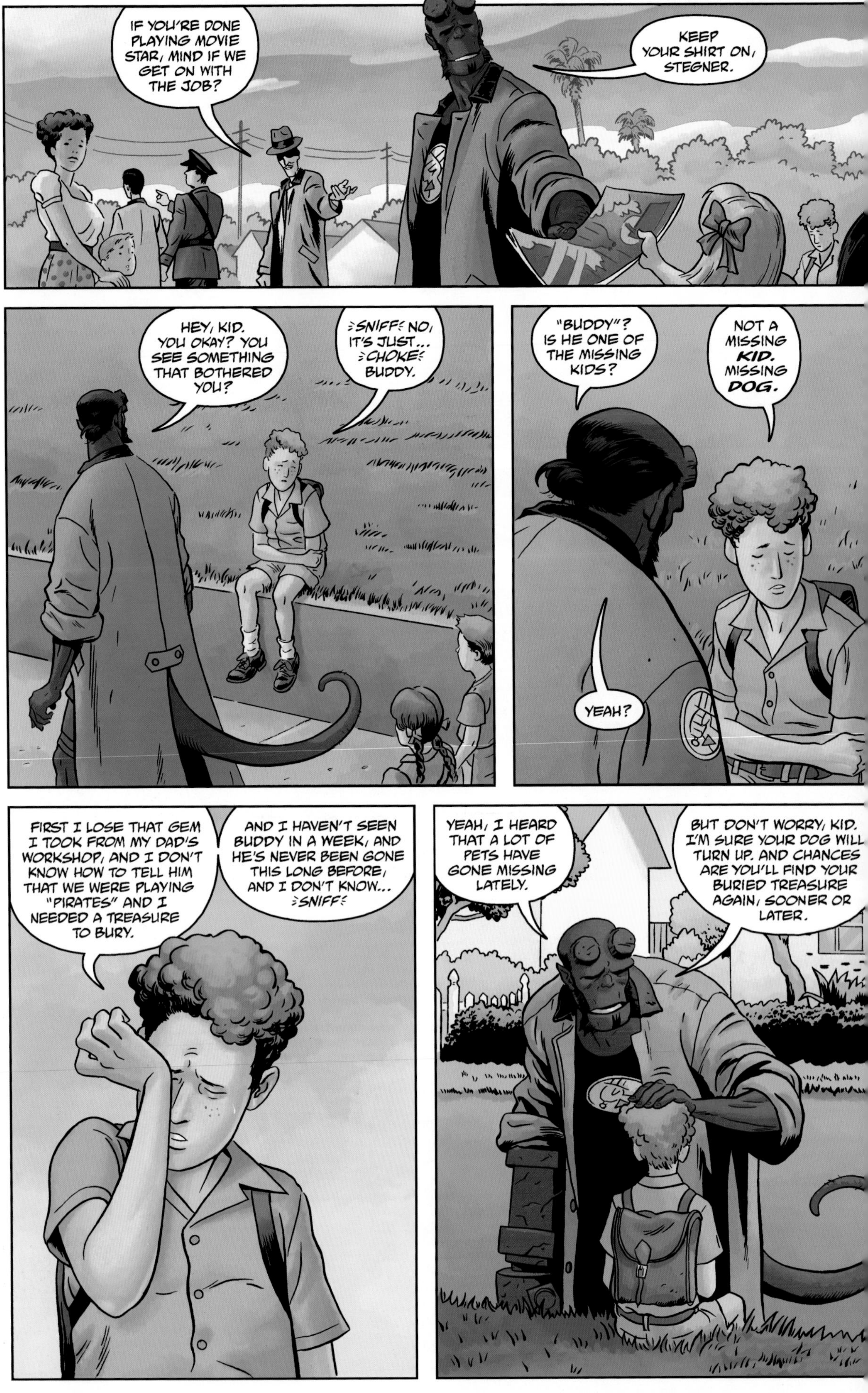
IF YOU'RE DONE PLAYING MOVIE STAR, MIND IF WE GET ON WITH THE JOB?
KEEP YOUR SHIRT ON, STEGNER.
HEY, KID. YOU OKAY? YOU SEE SOMETHING THAT BOTHERED YOU?
SNIFF NO, IT'S JUST... CHOKE BUDDY.
"BUDDY"? IS HE ONE OF THE MISSING KIDS?
NOT A MISSING KID. MISSING DOG.
YEAH?
FIRST I LOSE THAT GEM I TOOK FROM MY DAD'S WORKSHOP, AND I DON'T KNOW HOW TO TELL HIM THAT WE WERE PLAYING "PIRATES" AND I NEEDED A TREASURE TO BURY.
AND I HAVEN'T SEEN BUDDY IN A WEEK, AND HE'S NEVER BEEN GONE THIS LONG BEFORE, AND I DON'T KNOW... SNIFF
YEAH, I HEARD THAT A LOT OF PETS HAVE GONE MISSING LATELY.
BUT DON'T WORRY, KID. I'M SURE YOUR DOG WILL TURN UP. AND CHANCES ARE YOU'LL FIND YOUR BURIED TREASURE AGAIN, SOONER OR LATER.

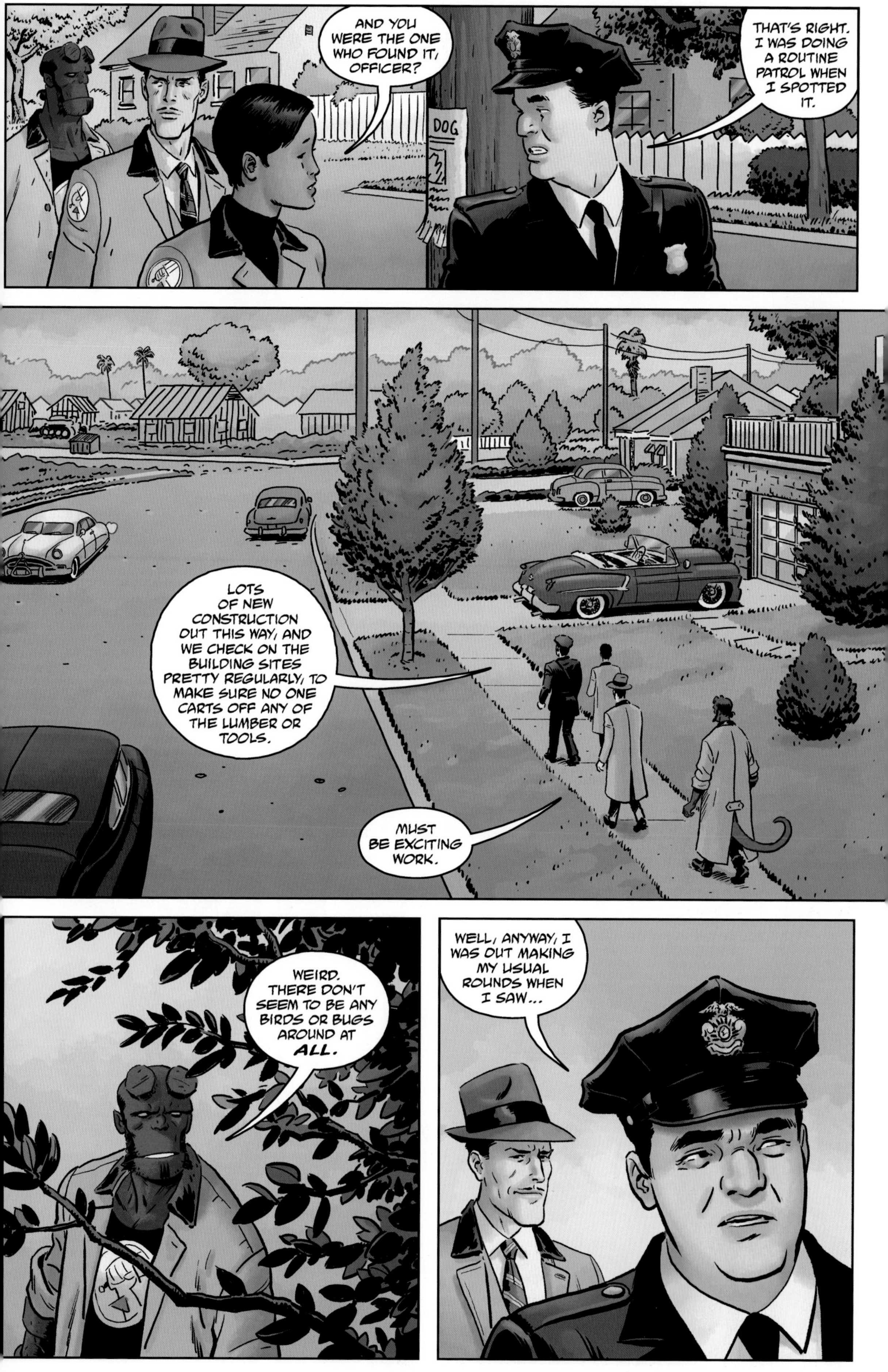
AND YOU WERE THE ONE WHO FOUND IT, OFFICER?
THAT'S RIGHT. I WAS DOING A ROUTINE PATROL WHEN I SPOTTED IT.
DOG
LOTS OF NEW CONSTRUCTION OUT THIS WAY, AND WE CHECK ON THE BUILDING SITES PRETTY REGULARLY, TO MAKE SURE NO ONE CARTS OFF ANY OF THE LUMBER OR TOOLS.
MUST BE EXCITING WORK.
WEIRD. THERE DON'T SEEM TO BE ANY BIRDS OR BUGS AROUND AT ALL.
WELL, ANYWAY, I WAS OUT MAKING MY USUAL ROUNDS WHEN I SAW...

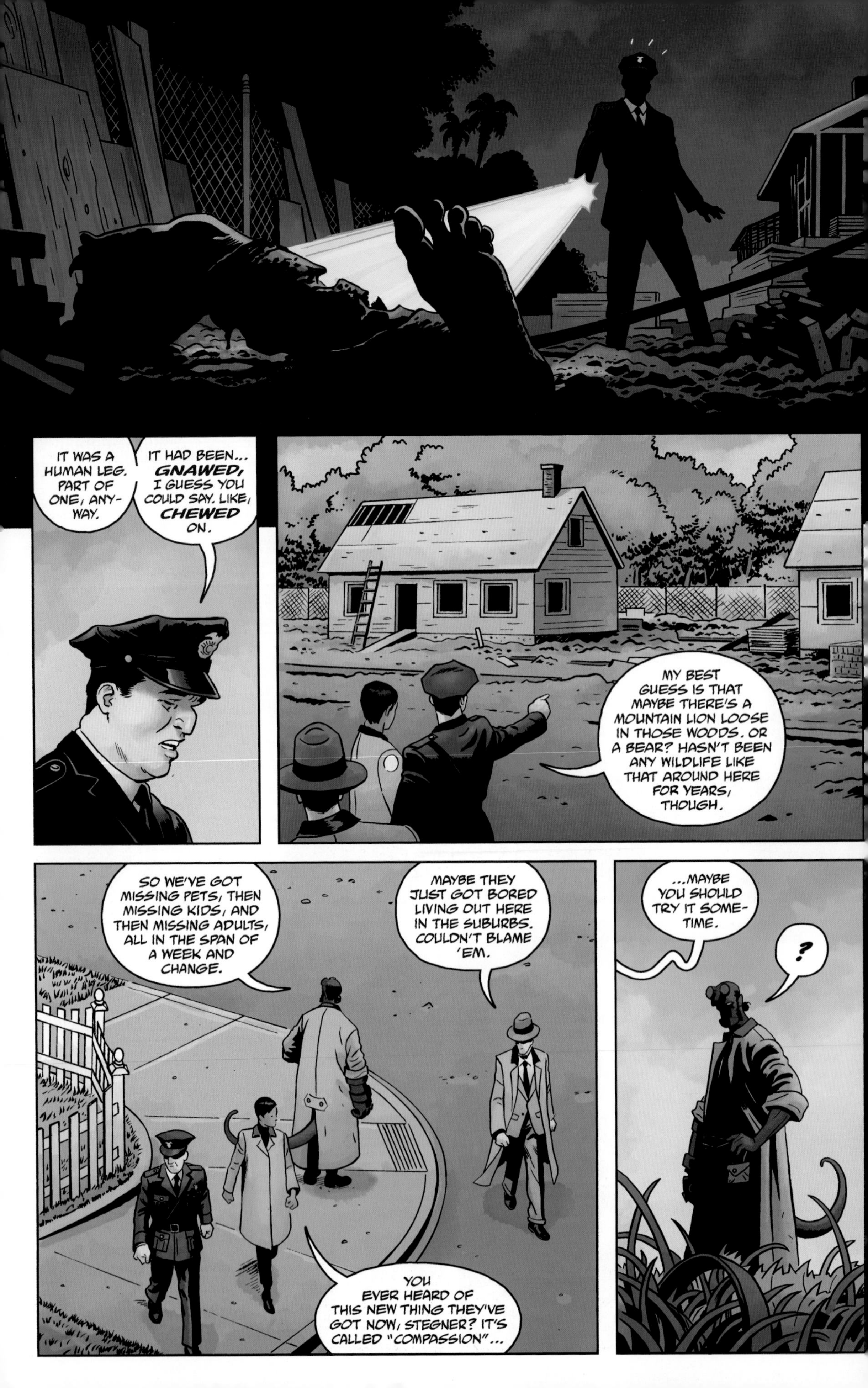
IT WAS A HUMAN LEG. PART OF ONE, ANY-WAY.
IT HAD BEEN... GNAWED, I GUESS YOU COULD SAY. LIKE, CHEWED ON.
MY BEST GUESS IS THAT MAYBE THERE'S A MOUNTAIN LION LOOSE IN THOSE WOODS. OR A BEAR? HASN'T BEEN ANY WILDLIFE LIKE THAT AROUND HERE FOR YEARS, THOUGH.
SO WE'VE GOT MISSING PETS, THEN MISSING KIDS, AND THEN MISSING ADULTS, ALL IN THE SPAN OF A WEEK AND CHANGE.
MAYBE THEY JUST GOT BORED LIVING OUT HERE IN THE SUBURBS. COULDN'T BLAME 'EM.
YOU EVER HEARD OF THIS NEW THING THEY'VE GOT NOW, STEGNER? IT'S CALLED "COMPASSION"...
...MAYBE YOU SHOULD TRY IT SOME-TIME.
?

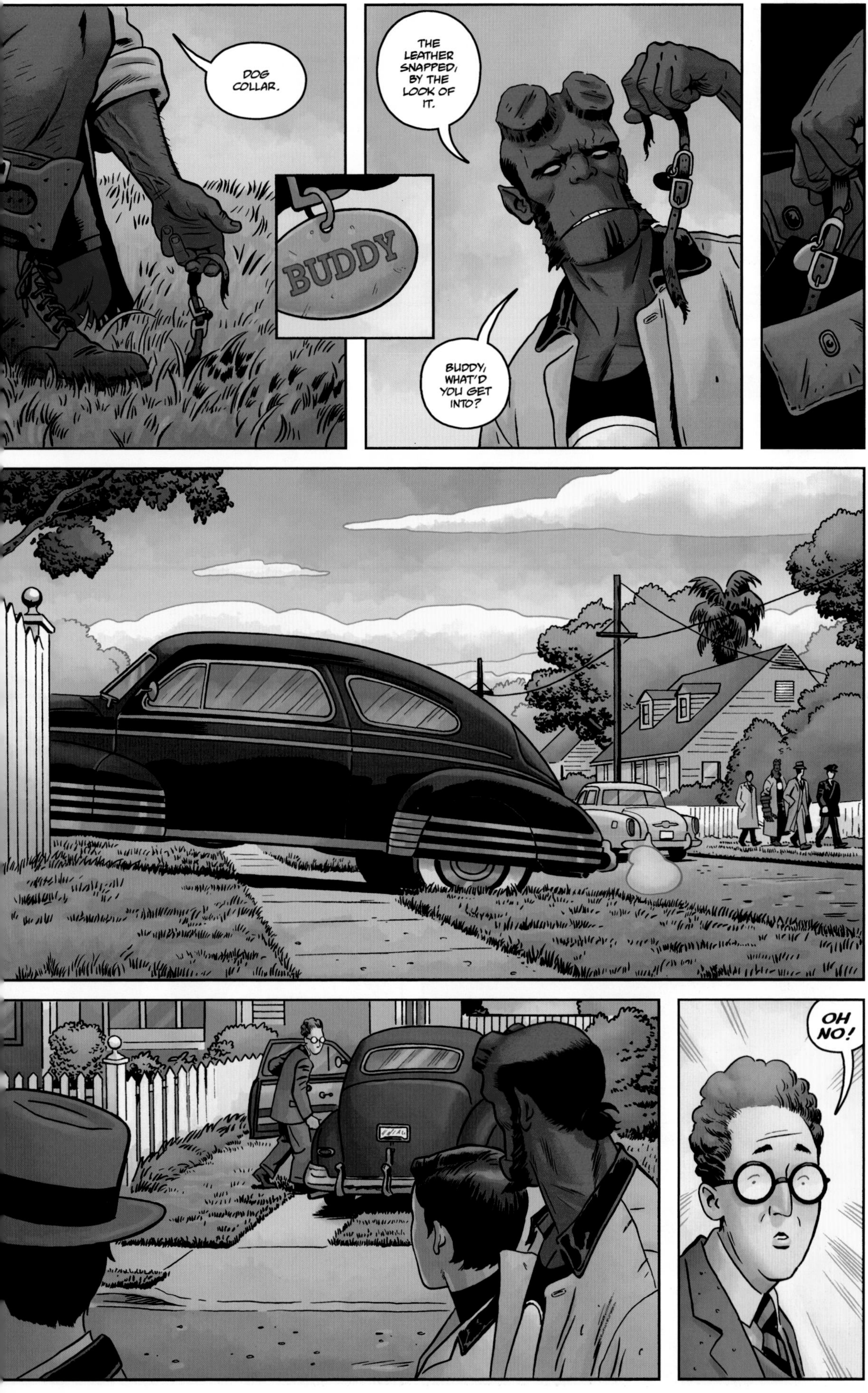
DOG COLLAR.
BUDDY
THE LEATHER SNAPPED, BY THE LOOK OF IT.
BUDDY, WHAT'D YOU GET INTO?
OH NO!

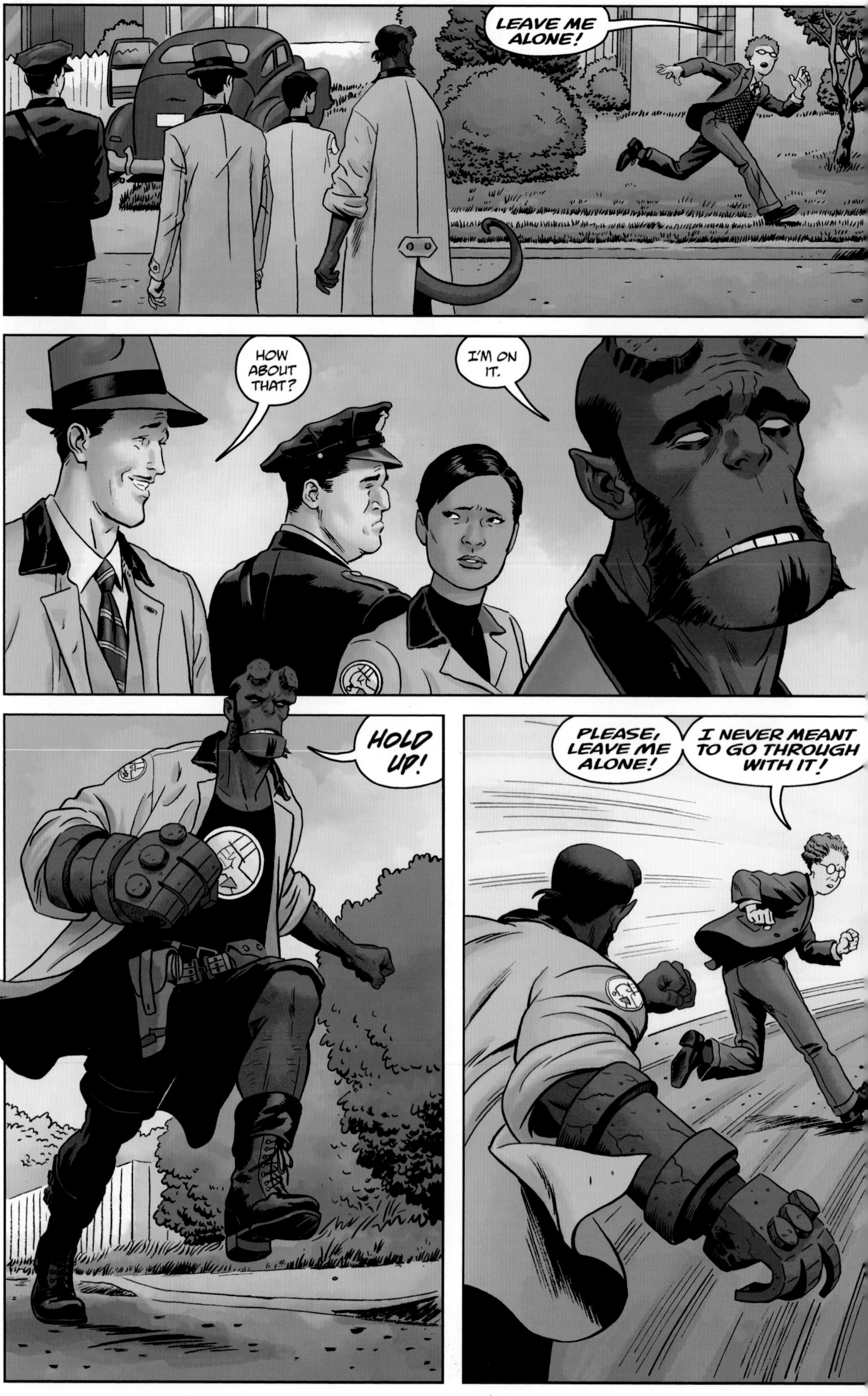
LEAVE ME ALONE!
HOW ABOUT THAT?
I'M ON IT.
HOLD UP!
PLEASE, LEAVE ME ALONE!
I NEVER MEANT TO GO THROUGH WITH IT!

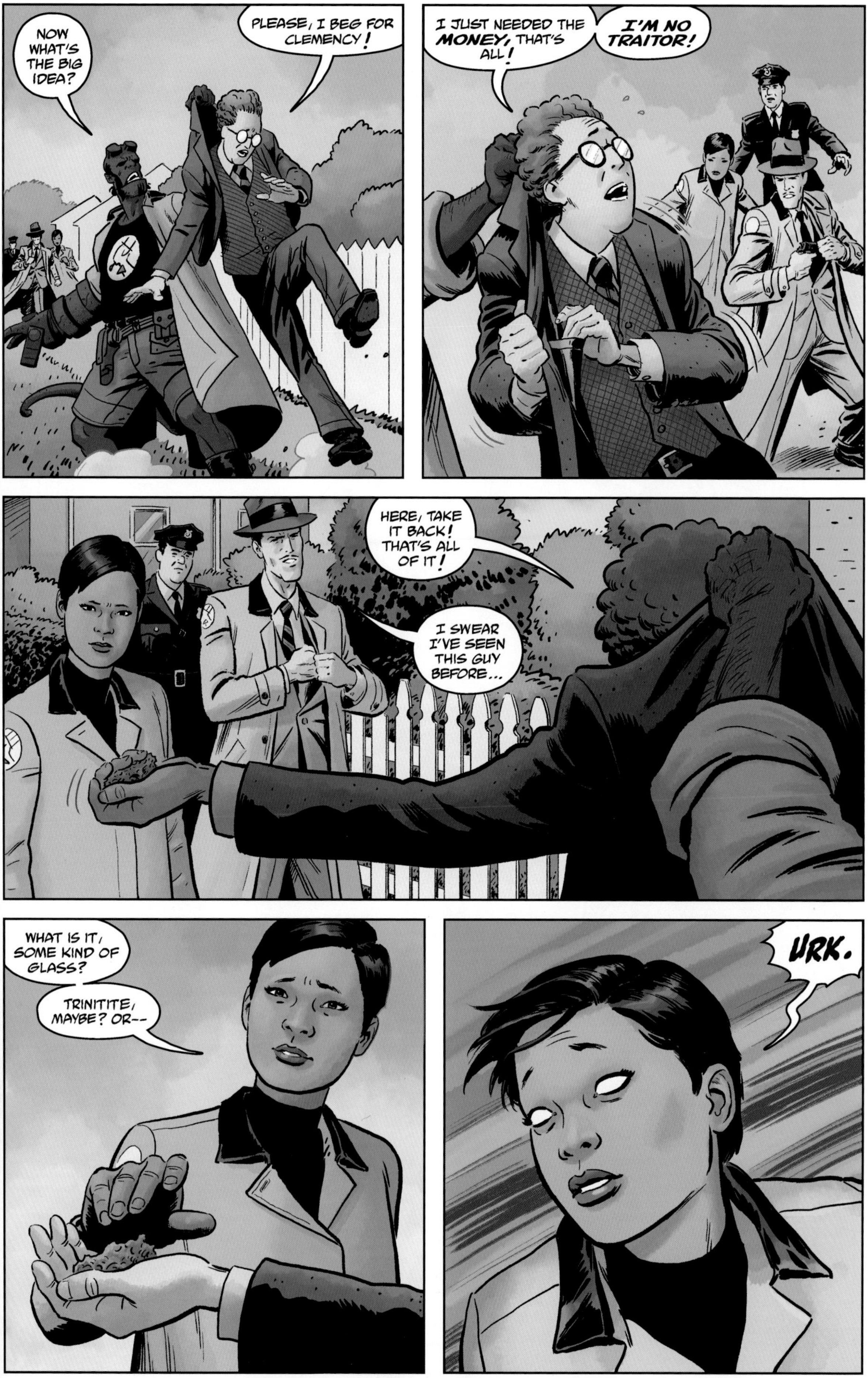

NOW WHAT'S THE BIG IDEA?
PLEASE, I BEG FOR CLEMENCY!
I JUST NEEDED THE MONEY, THAT'S ALL!
I'M NO TRAITOR!
HERE, TAKE IT BACK! THAT'S ALL OF IT!
I SWEAR I'VE SEEN THIS GUY BEFORE...
WHAT IS IT, SOME KIND OF GLASS?
TRINITITE, MAYBE? OR--
URK.

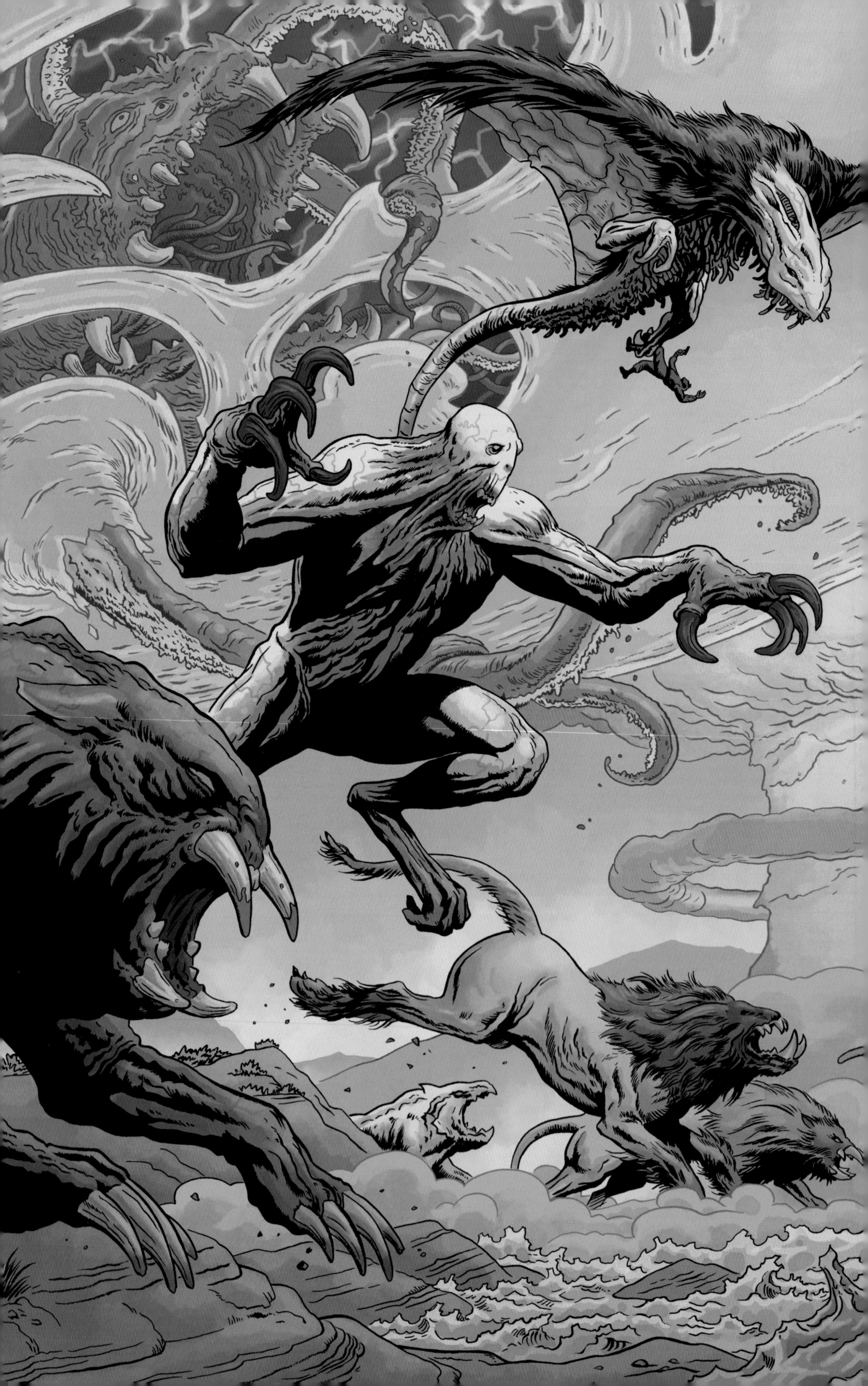

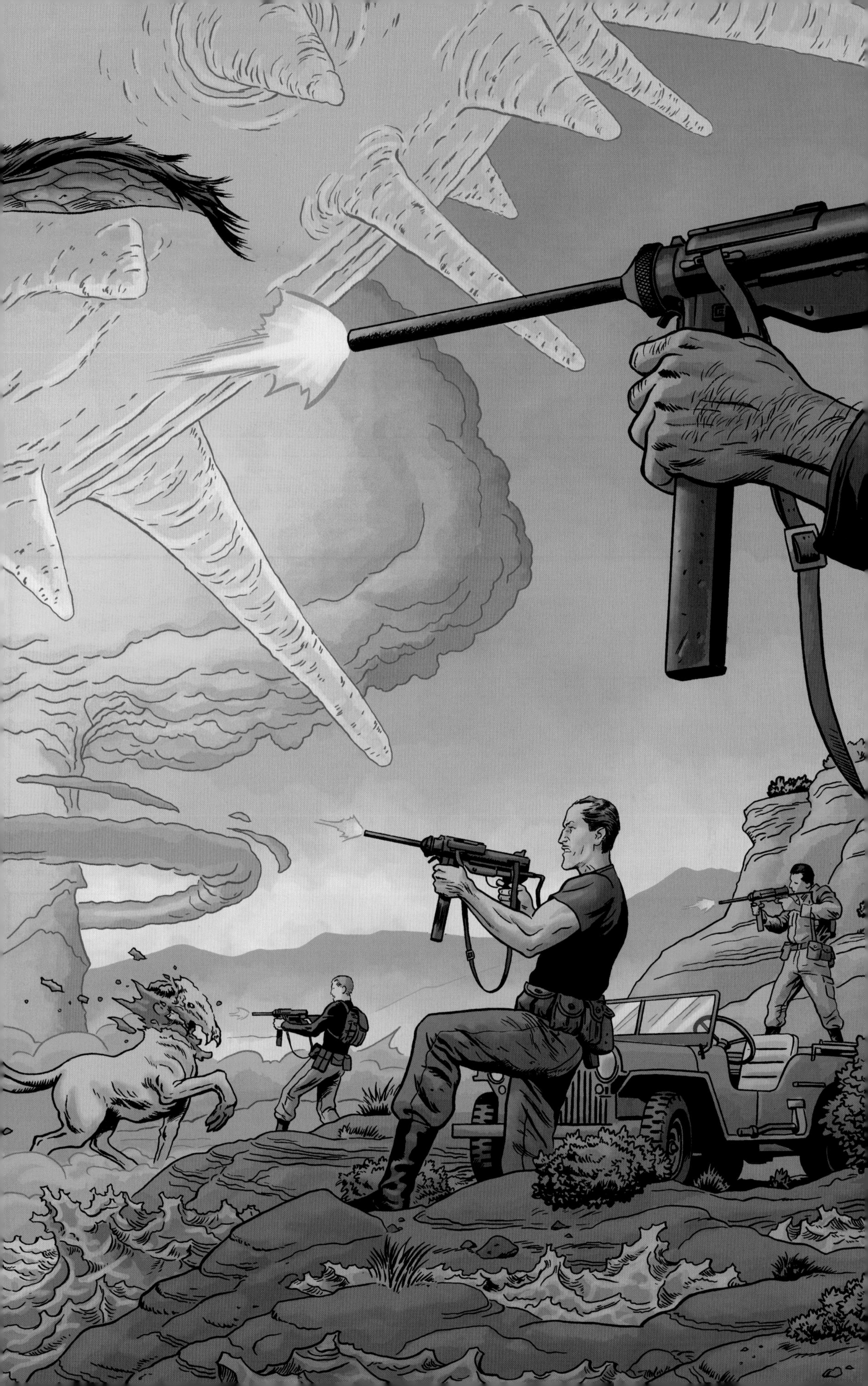

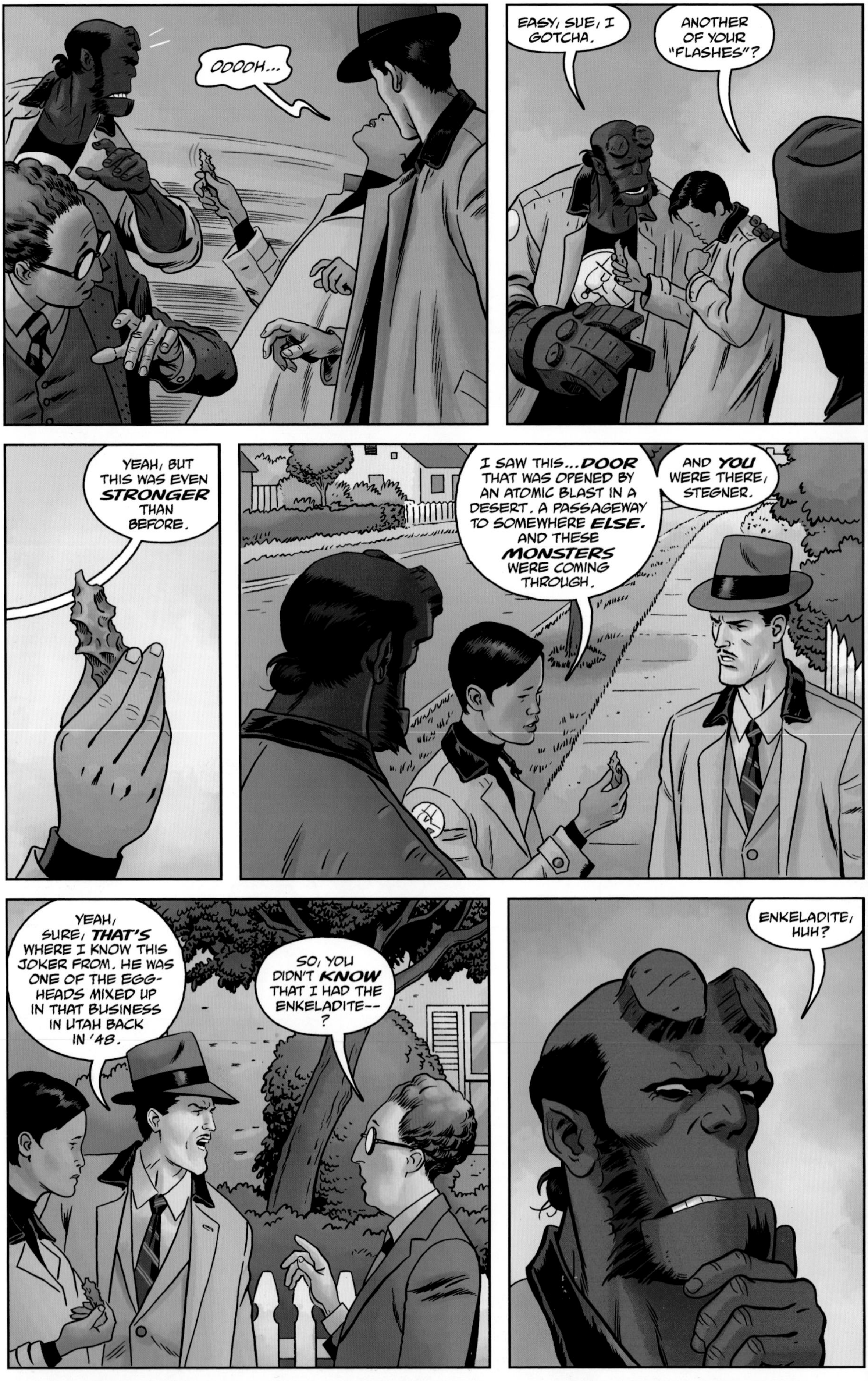
OOOOH...
EASY, SUE, I GOTCHA.
ANOTHER OF YOUR "FLASHES"?
YEAH, BUT THIS WAS EVEN STRONGER THAN BEFORE.
I SAW THIS... DOOR THAT WAS OPENED BY AN ATOMIC BLAST IN A DESERT. A PASSAGEWAY TO SOMEWHERE ELSE. AND THESE MONSTERS WERE COMING THROUGH.
AND YOU WERE THERE, STEGNER.
YEAH, SURE, THAT'S WHERE I KNOW THIS JOKER FROM. HE WAS ONE OF THE EGG-HEADS MIXED UP IN THAT BUSINESS IN UTAH BACK IN '48.
SO, YOU DIDN'T KNOW THAT I HAD THE ENKELADITE-- ?
ENKELADITE, HUH?

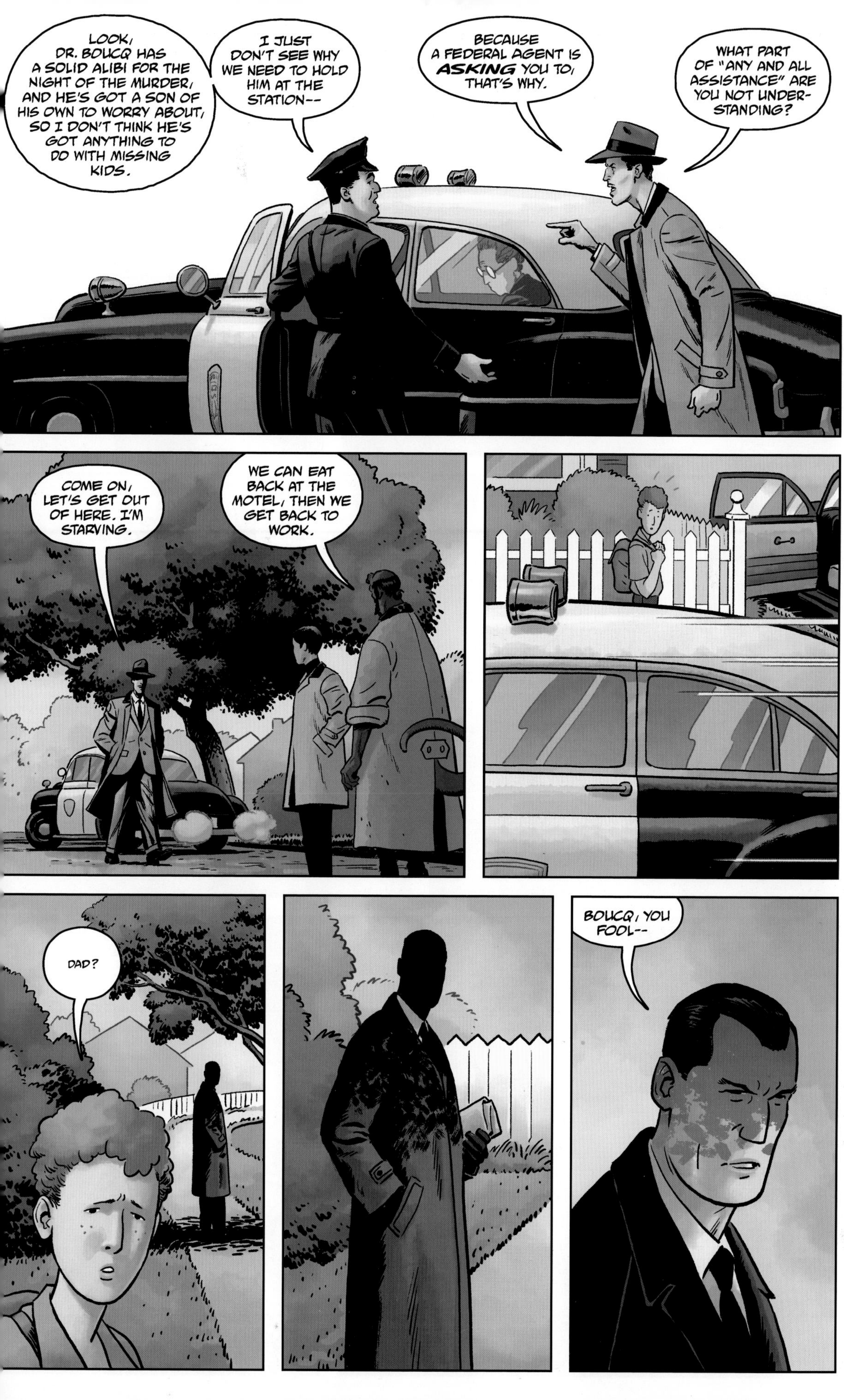
LOOK, DR. BOUCQ HAS A SOLID ALIBI FOR THE NIGHT OF THE MURDER, AND HE'S GOT A SON OF HIS OWN TO WORRY ABOUT, SO I DON'T THINK HE'S GOT ANYTHING TO DO WITH MISSING KIDS.
I JUST DON'T SEE WHY WE NEED TO HOLD HIM AT THE STATION--
BECAUSE A FEDERAL AGENT IS ASKING YOU TO, THAT'S WHY.
WHAT PART OF "ANY AND ALL ASSISTANCE" ARE YOU NOT UNDERSTANDING?
COME ON, LET'S GET OUT OF HERE. I'M STARVING.
WE CAN EAT BACK AT THE MOTEL, THEN WE GET BACK TO WORK.
DAD?
BOUCQ, YOU FOOL--

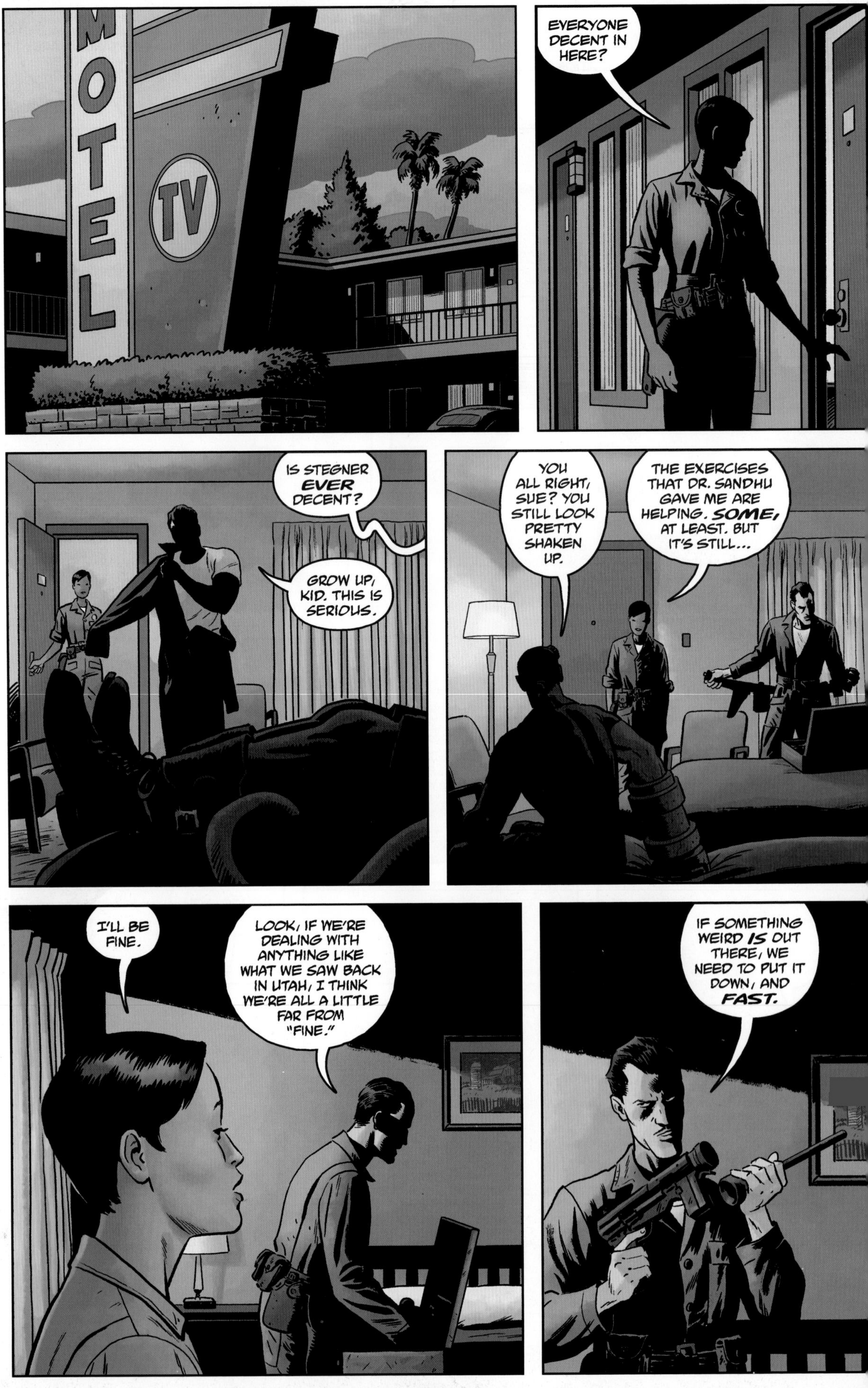
MOTEL
TV
EVERYONE DECENT IN HERE?
IS STEGNER EVER DECENT?
GROW UP, KID. THIS IS SERIOUS.
YOU ALL RIGHT, SUE? YOU STILL LOOK PRETTY SHAKEN UP.
THE EXERCISES THAT DR. SANDHU GAVE ME ARE HELPING. SOME, AT LEAST. BUT IT'S STILL...
I'LL BE FINE.
LOOK, IF WE'RE DEALING WITH ANYTHING LIKE WHAT WE SAW BACK IN UTAH, I THINK WE'RE ALL A LITTLE FAR FROM "FINE."
IF SOMETHING WEIRD IS OUT THERE, WE NEED TO PUT IT DOWN, AND FAST.

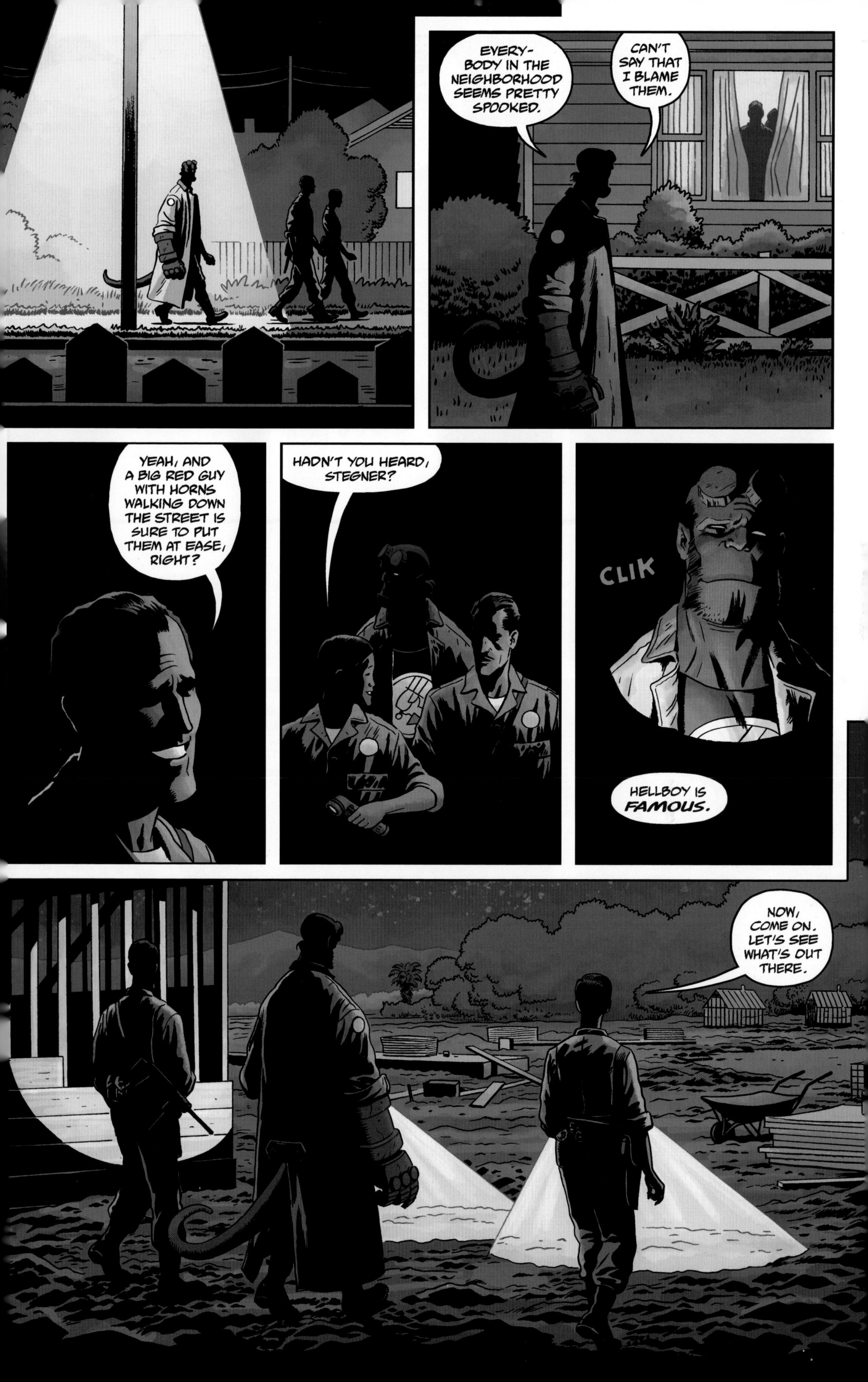
EVERY-BODY IN THE NEIGHBORHOOD SEEMS PRETTY SPOOKED.
CAN'T SAY THAT I BLAME THEM.
YEAH, AND A BIG RED GUY WITH HORNS WALKING DOWN THE STREET IS SURE TO PUT THEM AT EASE, RIGHT?
HADN'T YOU HEARD, STEGNER?
CLIK
HELLBOY IS *FAMOUS.*
NOW, COME ON. LET'S SEE WHAT'S OUT THERE.

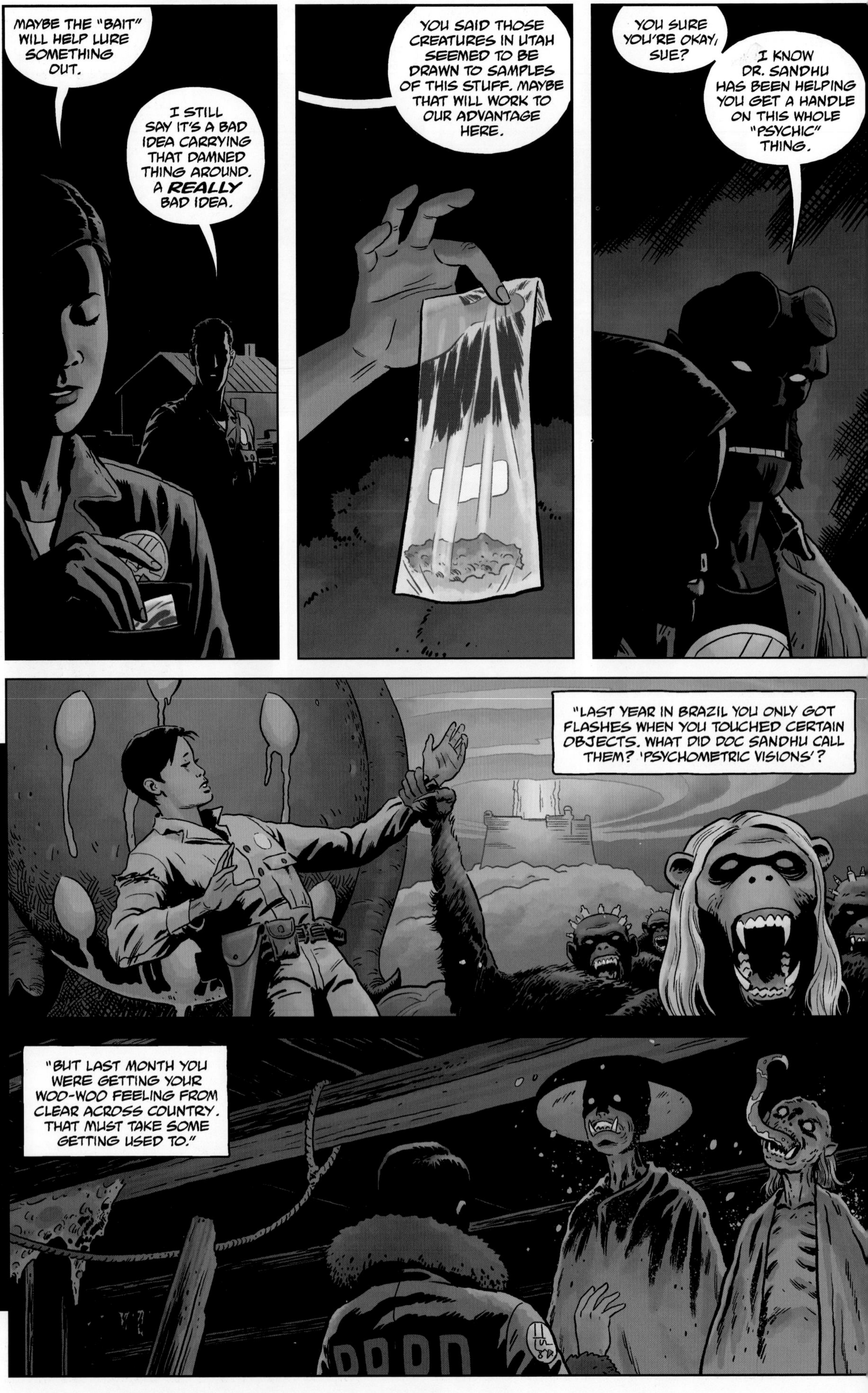
MAYBE THE "BAIT" WILL HELP LURE SOMETHING OUT.
I STILL SAY IT'S A BAD IDEA CARRYING THAT DAMNED THING AROUND. A REALLY BAD IDEA.
YOU SAID THOSE CREATURES IN UTAH SEEMED TO BE DRAWN TO SAMPLES OF THIS STUFF. MAYBE THAT WILL WORK TO OUR ADVANTAGE HERE.
YOU SURE YOU'RE OKAY, SUE?
I KNOW DR. SANDHU HAS BEEN HELPING YOU GET A HANDLE ON THIS WHOLE "PSYCHIC" THING.
"LAST YEAR IN BRAZIL YOU ONLY GOT FLASHES WHEN YOU TOUCHED CERTAIN OBJECTS. WHAT DID DOC SANDHU CALL THEM? 'PSYCHOMETRIC VISIONS'?
"BUT LAST MONTH YOU WERE GETTING YOUR WOO-WOO FEELING FROM CLEAR ACROSS COUNTRY. THAT MUST TAKE SOME GETTING USED TO."

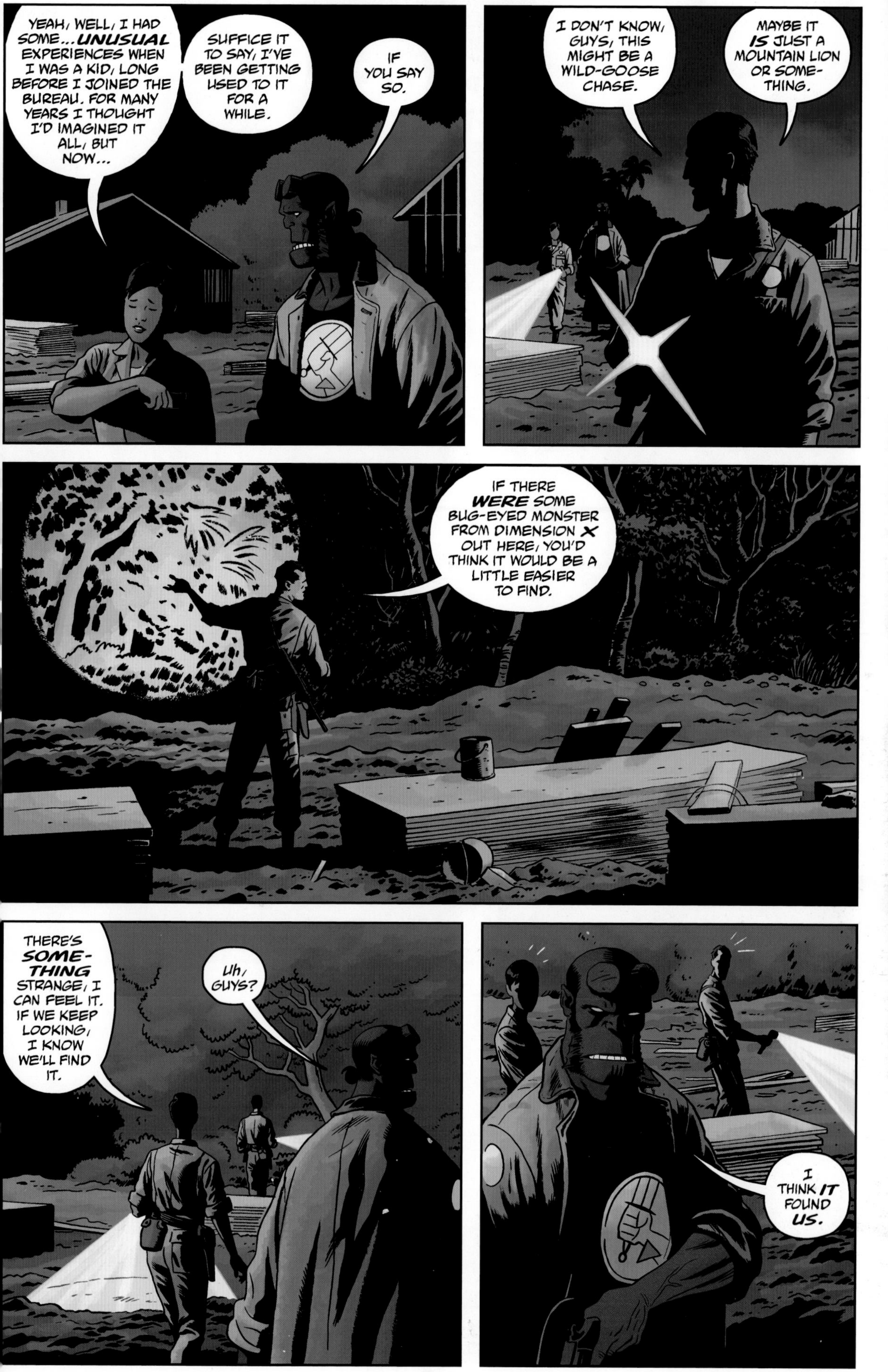
YEAH, WELL, I HAD SOME... UNUSUAL EXPERIENCES WHEN I WAS A KID, LONG BEFORE I JOINED THE BUREAU. FOR MANY YEARS I THOUGHT I'D IMAGINED IT ALL, BUT NOW...
SUFFICE IT TO SAY, I'VE BEEN GETTING USED TO IT FOR A WHILE.
IF YOU SAY SO.
I DON'T KNOW, GUYS, THIS MIGHT BE A WILD-GOOSE CHASE.
MAYBE IT IS JUST A MOUNTAIN LION OR SOME-THING.
IF THERE WERE SOME BUG-EYED MONSTER FROM DIMENSION X OUT HERE, YOU'D THINK IT WOULD BE A LITTLE EASIER TO FIND.
THERE'S SOME-THING STRANGE, I CAN FEEL IT. IF WE KEEP LOOKING, I KNOW WE'LL FIND IT.
UH, GUYS?
I THINK IT FOUND US.

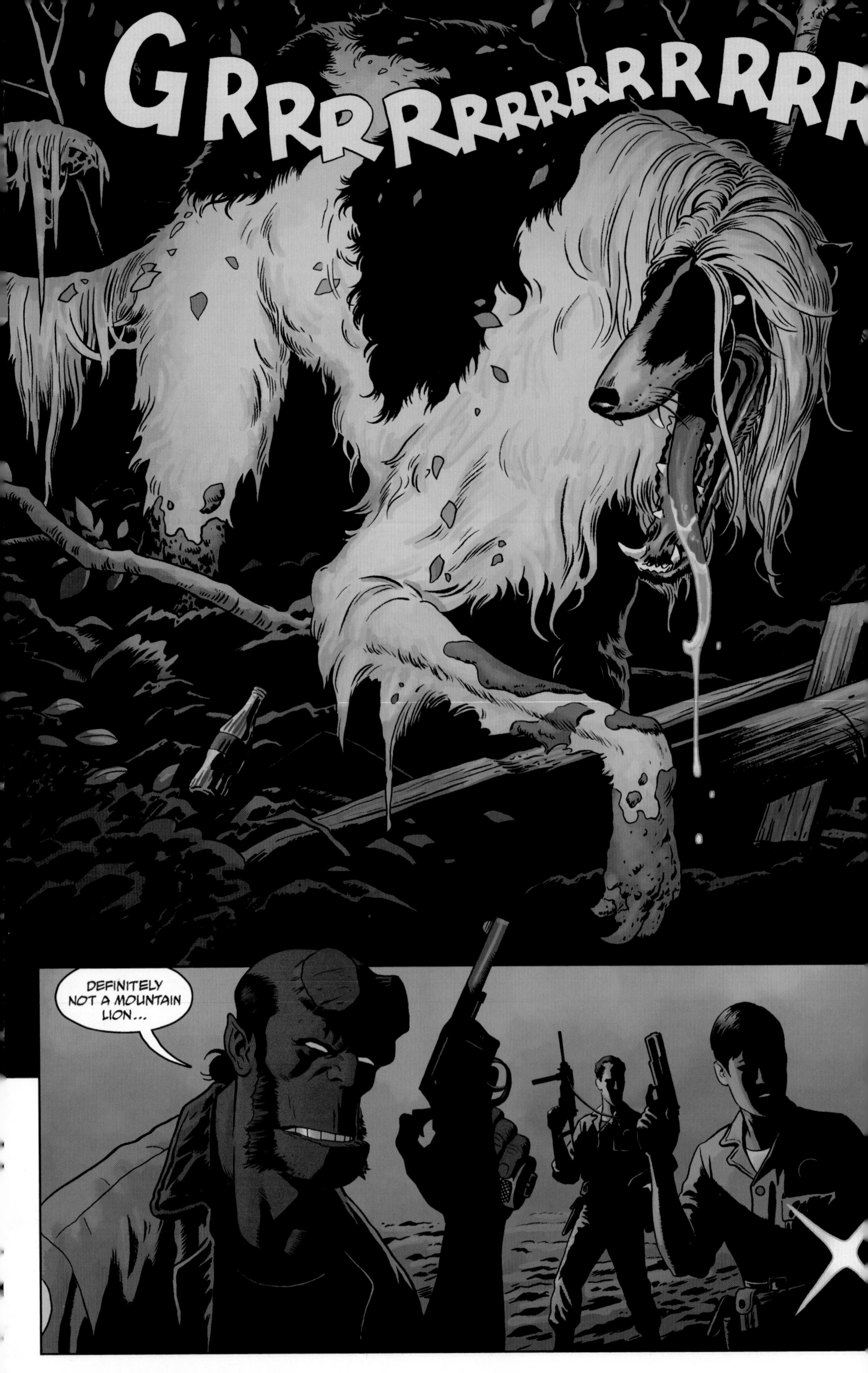
GRRRRRRRRRRRRR
DEFINITELY NOT A MOUNTAIN LION...

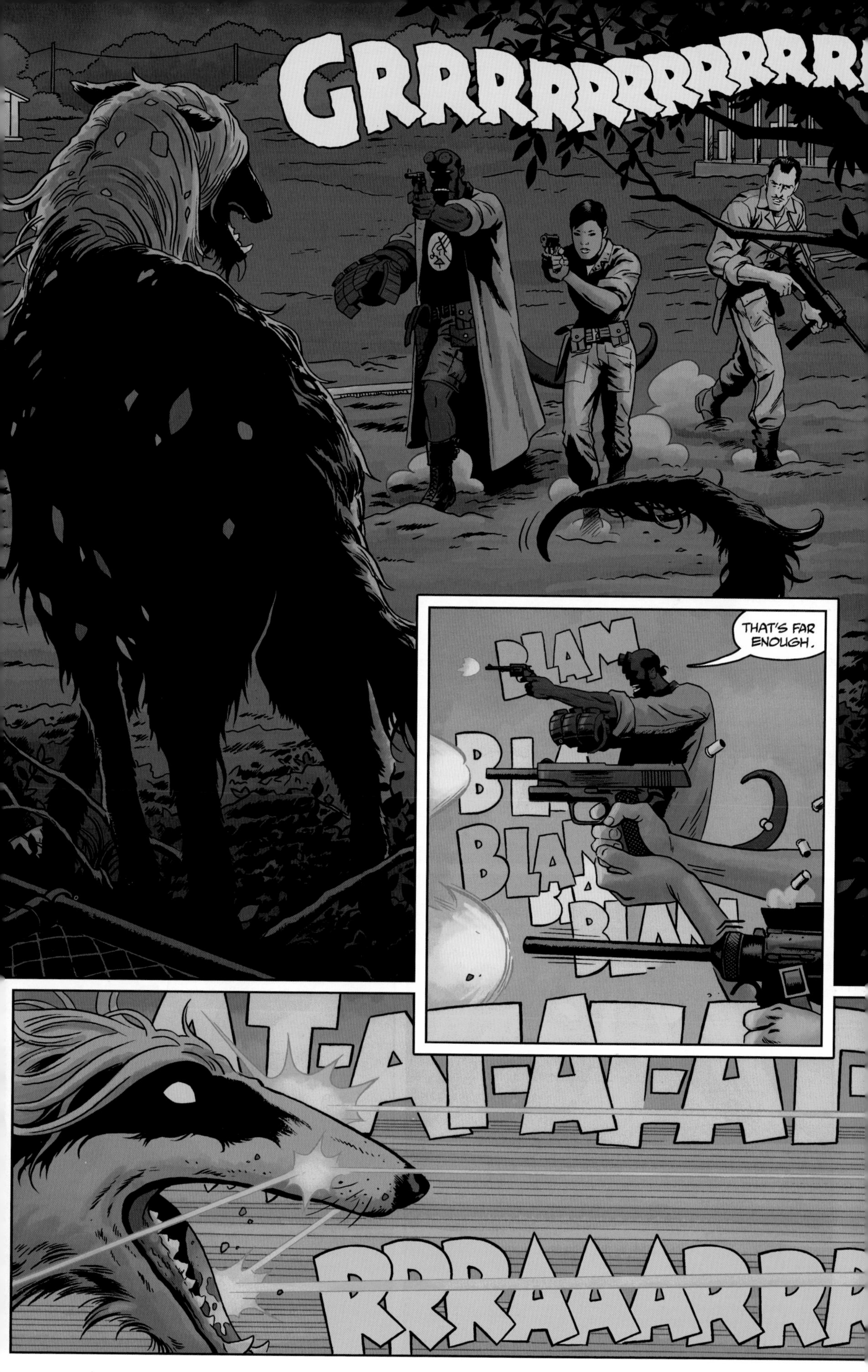

GRRRRRRRRRR
BLAM
THAT'S FAR ENOUGH.
BLAM
RRRAAARRR

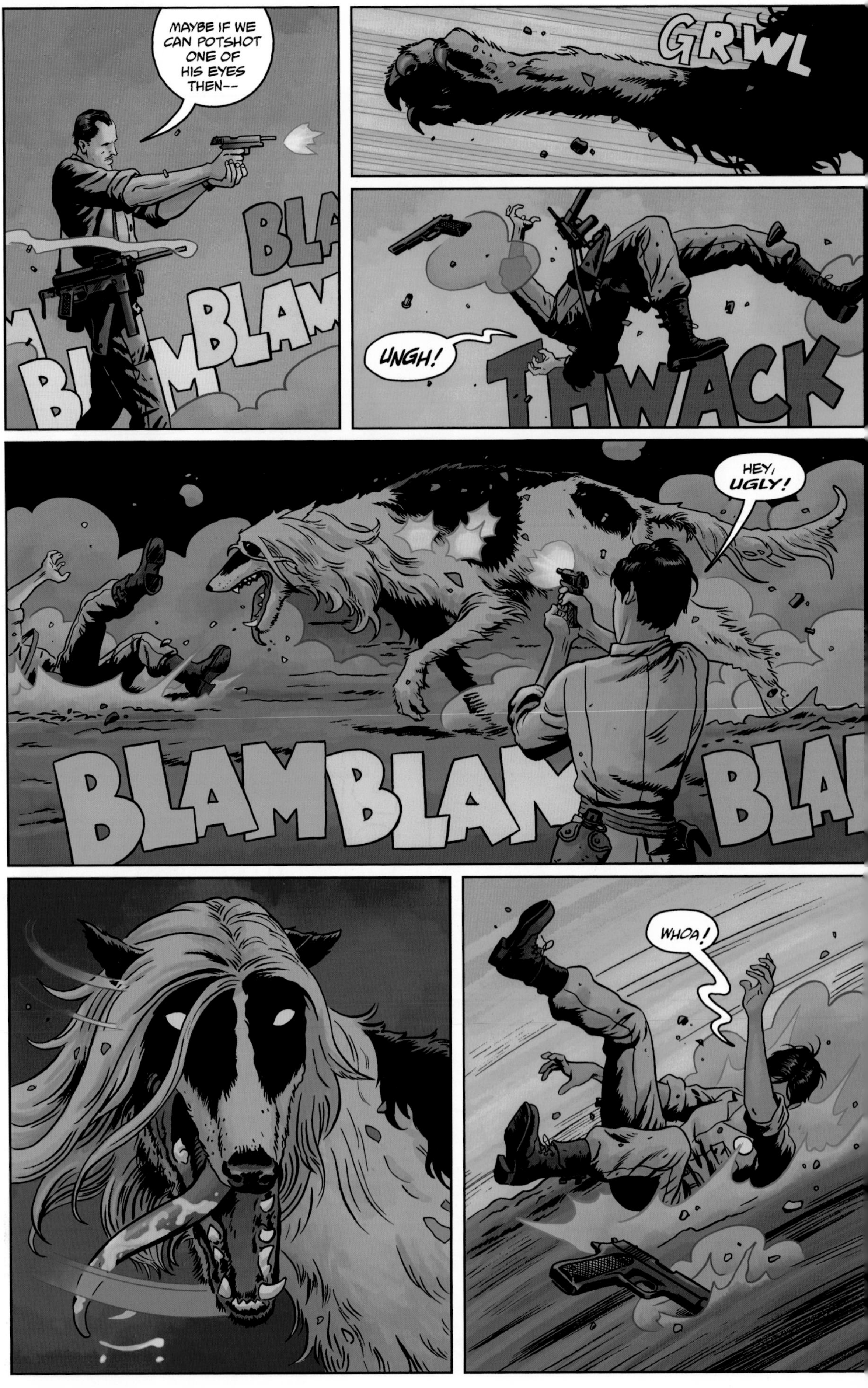
MAYBE IF WE CAN POTSHOT ONE OF HIS EYES THEN--
BLA
BLAMBLAM
GRWL
UNGH!
THWACK
HEY, UGLY!
BLAMBLAM
BLA
WHOA!

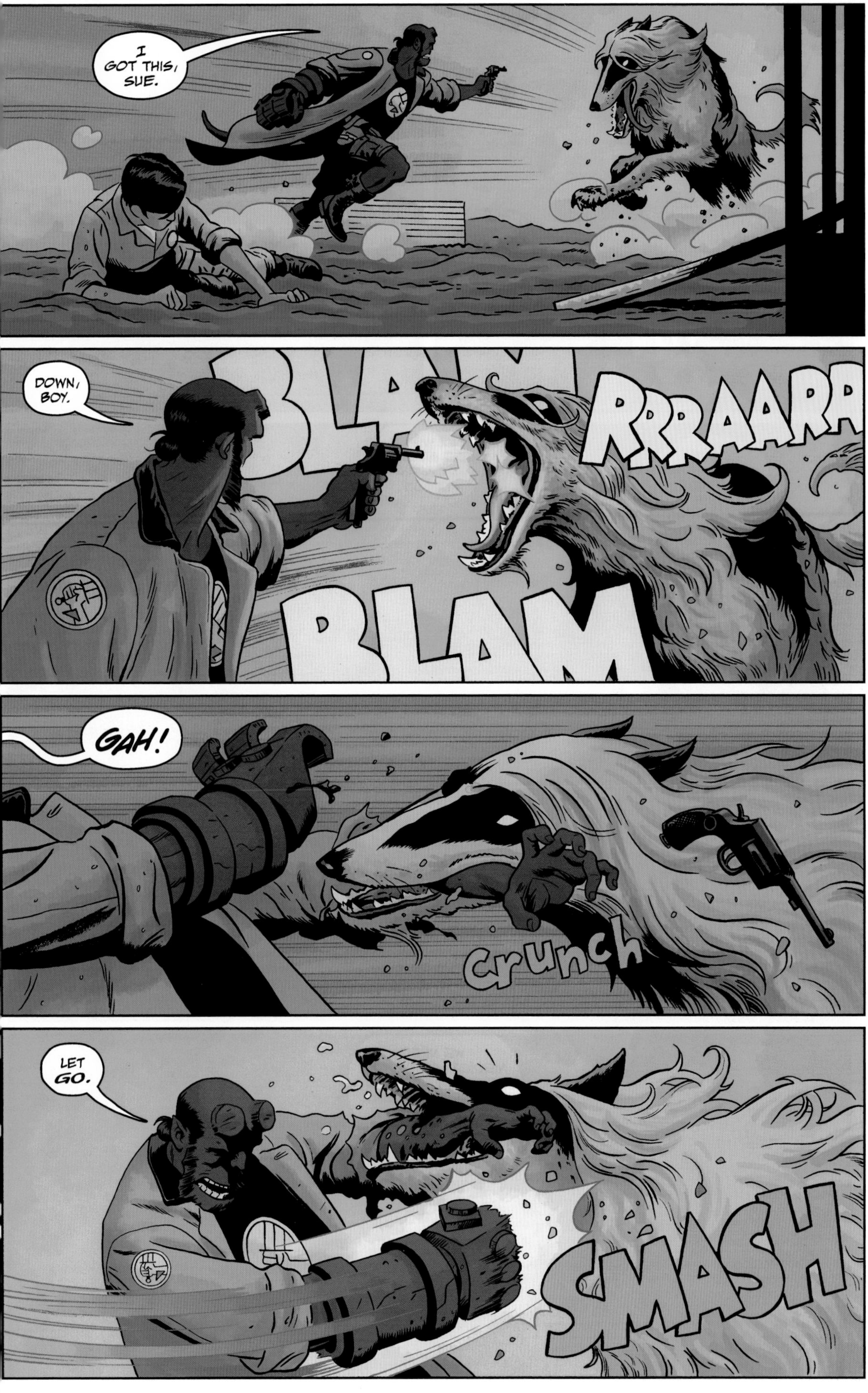
I GOT THIS, SUE.
DOWN, BOY.
BLAM
RRRAARR
BLAM
GAH!
crunch
LET GO.
SMASH

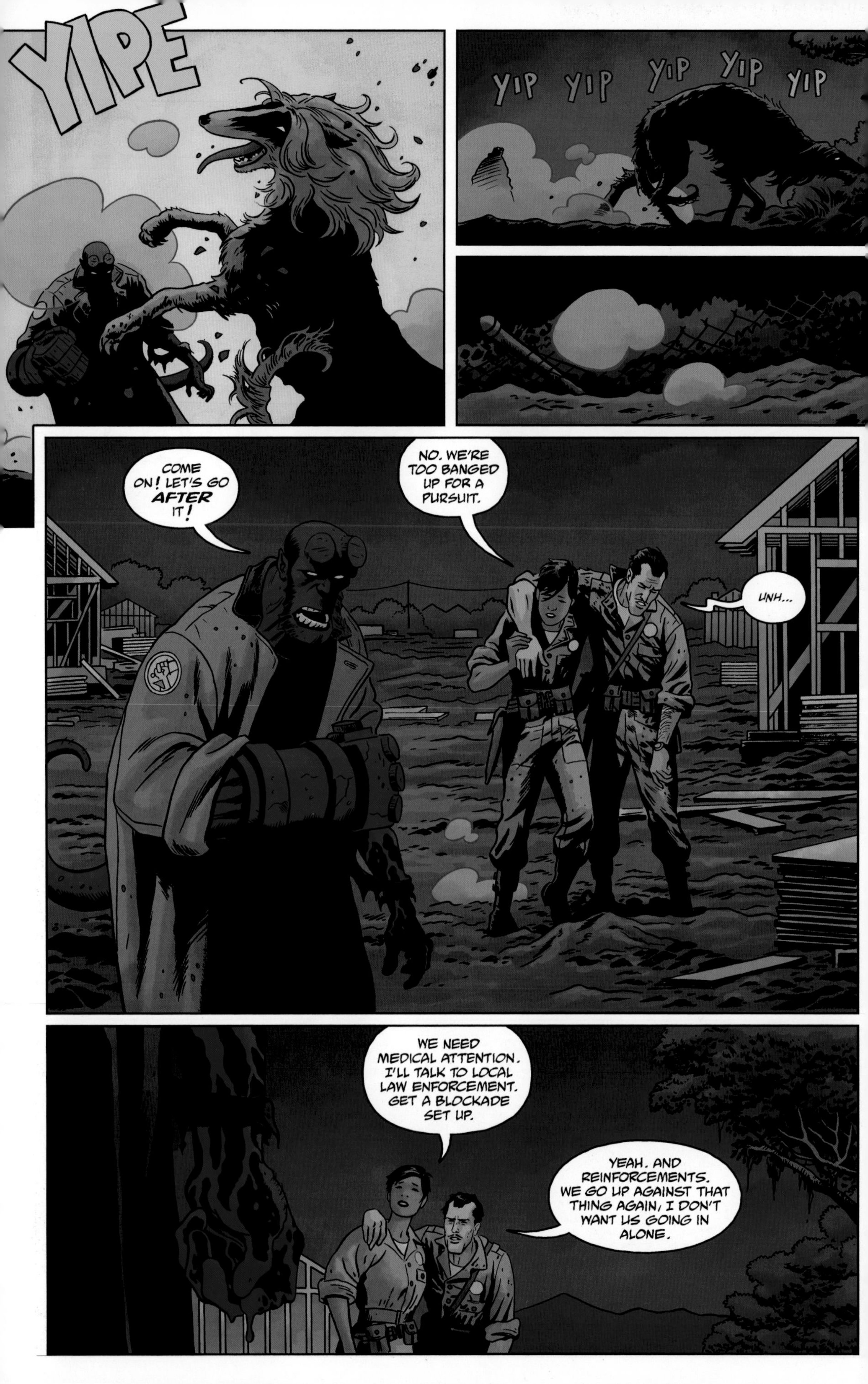
YIPE
YIP YIP YIP YIP YIP
COME ON! LET'S GO AFTER IT!
NO. WE'RE TOO BANGED UP FOR A PURSUIT.
UNH...
WE NEED MEDICAL ATTENTION. I'LL TALK TO LOCAL LAW ENFORCEMENT. GET A BLOCKADE SET UP.
YEAH. AND REINFORCEMENTS. WE GO UP AGAINST THAT THING AGAIN, I DON'T WANT US GOING IN ALONE.

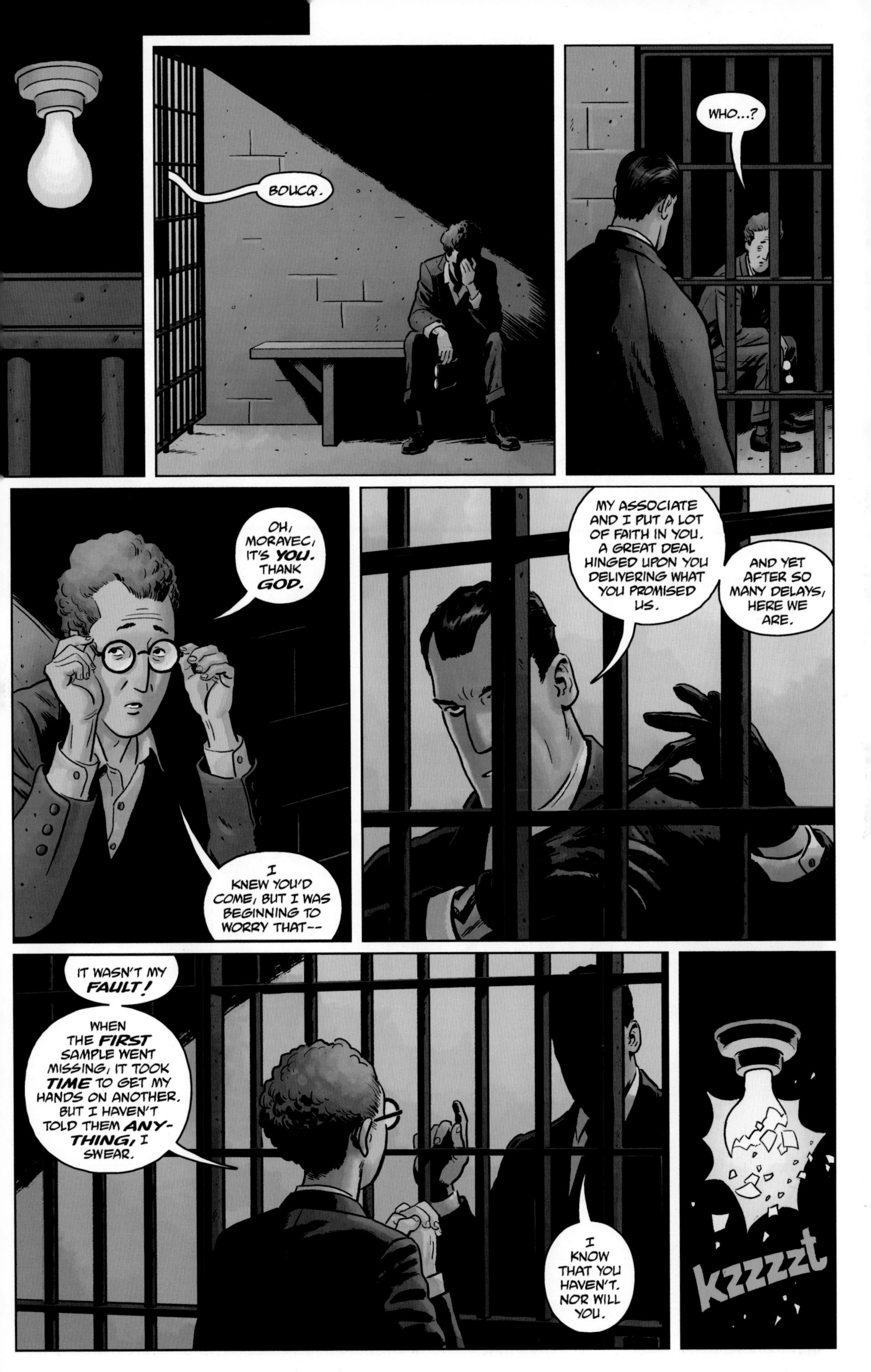
BOUCQ.
WHO...?
OH, MORAVEC, IT'S YOU. THANK GOD.
I KNEW YOU'D COME, BUT I WAS BEGINNING TO WORRY THAT--
MY ASSOCIATE AND I PUT A LOT OF FAITH IN YOU. A GREAT DEAL HINGED UPON YOU DELIVERING WHAT YOU PROMISED US.
AND YET AFTER SO MANY DELAYS, HERE WE ARE.
IT WASN'T MY FAULT!
WHEN THE FIRST SAMPLE WENT MISSING, IT TOOK TIME TO GET MY HANDS ON ANOTHER. BUT I HAVEN'T TOLD THEM ANYTHING, I SWEAR.
I KNOW THAT YOU HAVEN'T. NOR WILL YOU.
kzzzzt

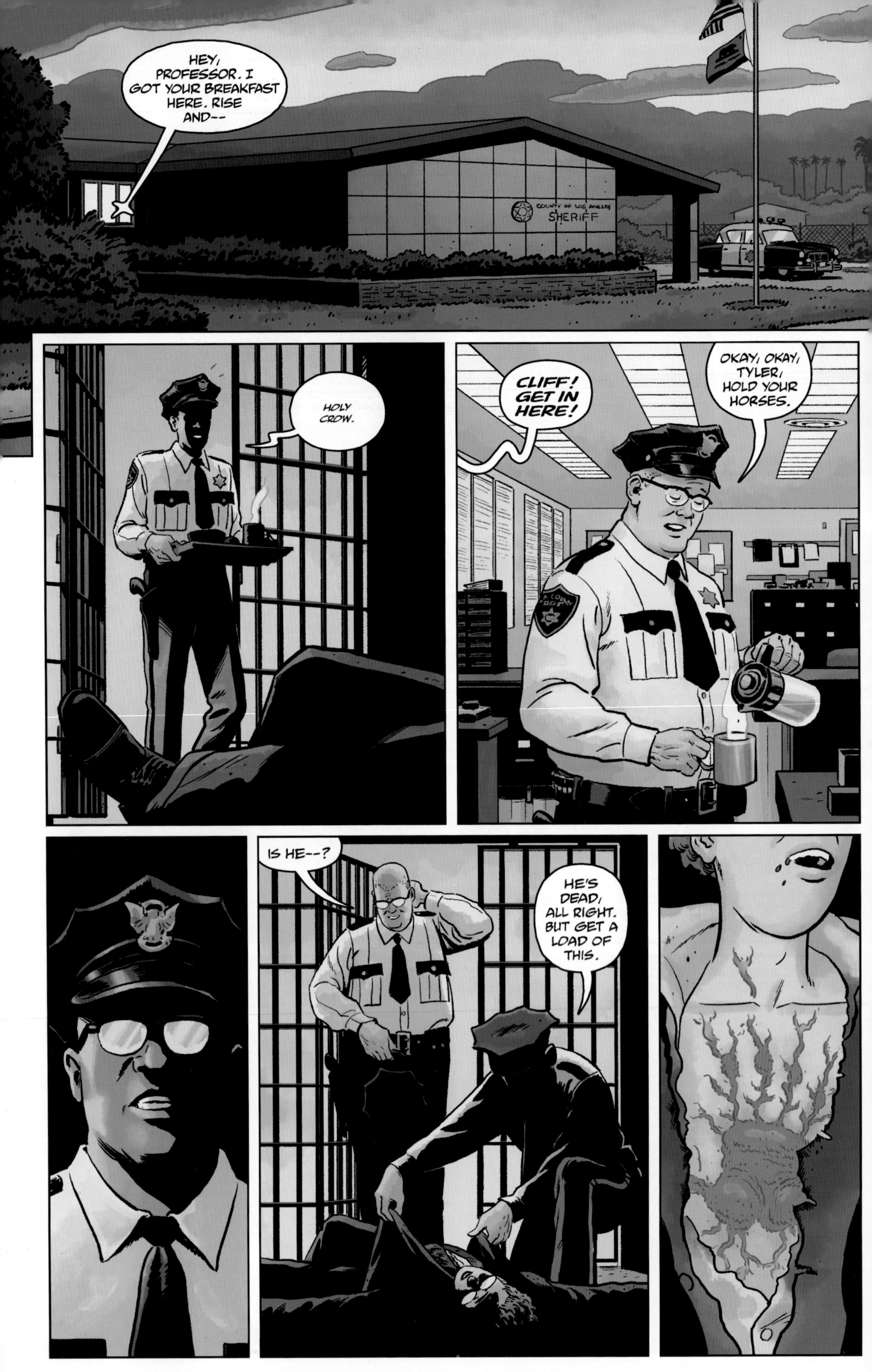
HEY, PROFESSOR. I GOT YOUR BREAKFAST HERE. RISE AND--
COUNTY OF LOS ANGELES SHERIFF
HOLY CROW.
CLIFF! GET IN HERE!
OKAY, OKAY, TYLER, HOLD YOUR HORSES.
IS HE--?
HE'S DEAD, ALL RIGHT. BUT GET A LOAD OF THIS.

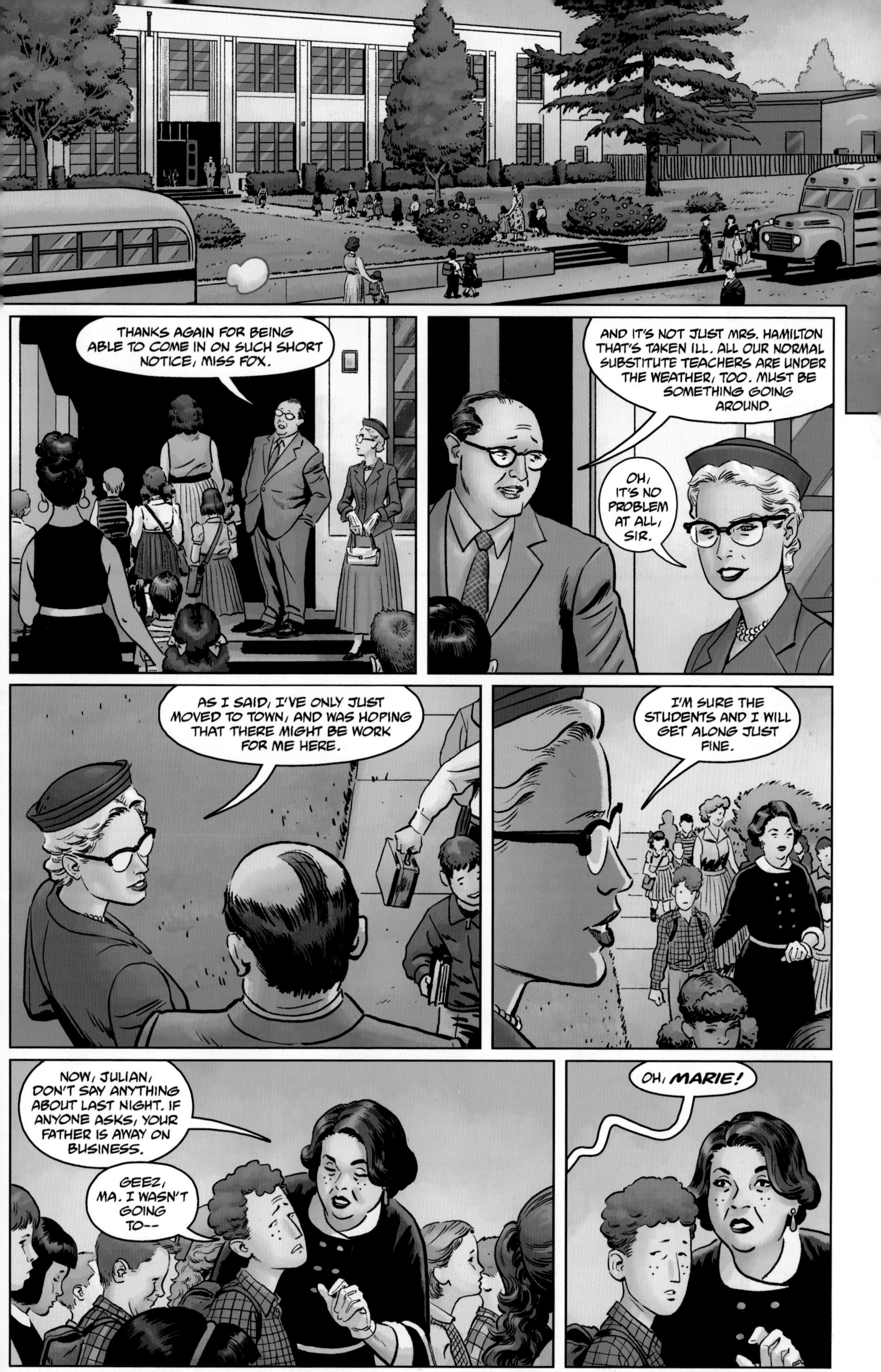
THANKS AGAIN FOR BEING ABLE TO COME IN ON SUCH SHORT NOTICE, MISS FOX.
AND IT'S NOT JUST MRS. HAMILTON THAT'S TAKEN ILL. ALL OUR NORMAL SUBSTITUTE TEACHERS ARE UNDER THE WEATHER, TOO. MUST BE SOMETHING GOING AROUND.
OH, IT'S NO PROBLEM AT ALL, SIR.
AS I SAID, I'VE ONLY JUST MOVED TO TOWN, AND WAS HOPING THAT THERE MIGHT BE WORK FOR ME HERE.
I'M SURE THE STUDENTS AND I WILL GET ALONG JUST FINE.
NOW, JULIAN, DON'T SAY ANYTHING ABOUT LAST NIGHT. IF ANYONE ASKS, YOUR FATHER IS AWAY ON BUSINESS.
GEEZ, MA. I WASN'T GOING TO--
OH, MARIE!

DID I SEE YOUR HUSBAND LEAVING WITH THE **POLICE** LAST NIGHT?

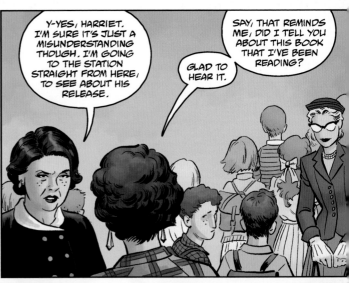

Y-YES, HARRIET. I'M SURE IT'S JUST A MISUNDERSTANDING THOUGH. I'M GOING TO THE STATION STRAIGHT FROM HERE, TO SEE ABOUT HIS RELEASE.

GLAD TO HEAR IT.

SAY, THAT REMINDS ME, DID I TELL YOU ABOUT THIS BOOK THAT I'VE BEEN READING?

IT'S CALLED BABYLON RISING, AND IT'S ALL ABOUT HOW **LEARNING** IS OUR **REAL** PROBLEM, AND THAT THE TRICK IS **UNLEARNING**...

HELLO, CHILDREN. I'M MISS FOX.

brrrinnggg

I'M AS WORRIED ABOUT THOSE MISSING CHILDREN AS ANYONE, BUT HOW AM I SUPPOSED TO RUN A SCHOOL WITH ALL THIS **CHAOS** ABOUT?

FIRST THE POLICE SET UP THAT BARRICADE, AND NOW THE **ARMY** IS MOVING IN?

NOT THE ARMY...

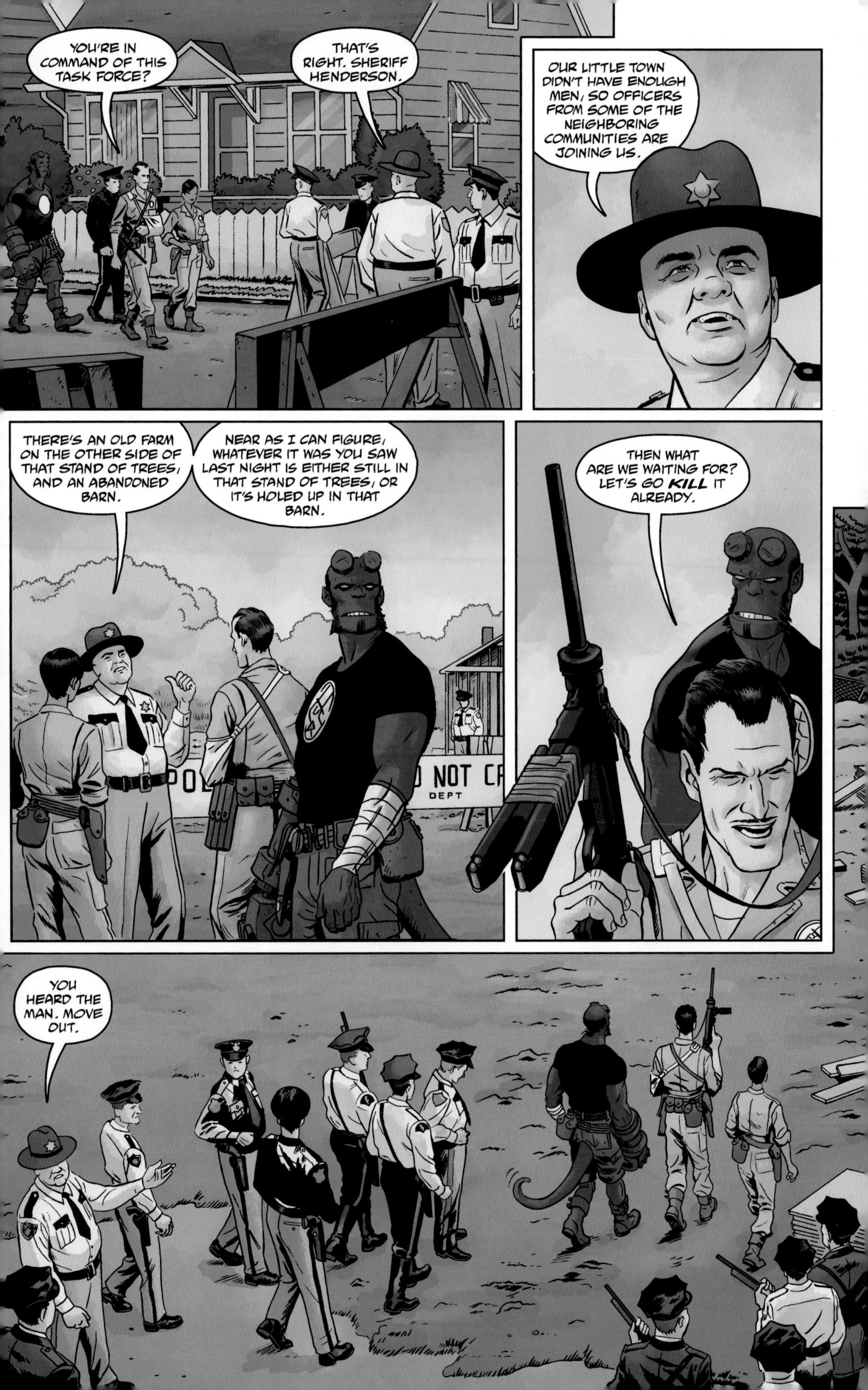
YOU'RE IN COMMAND OF THIS TASK FORCE?
THAT'S RIGHT. SHERIFF HENDERSON.
OUR LITTLE TOWN DIDN'T HAVE ENOUGH MEN, SO OFFICERS FROM SOME OF THE NEIGHBORING COMMUNITIES ARE JOINING US.
THERE'S AN OLD FARM ON THE OTHER SIDE OF THAT STAND OF TREES, AND AN ABANDONED BARN.
NEAR AS I CAN FIGURE, WHATEVER IT WAS YOU SAW LAST NIGHT IS EITHER STILL IN THAT STAND OF TREES, OR IT'S HOLED UP IN THAT BARN.
DEPT
THEN WHAT ARE WE WAITING FOR? LET'S GO KILL IT ALREADY.
YOU HEARD THE MAN. MOVE OUT.

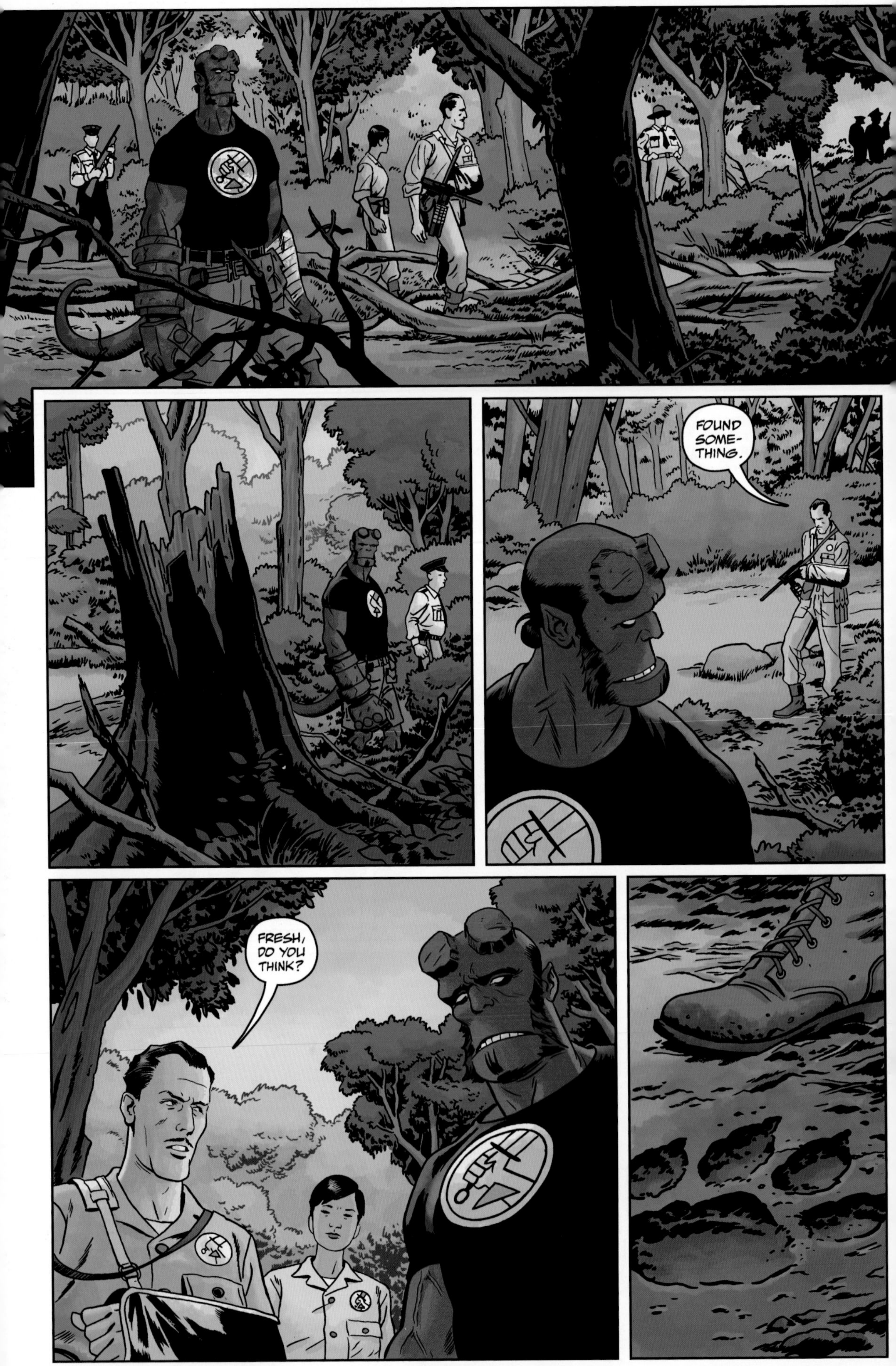
FOUND SOME-THING.
FRESH, DO YOU THINK?

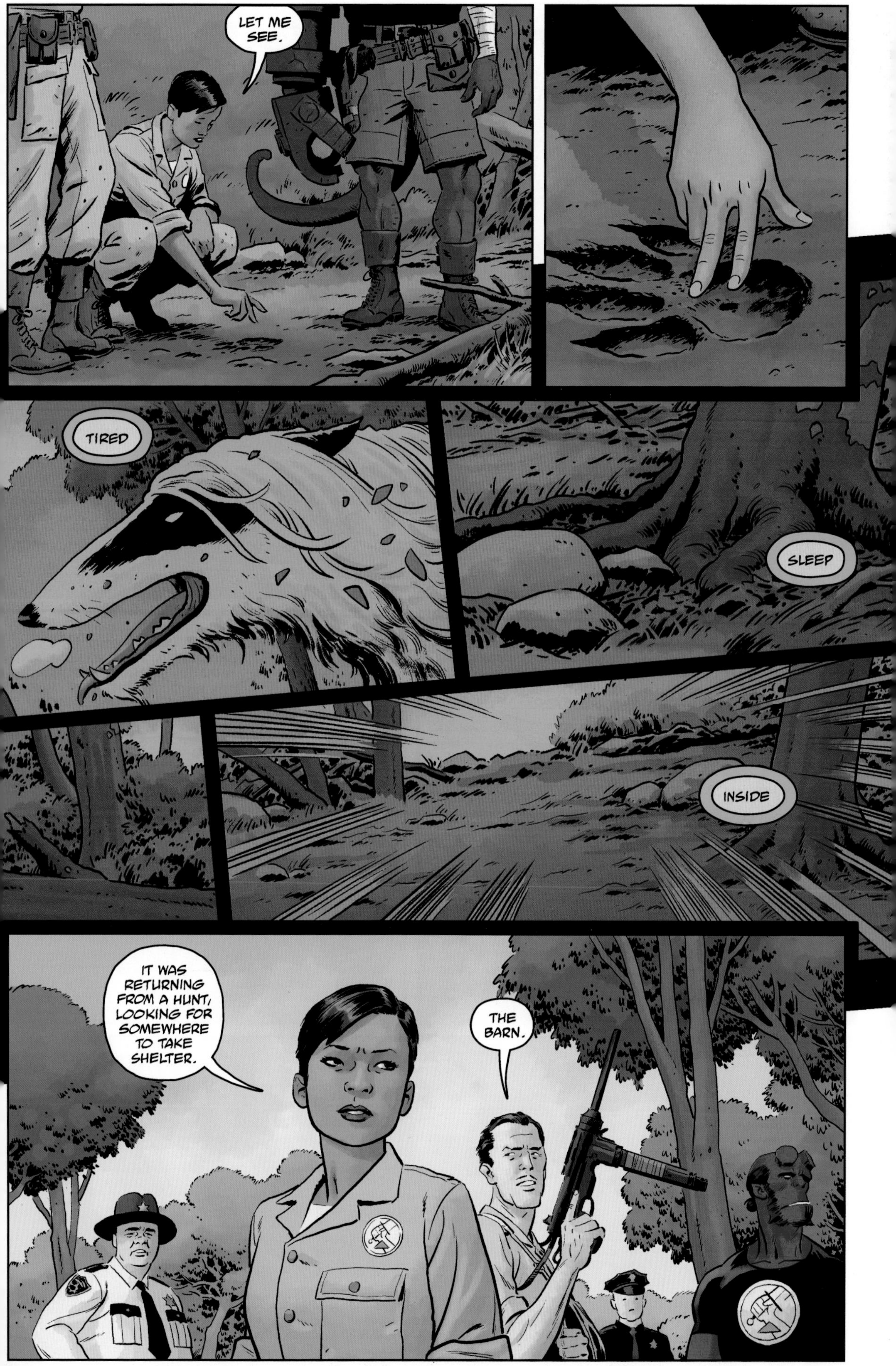
LET ME SEE.
TIRED
SLEEP
INSIDE
IT WAS RETURNING FROM A HUNT, LOOKING FOR SOMEWHERE TO TAKE SHELTER.
THE BARN.

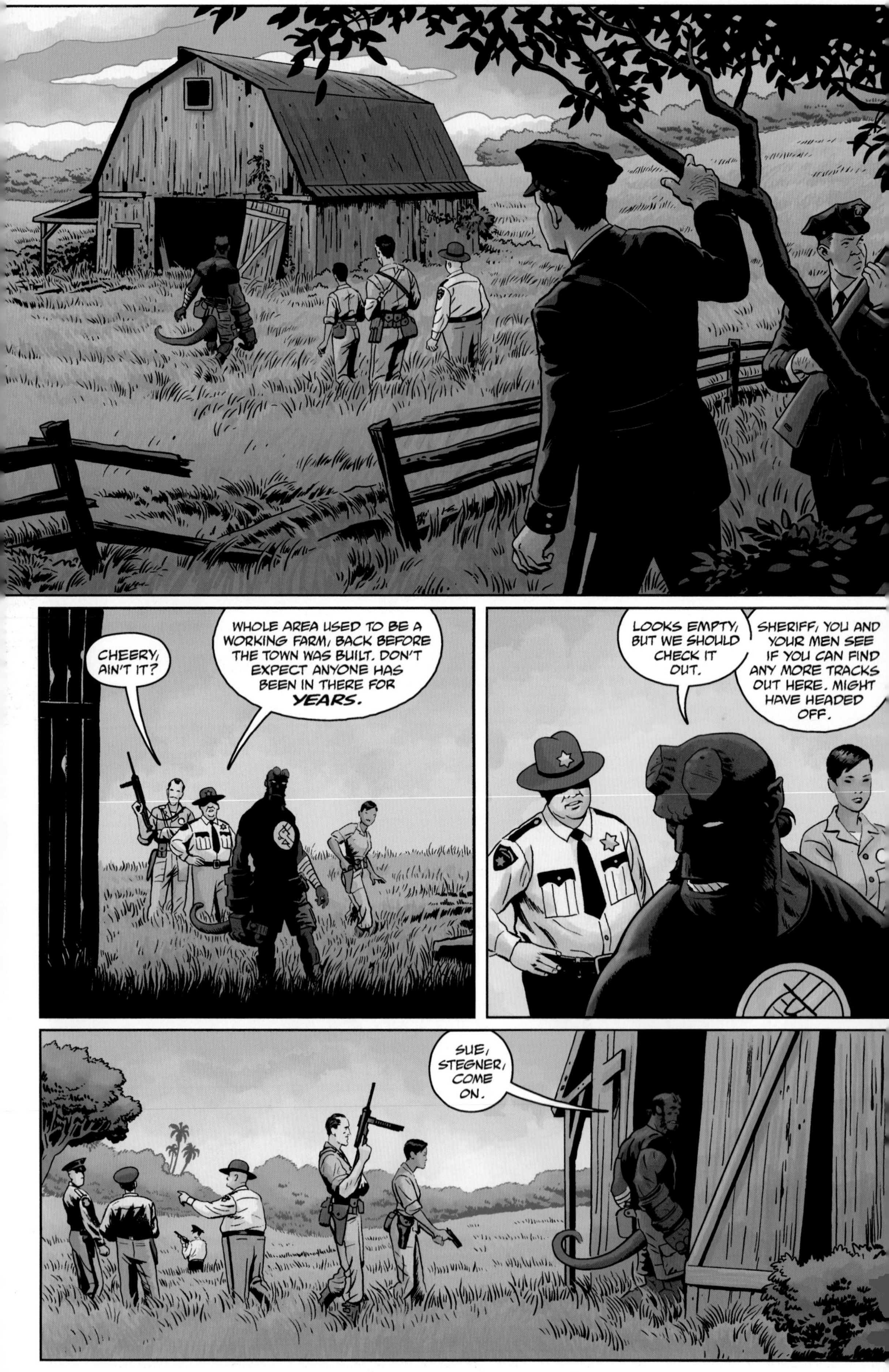
CHEERY, AIN'T IT?
WHOLE AREA USED TO BE A WORKING FARM, BACK BEFORE THE TOWN WAS BUILT. DON'T EXPECT ANYONE HAS BEEN IN THERE FOR *YEARS.*
LOOKS EMPTY, BUT WE SHOULD CHECK IT OUT.
SHERIFF, YOU AND YOUR MEN SEE IF YOU CAN FIND ANY MORE TRACKS OUT HERE. MIGHT HAVE HEADED OFF.
SUE, STEGNER, COME ON.

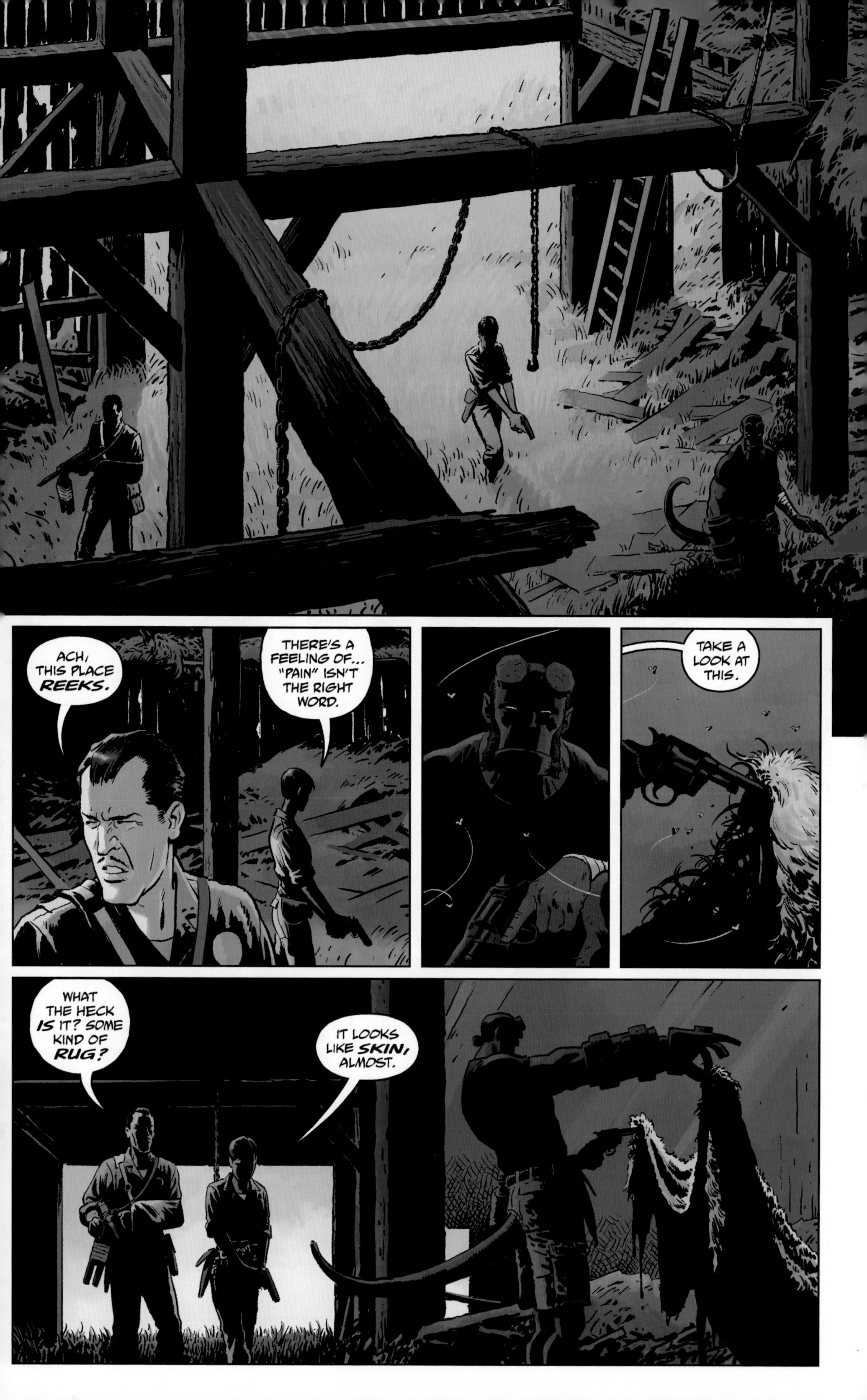
ACH, THIS PLACE REEKS.
THERE'S A FEELING OF... "PAIN" ISN'T THE RIGHT WORD.
TAKE A LOOK AT THIS.
WHAT THE HECK IS IT? SOME KIND OF RUG?
IT LOOKS LIKE SKIN, ALMOST.

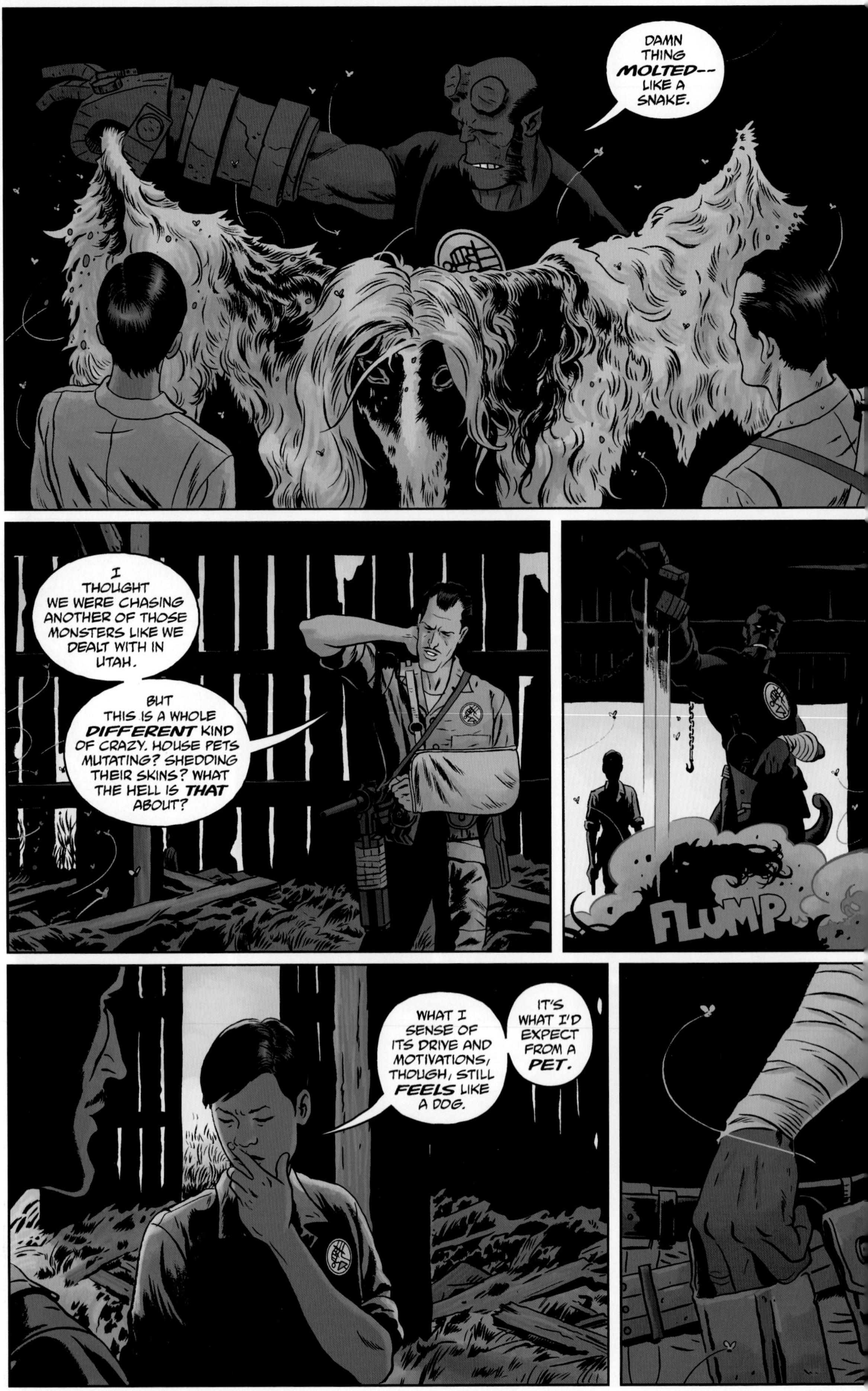
DAMN THING MOLTED-- LIKE A SNAKE.
I THOUGHT WE WERE CHASING ANOTHER OF THOSE MONSTERS LIKE WE DEALT WITH IN UTAH.
BUT THIS IS A WHOLE DIFFERENT KIND OF CRAZY. HOUSE PETS MUTATING? SHEDDING THEIR SKINS? WHAT THE HELL IS THAT ABOUT?
FLUMP
WHAT I SENSE OF ITS DRIVE AND MOTIVATIONS, THOUGH, STILL FEELS LIKE A DOG.
IT'S WHAT I'D EXPECT FROM A PET.

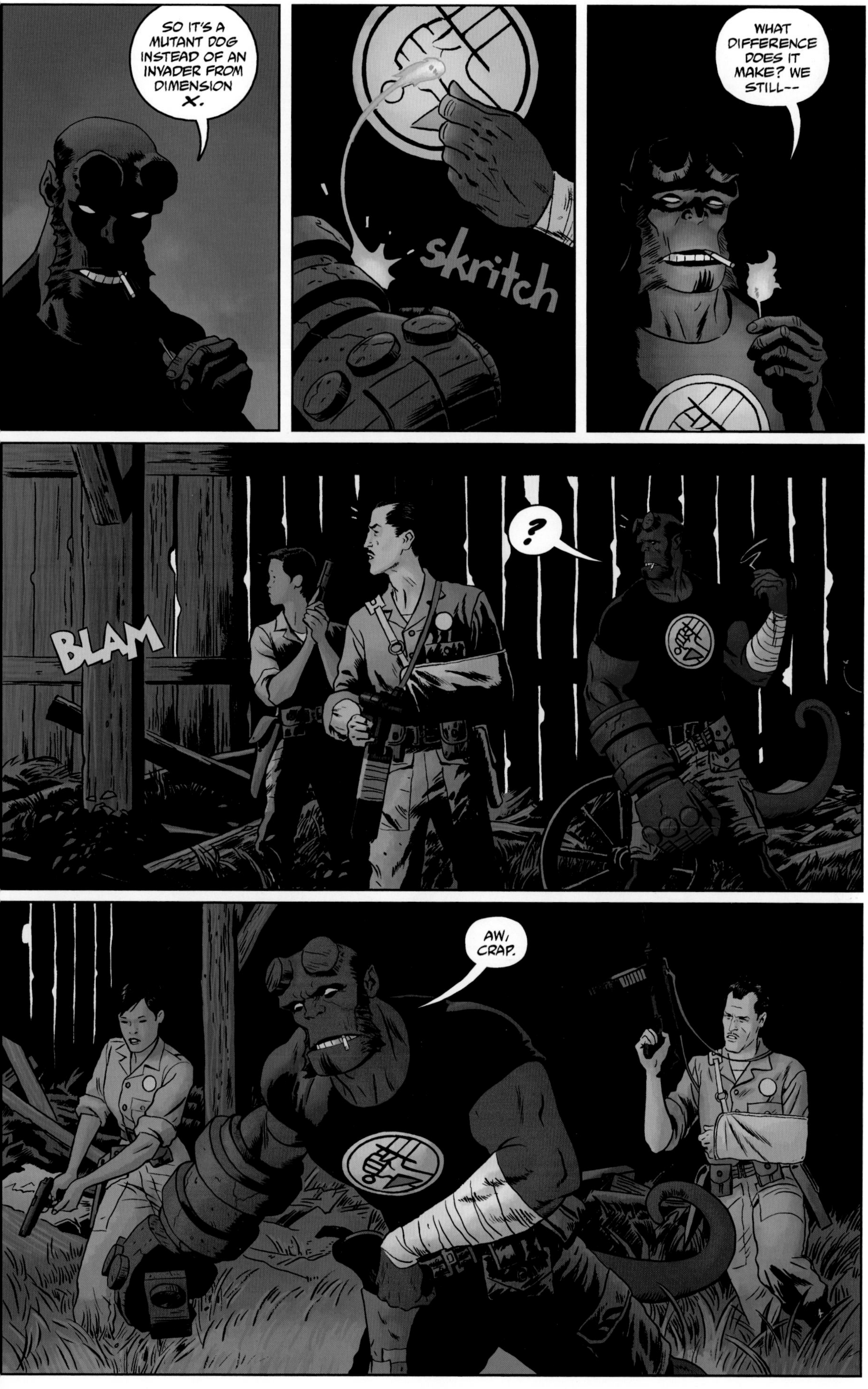
SO IT'S A MUTANT DOG INSTEAD OF AN INVADER FROM DIMENSION X.
skritch
WHAT DIFFERENCE DOES IT MAKE? WE STILL--
BLAM
?
AW, CRAP.

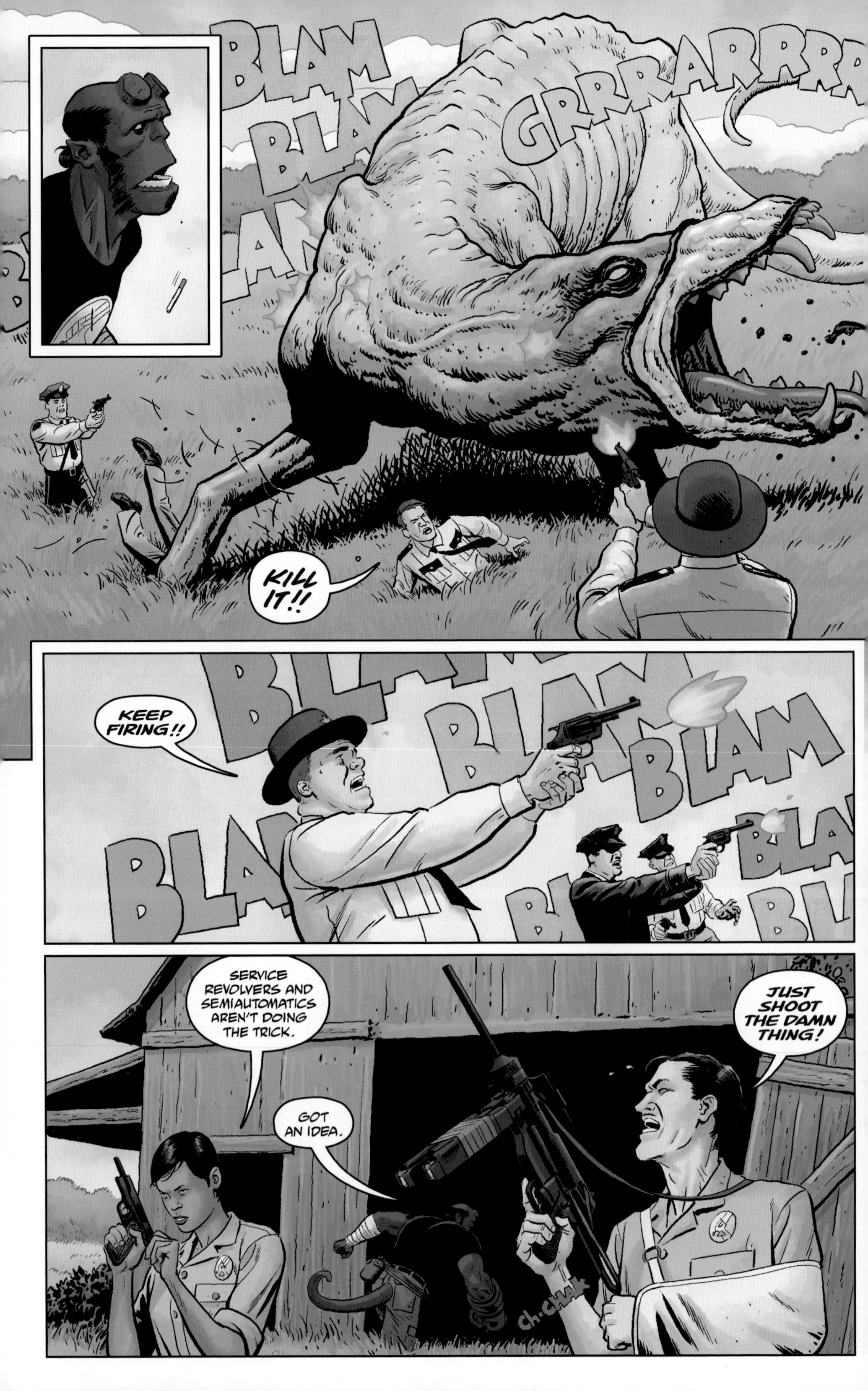
BLAM
BLAM
GRRRARRRR
KILL IT!!
KEEP FIRING!!
BLAM
BLAM
SERVICE REVOLVERS AND SEMIAUTOMATICS AREN'T DOING THE TRICK.
GOT AN IDEA.
JUST SHOOT THE DAMN THING!
CH-CHAK

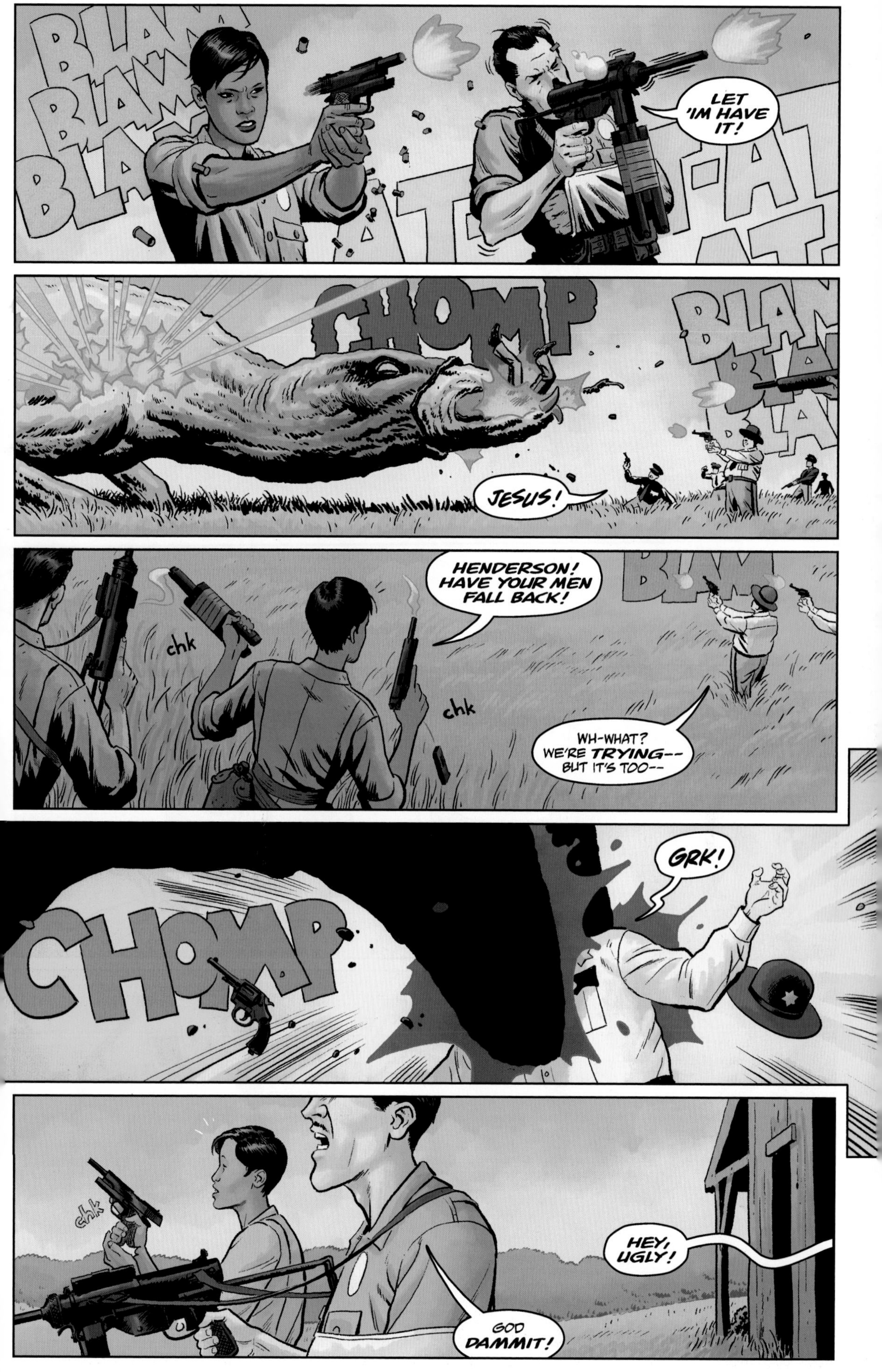
LET 'IM HAVE IT!
CHOMP
JESUS!
HENDERSON! HAVE YOUR MEN FALL BACK!
chk
chk
WH-WHAT? WE'RE TRYING-- BUT IT'S TOO--
GRK!
CHOMP
chk
HEY, UGLY!
GOD DAMMIT!

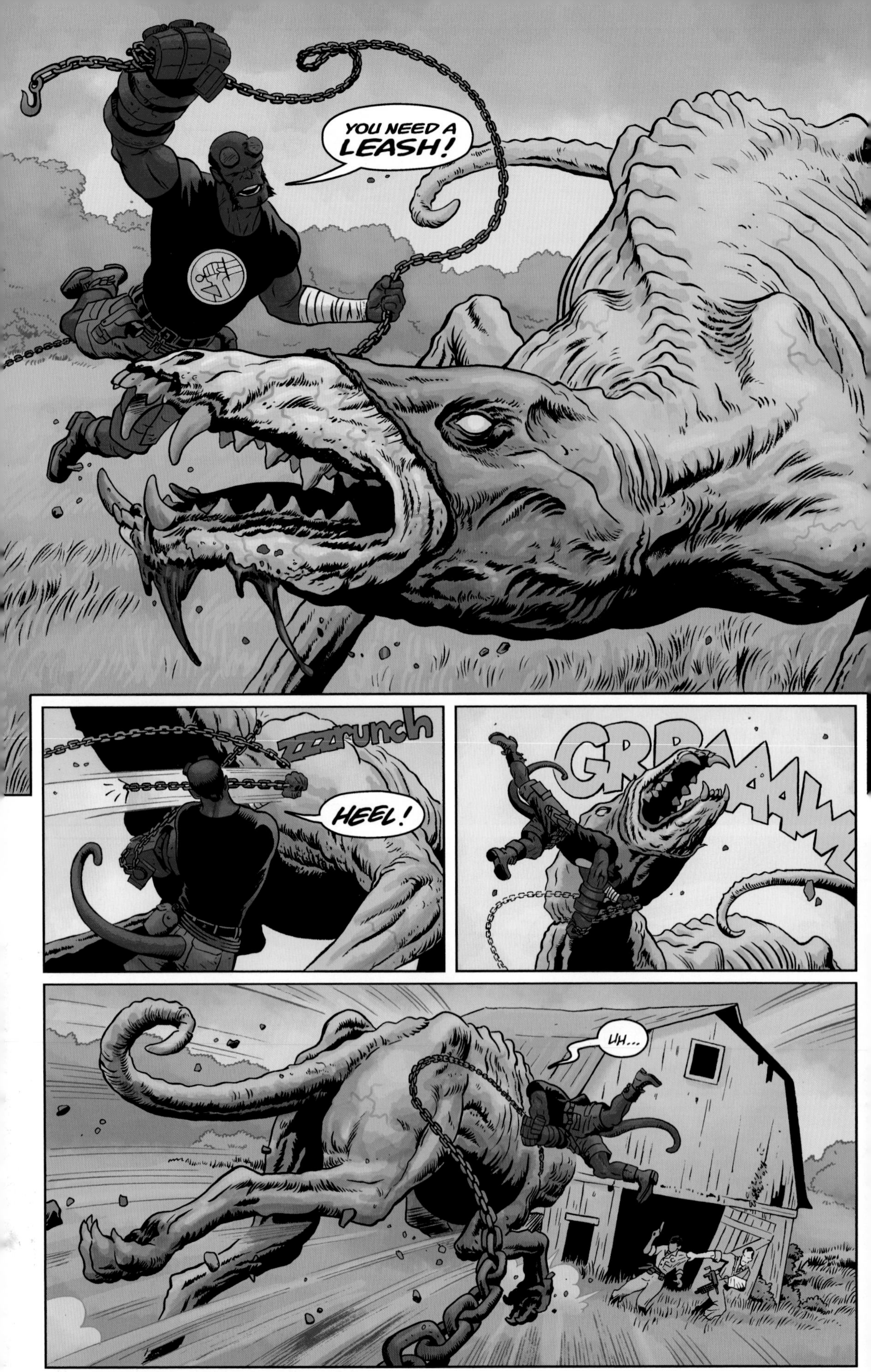
YOU NEED A LEASH!
ZZZRUNCH
HEEL!
UH...

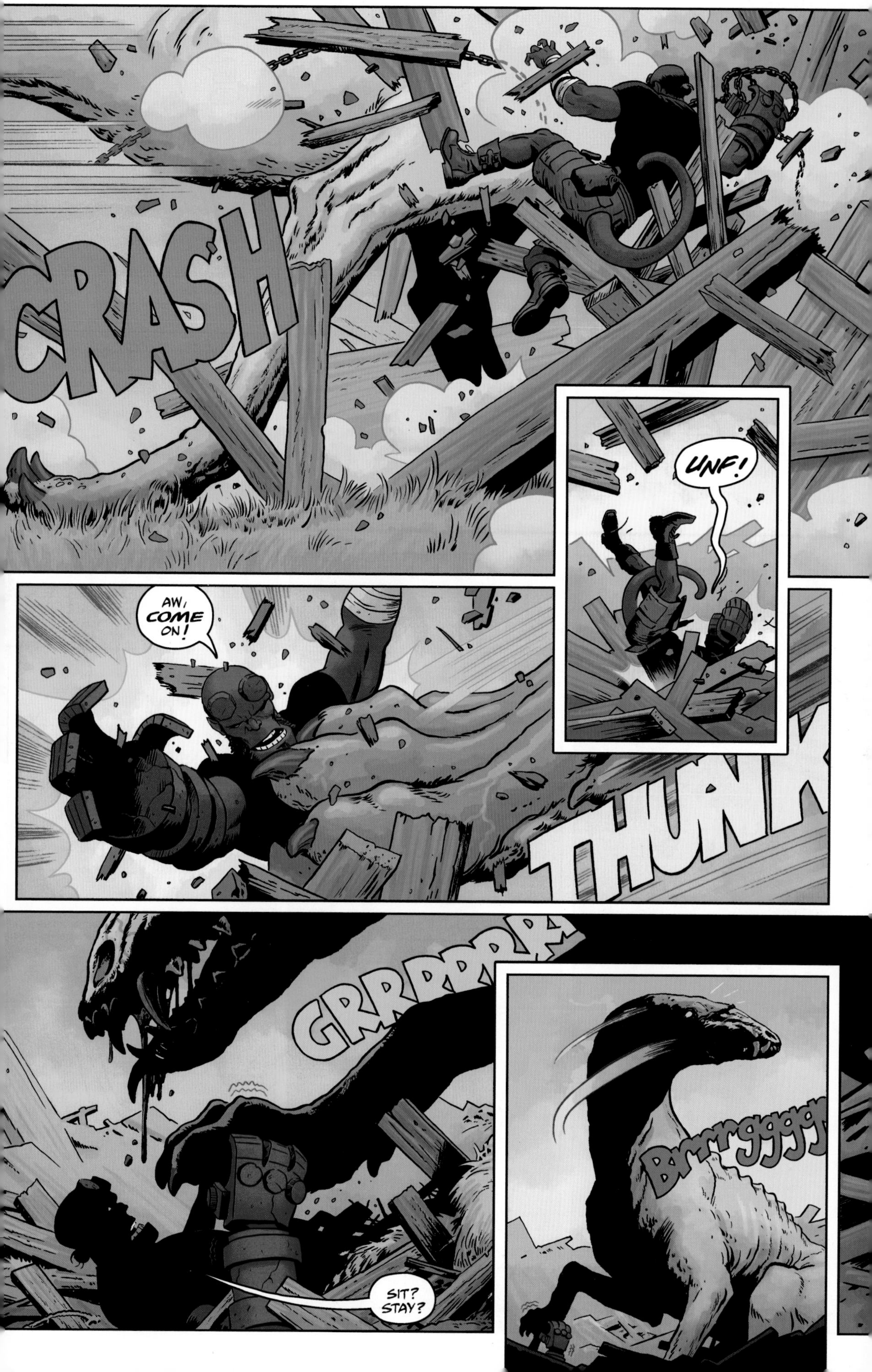
CRASH
UNF!
AW, COME ON!
THUNK
GRRRRR
SIT? STAY?
Brrrrgggg

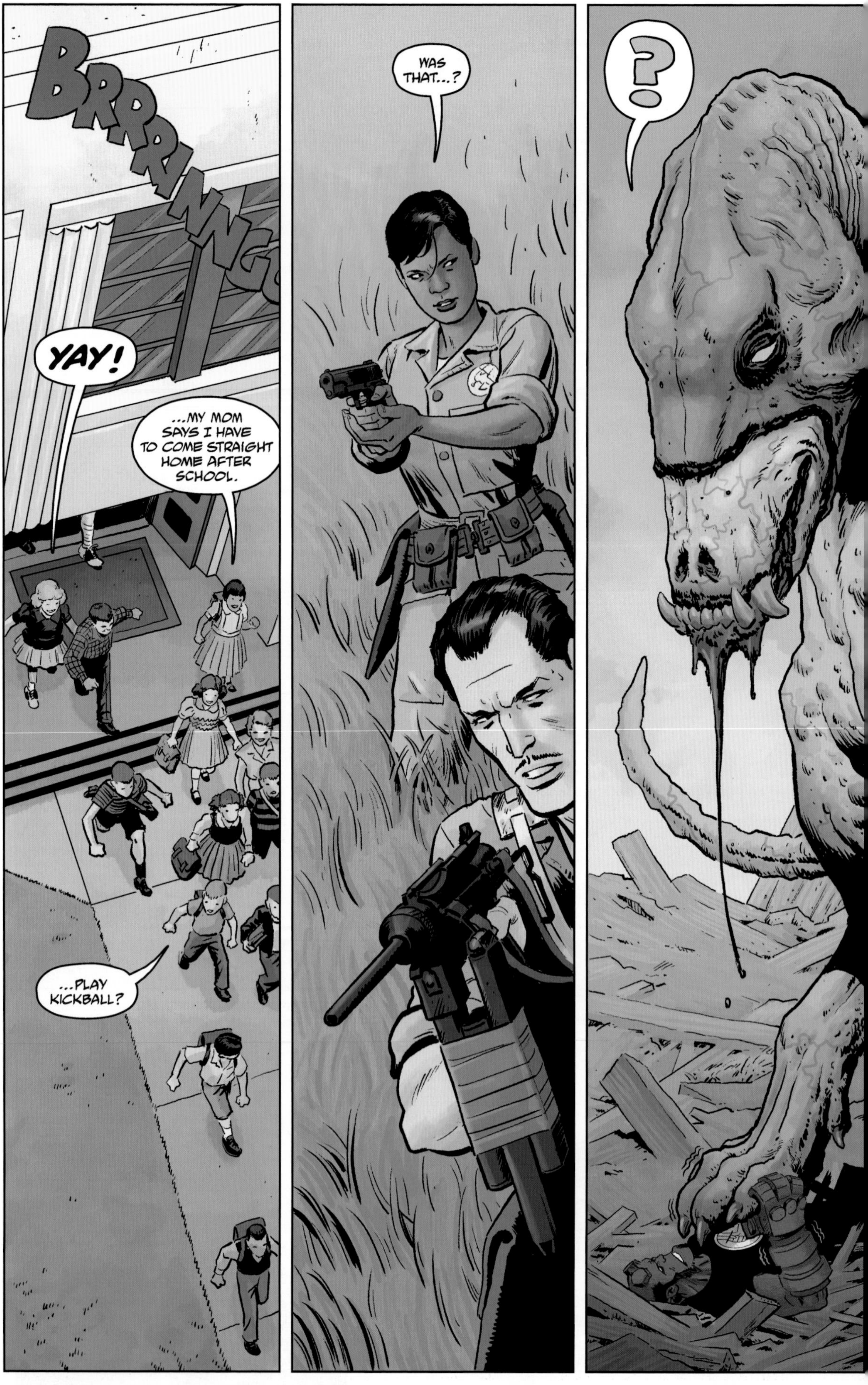
BRRRRANNNGG
YAY!
...MY MOM SAYS I HAVE TO COME STRAIGHT HOME AFTER SCHOOL.
...PLAY KICKBALL?
WAS THAT...?
?

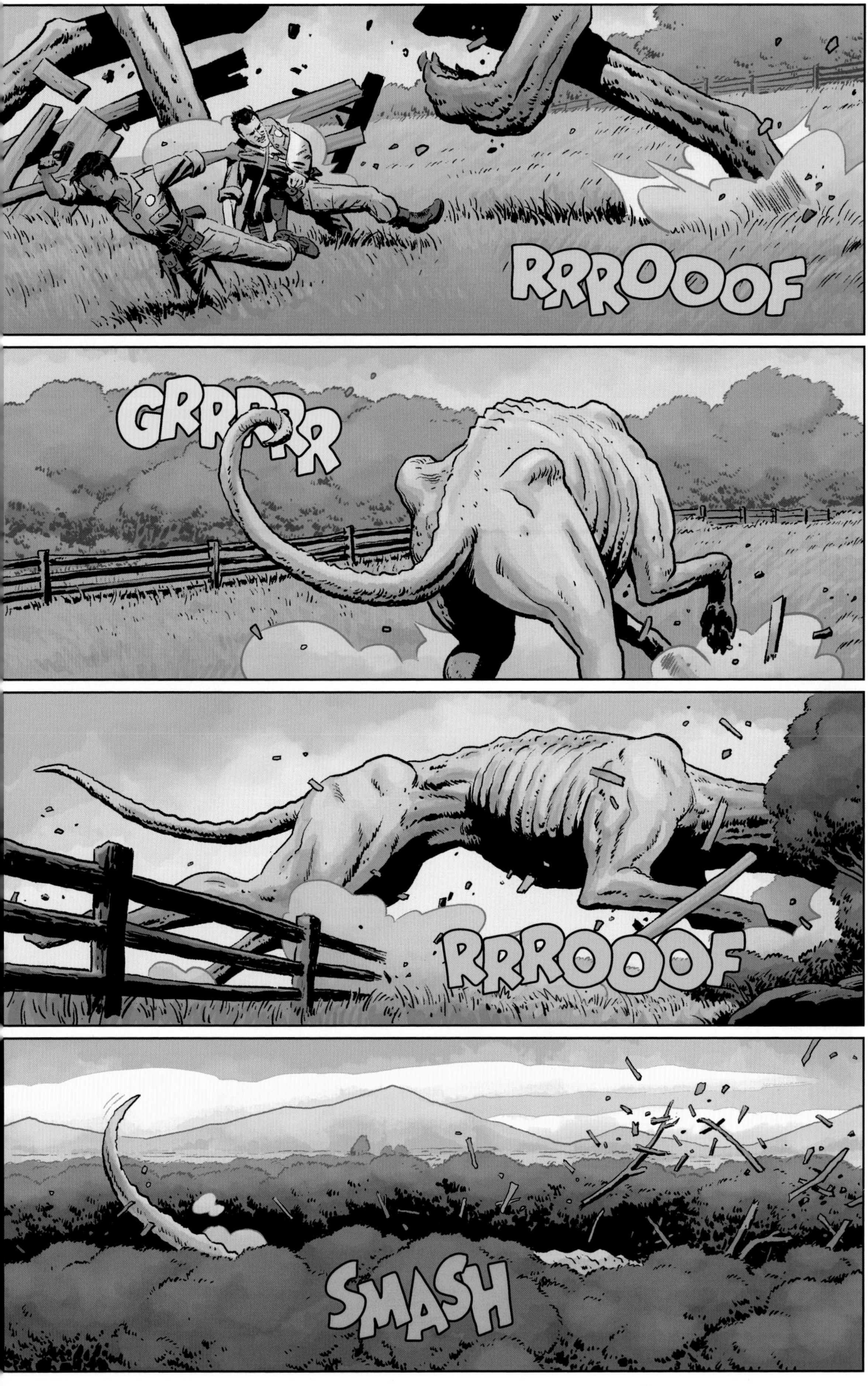
RRROOOF
GRRRRR
RRROOOF
SMASH

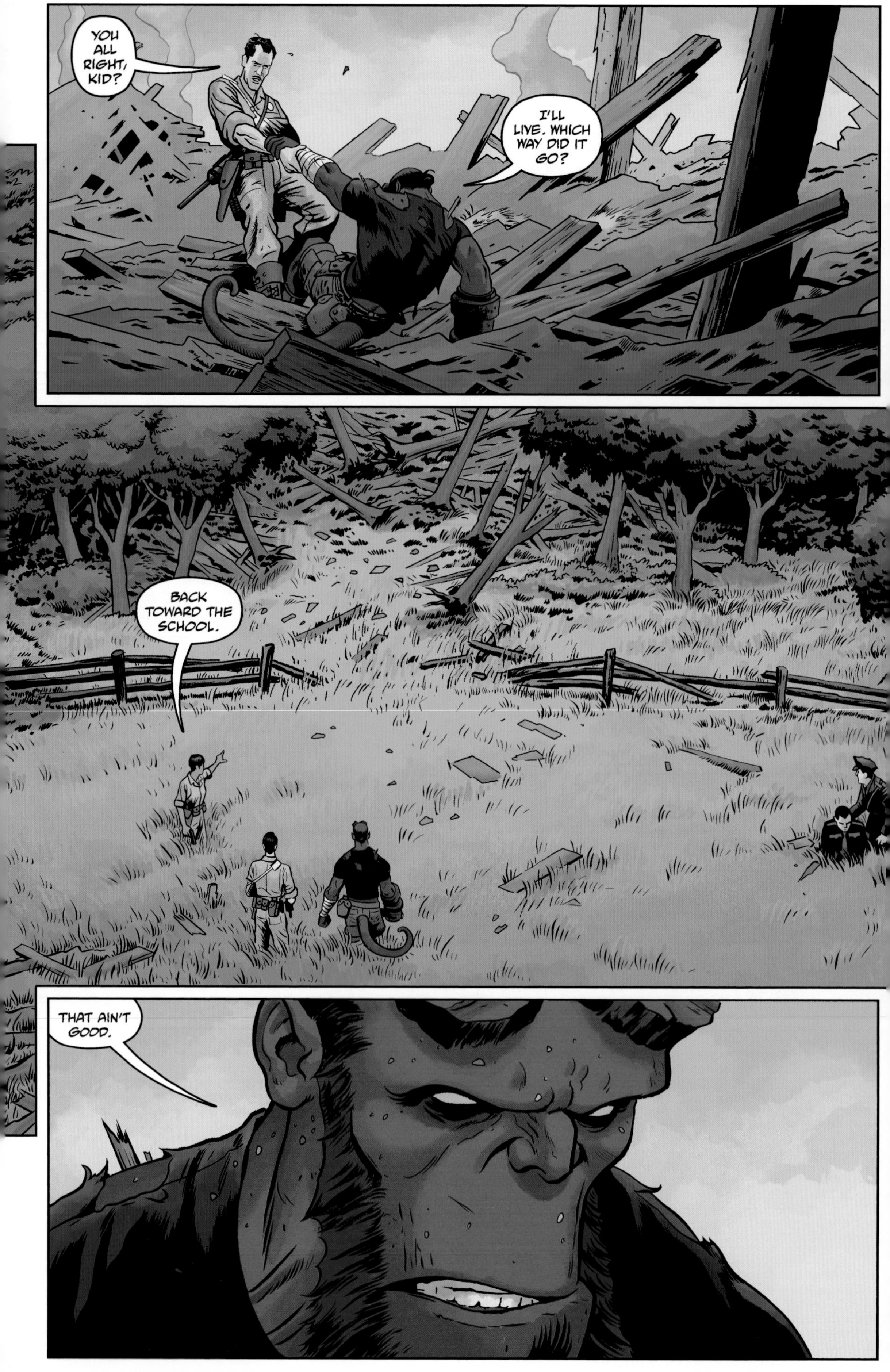
YOU ALL RIGHT, KID?
I'LL LIVE. WHICH WAY DID IT GO?
BACK TOWARD THE SCHOOL.
THAT AIN'T GOOD.

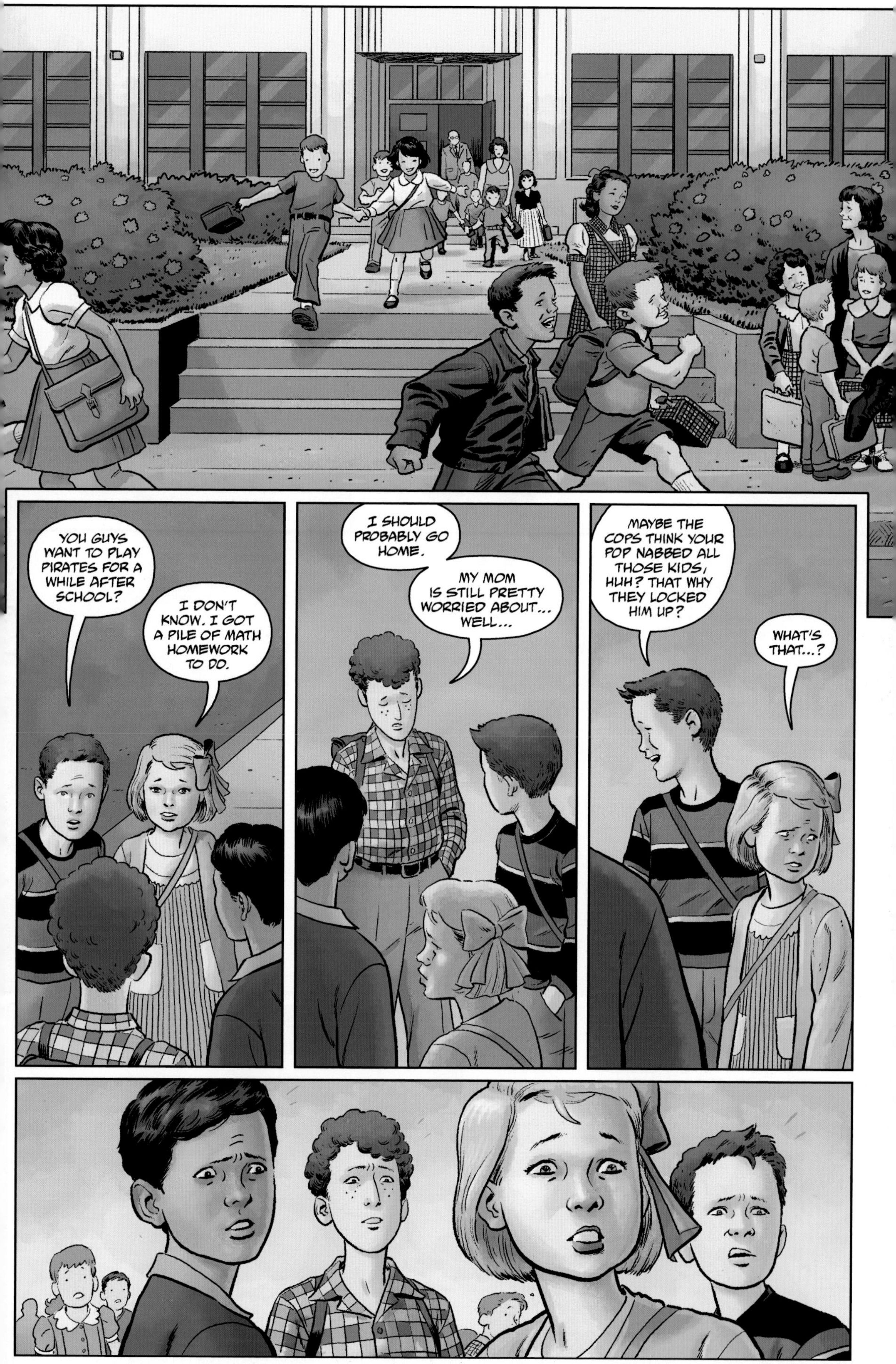
YOU GUYS WANT TO PLAY PIRATES FOR A WHILE AFTER SCHOOL?
I DON'T KNOW. I GOT A PILE OF MATH HOMEWORK TO DO.
I SHOULD PROBABLY GO HOME.
MY MOM IS STILL PRETTY WORRIED ABOUT... WELL...
MAYBE THE COPS THINK YOUR POP NABBED ALL THOSE KIDS, HUH? THAT WHY THEY LOCKED HIM UP?
WHAT'S THAT...?

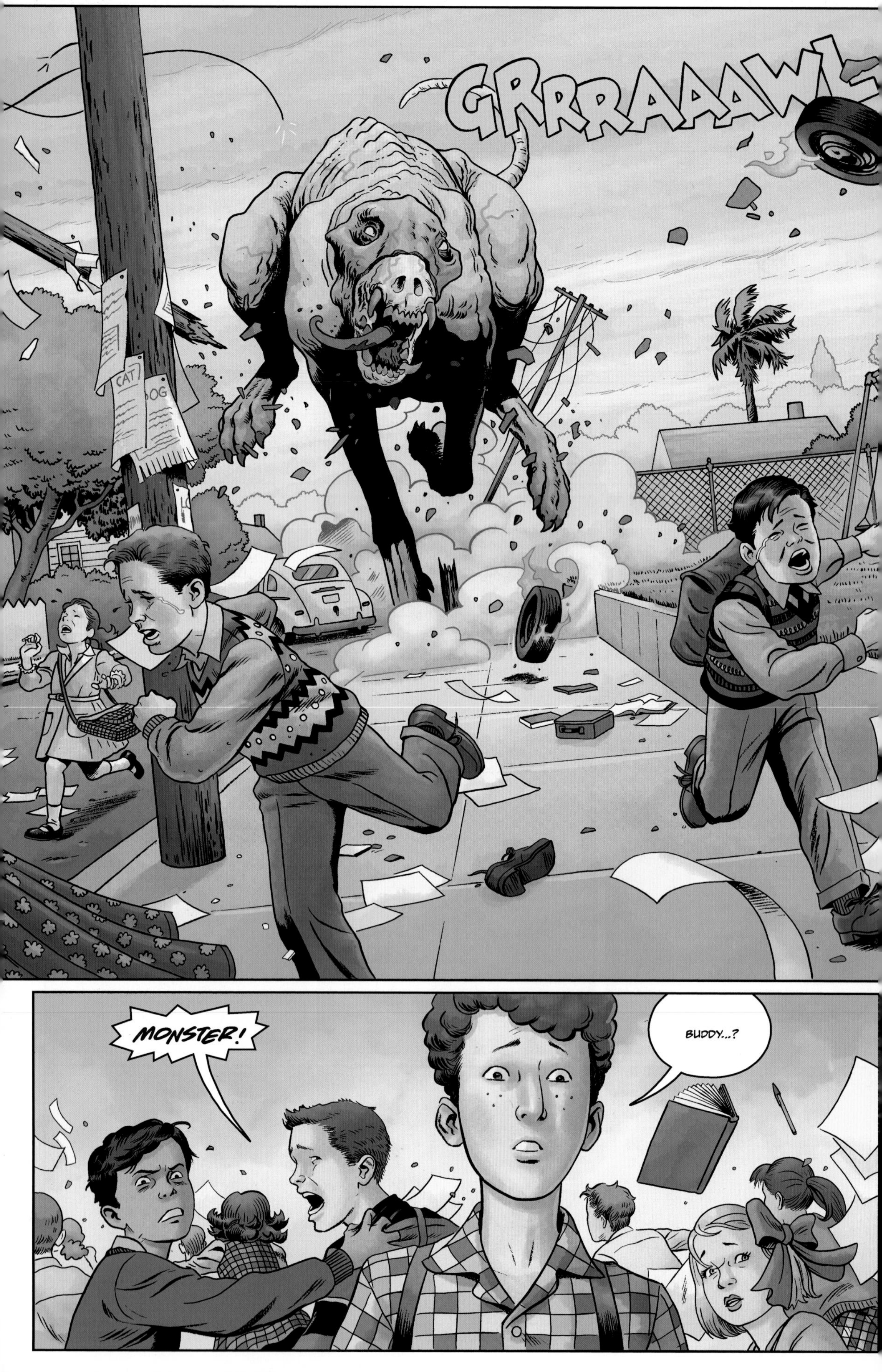
GRRRAAAWW
CAT
DOG
MONSTER!
BUDDY...?

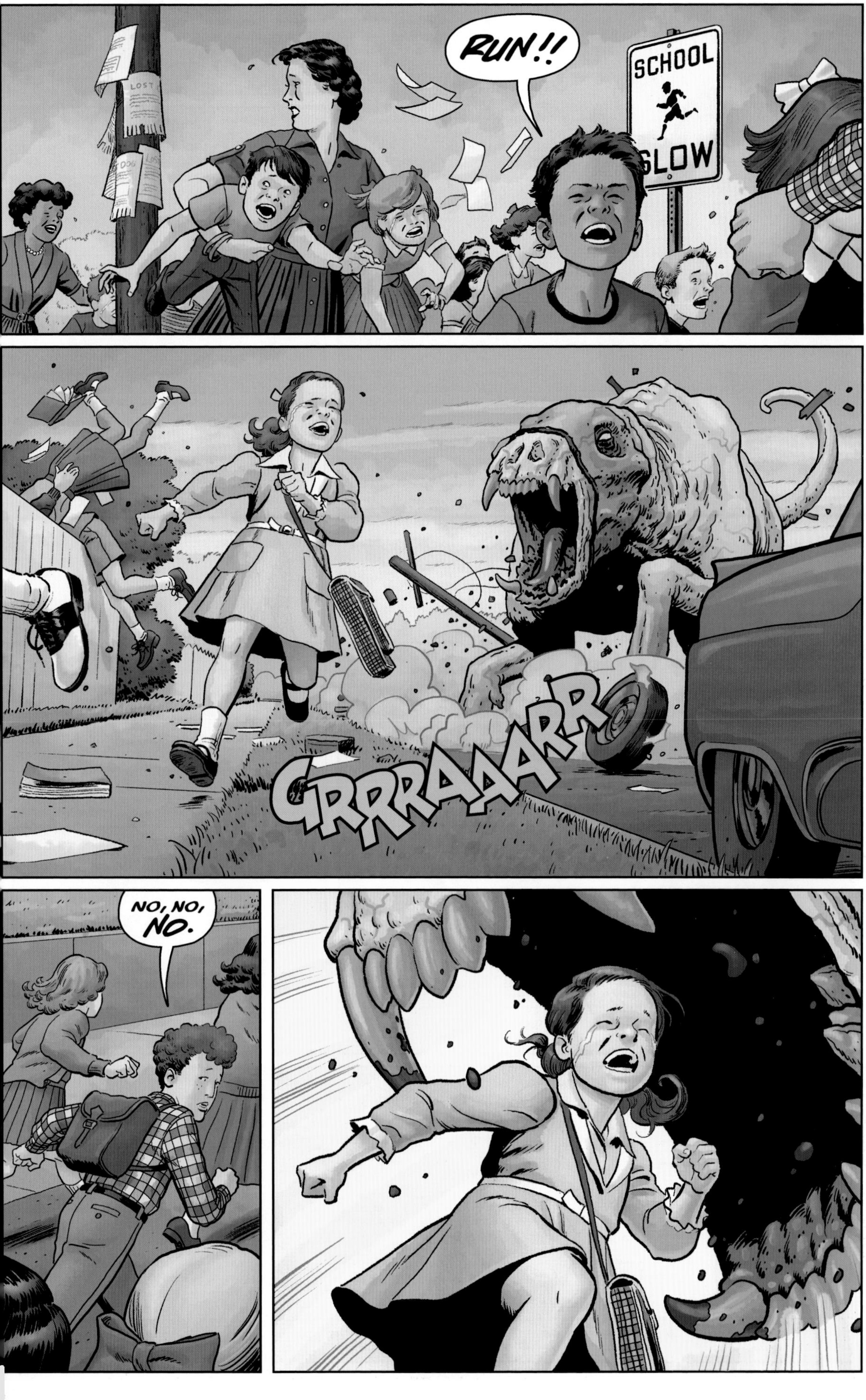
RUN!!
SCHOOL
SLOW
LOST
LOST
DOG
GRRRAAARR
NO, NO, NO.

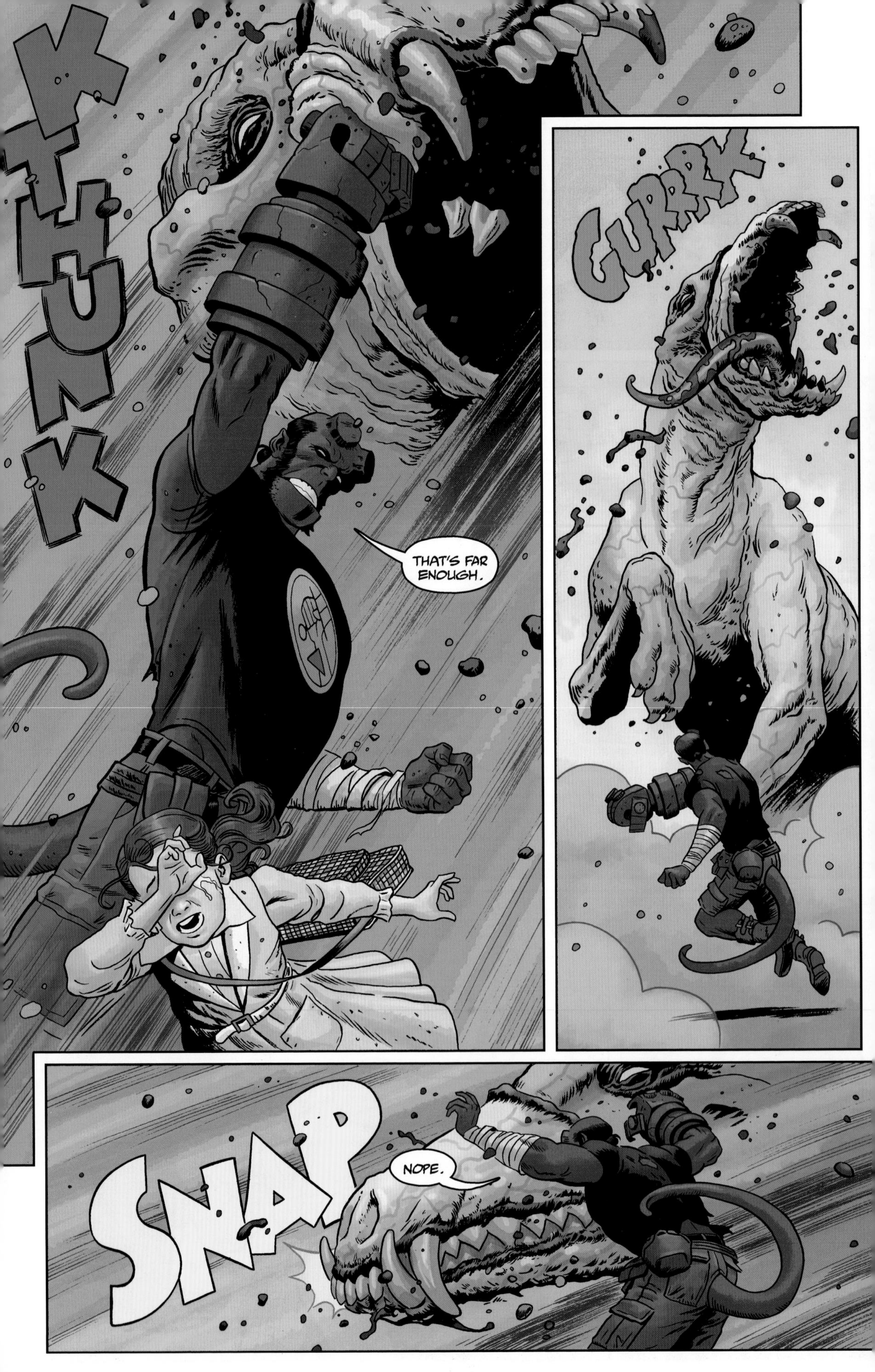
KTHUNK
THAT'S FAR ENOUGH.
GURRK
SNAP
NOPE.

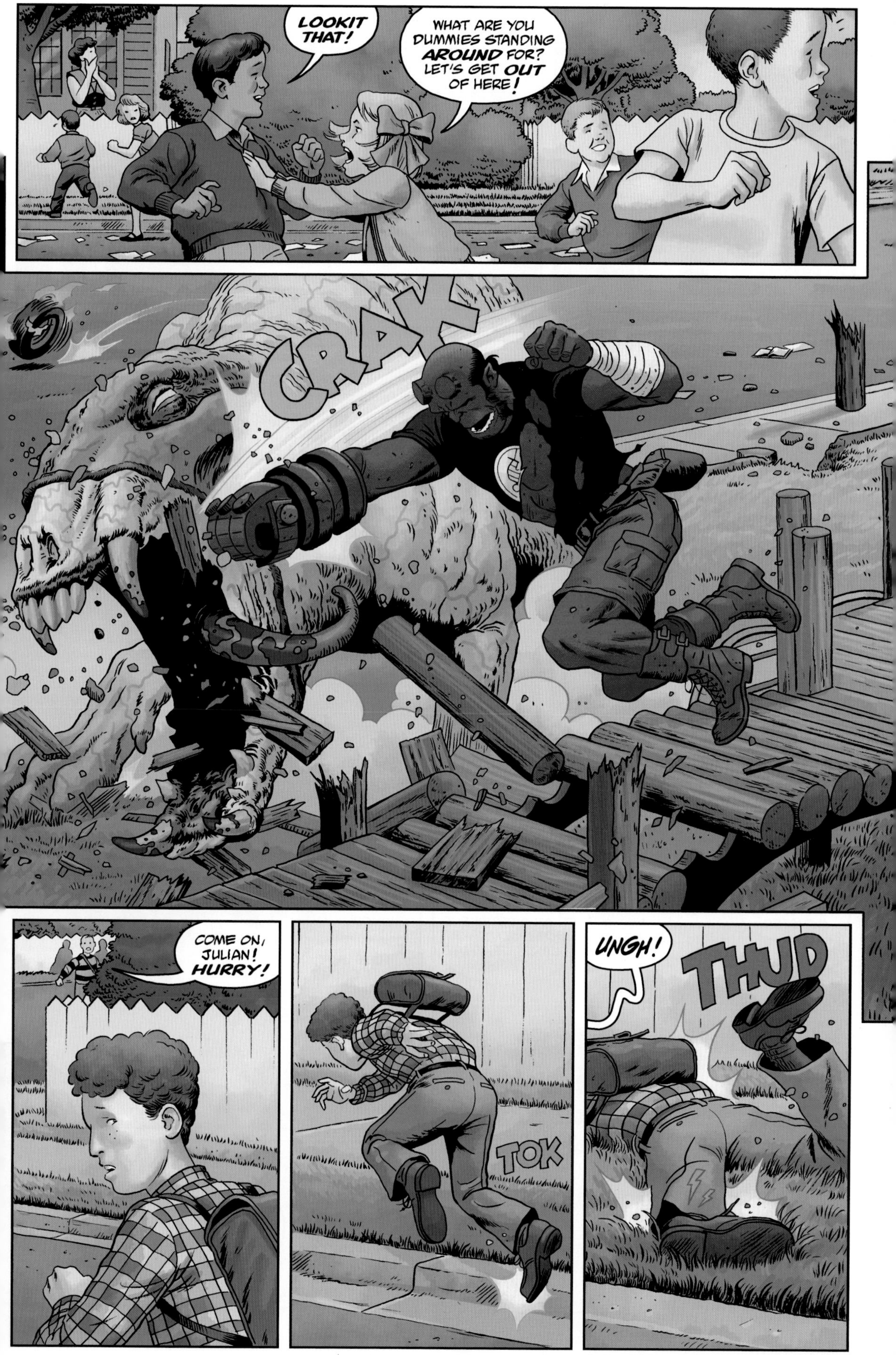
LOOKIT THAT!
WHAT ARE YOU DUMMIES STANDING AROUND FOR? LET'S GET OUT OF HERE!
CRAK
COME ON, JULIAN! HURRY!
TOK
UNGH!
THUD

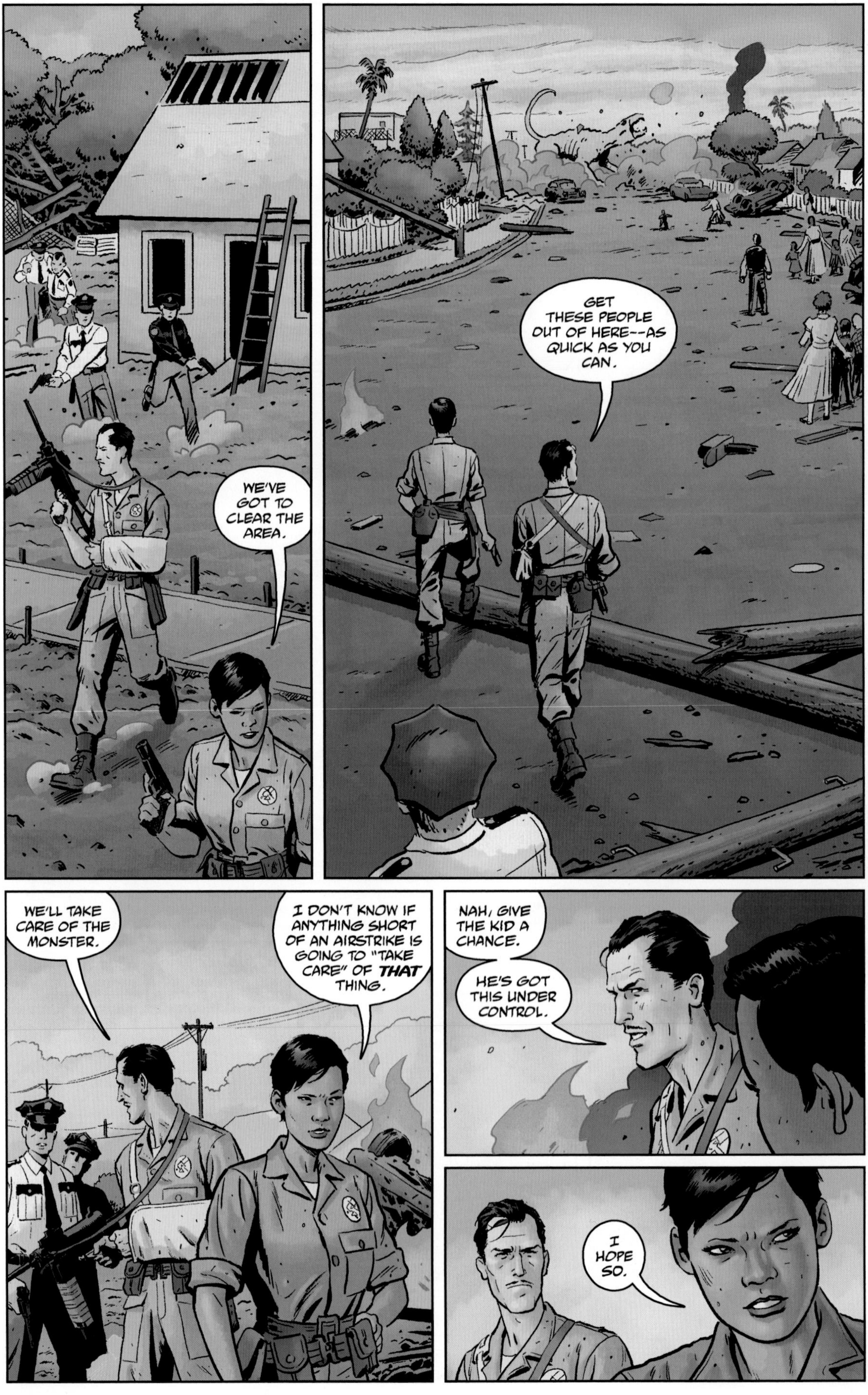
WE'VE GOT TO CLEAR THE AREA.
GET THESE PEOPLE OUT OF HERE--AS QUICK AS YOU CAN.
WE'LL TAKE CARE OF THE MONSTER.
I DON'T KNOW IF ANYTHING SHORT OF AN AIRSTRIKE IS GOING TO "TAKE CARE" OF THAT THING.
NAH, GIVE THE KID A CHANCE.
HE'S GOT THIS UNDER CONTROL.
I HOPE SO.

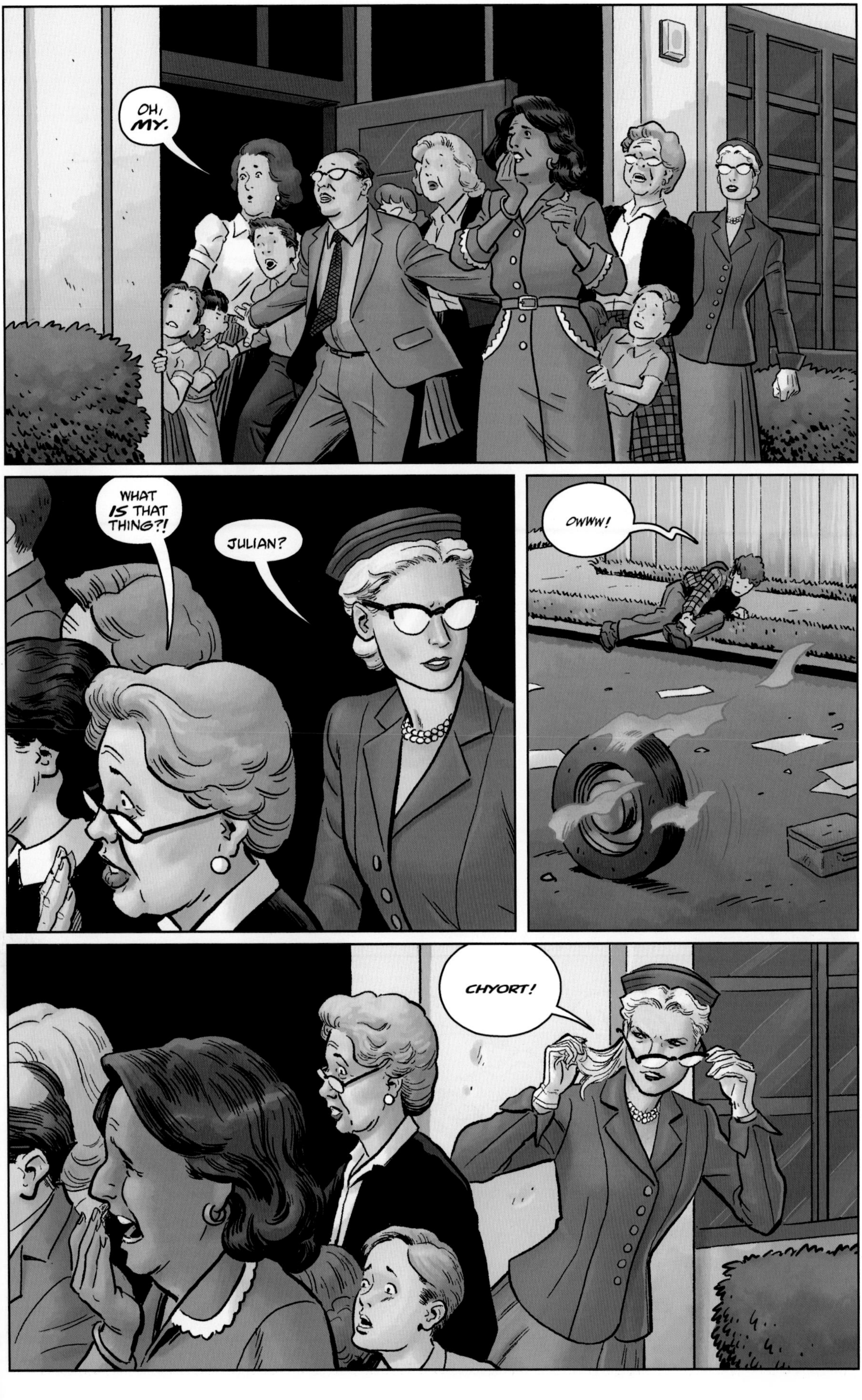
OH, MY.
WHAT IS THAT THING?!
JULIAN?
OWWW!
CHYORT!

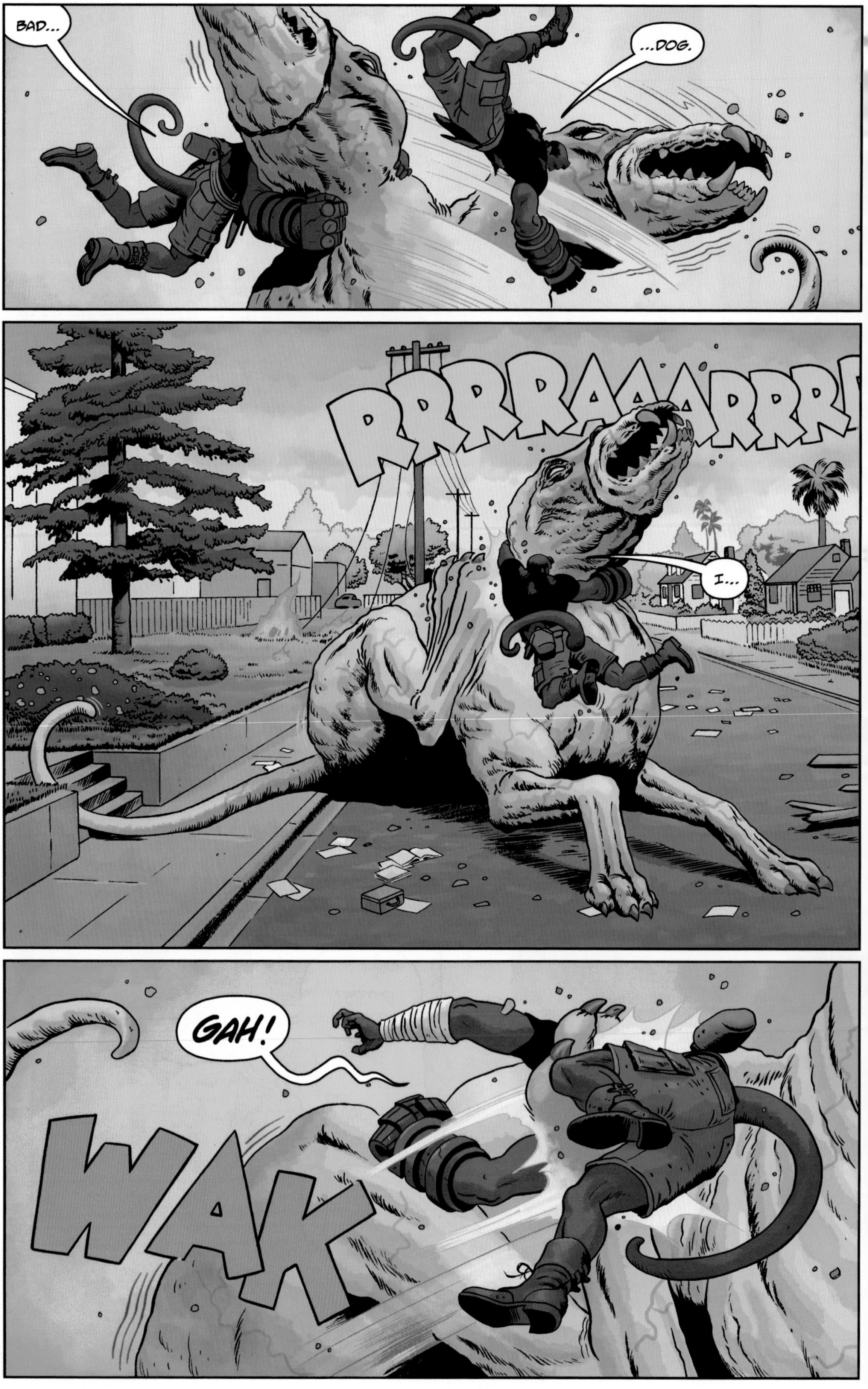
BAD...
...DOG.
RRRRAAARRRR
I...
GAH!
WAK

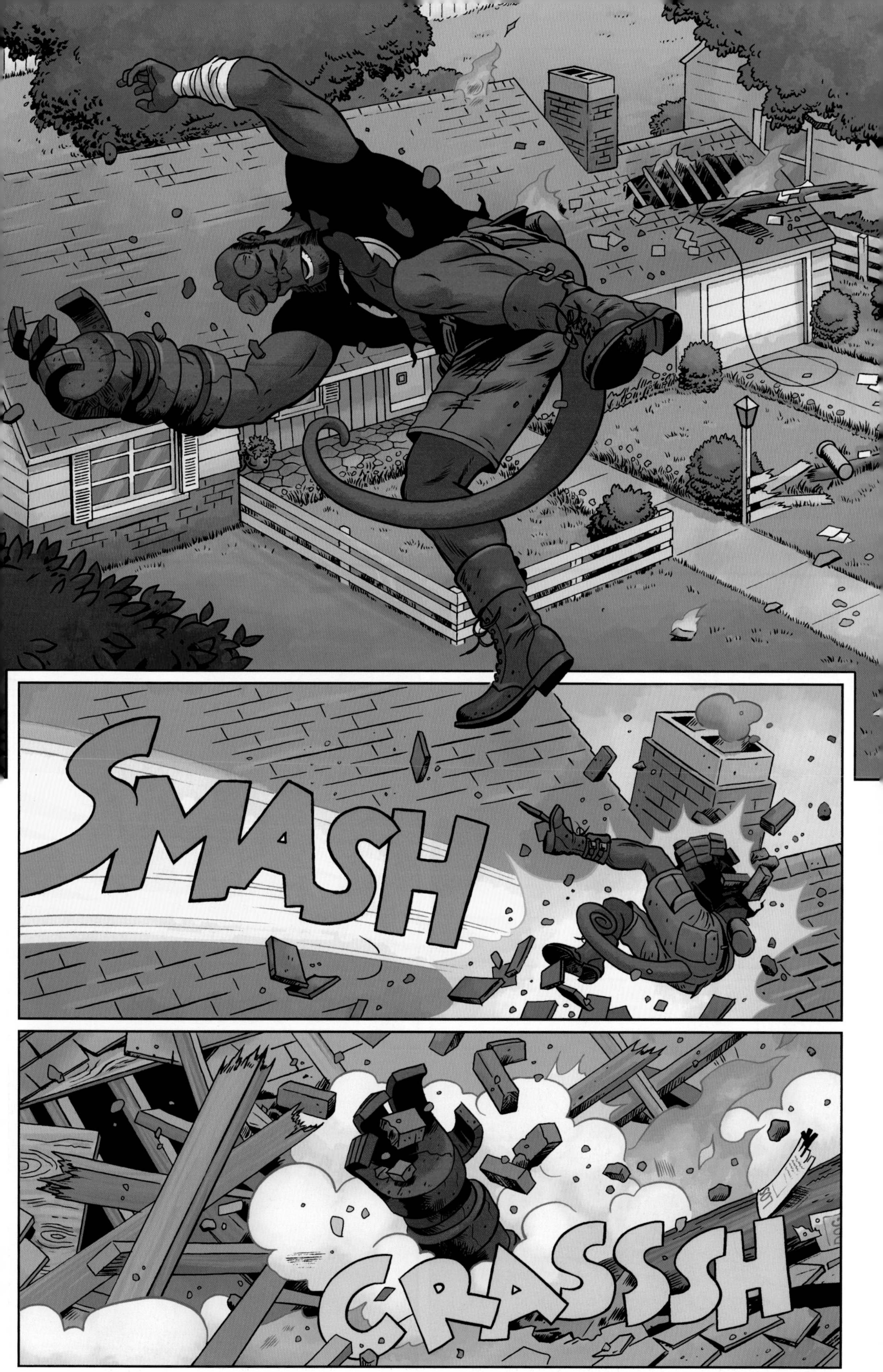
SMASH
CRASSSH

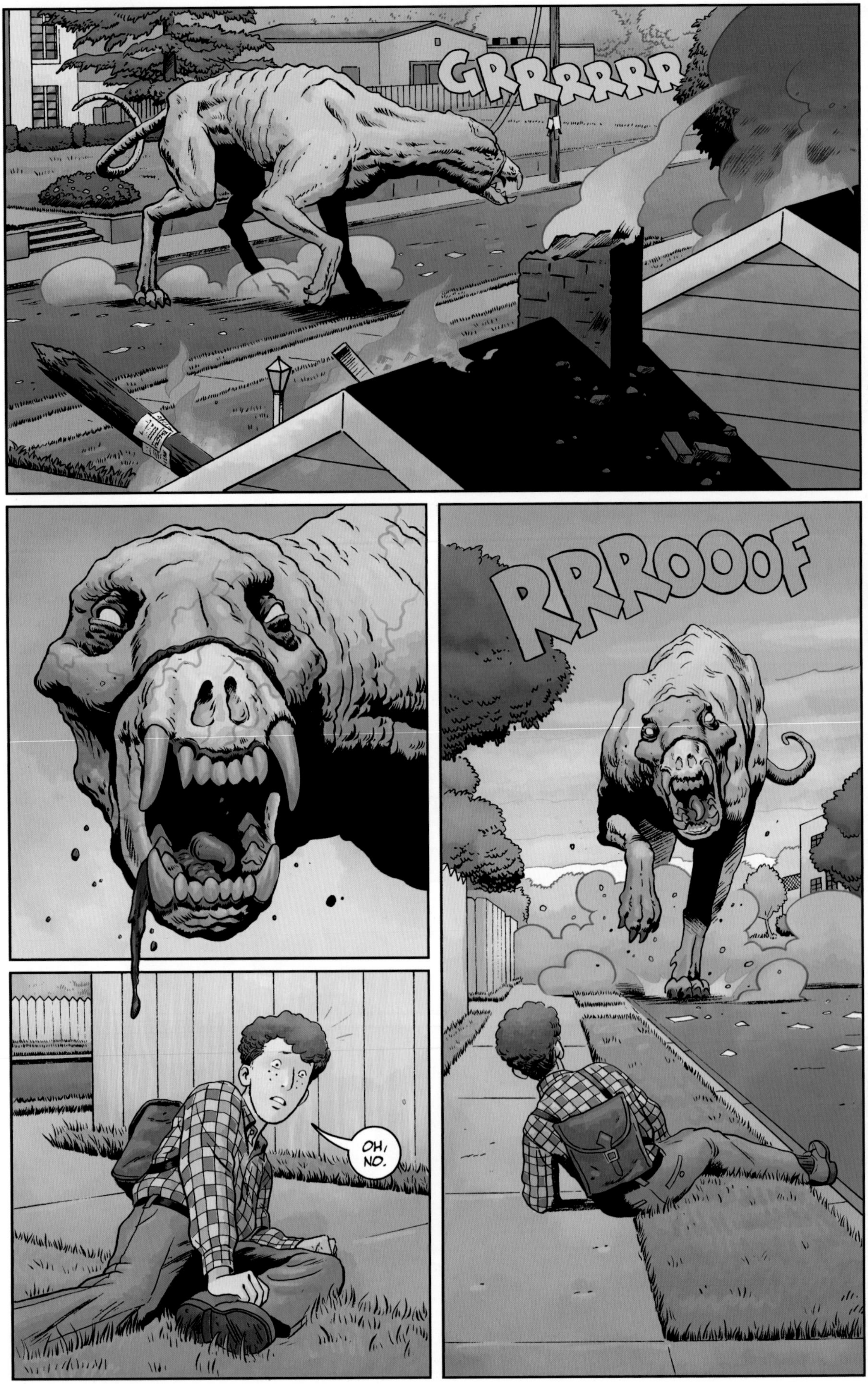
GRRRRRR
RRROOOF
OH, NO.

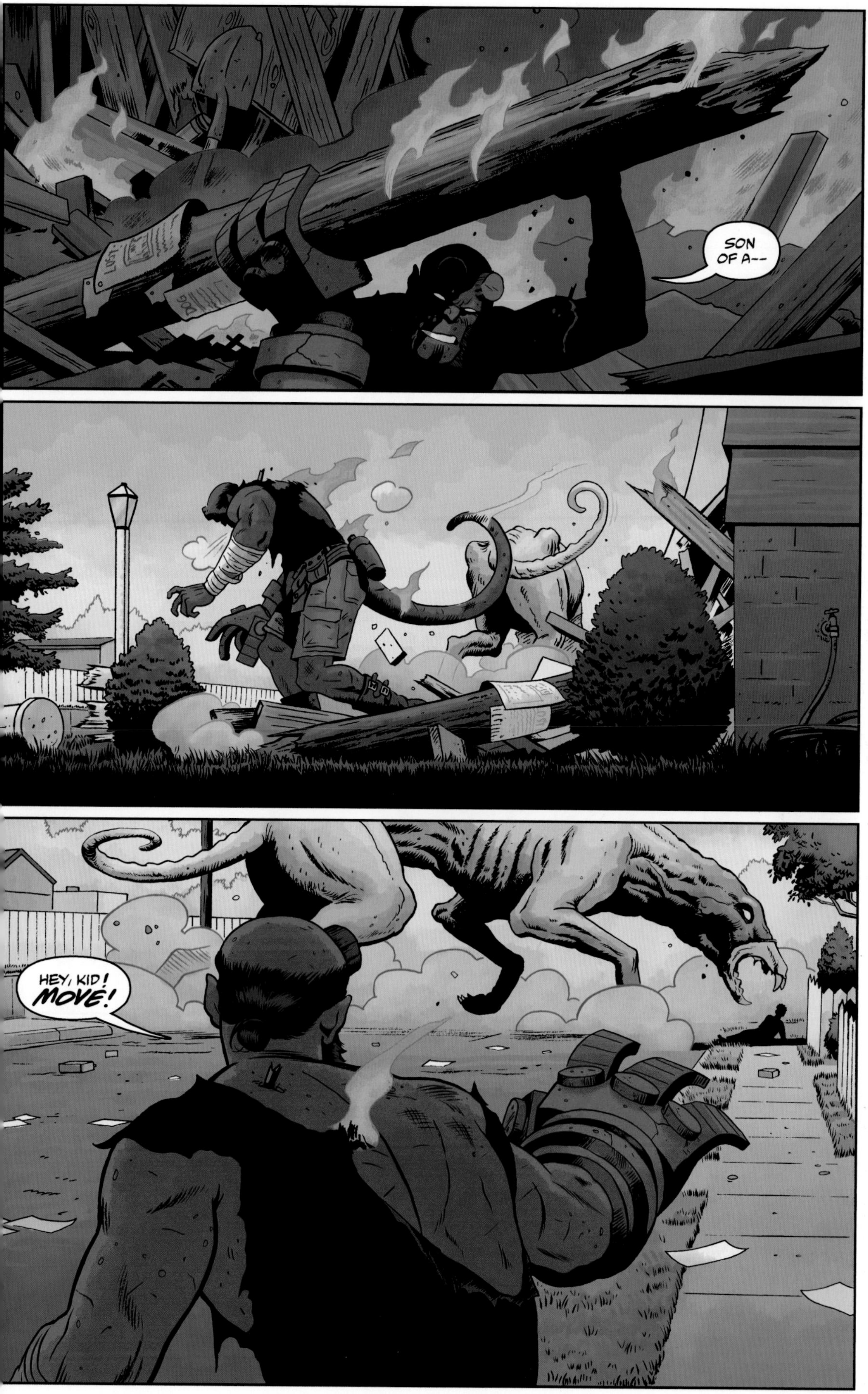
SON OF A--
HEY, KID! MOVE!

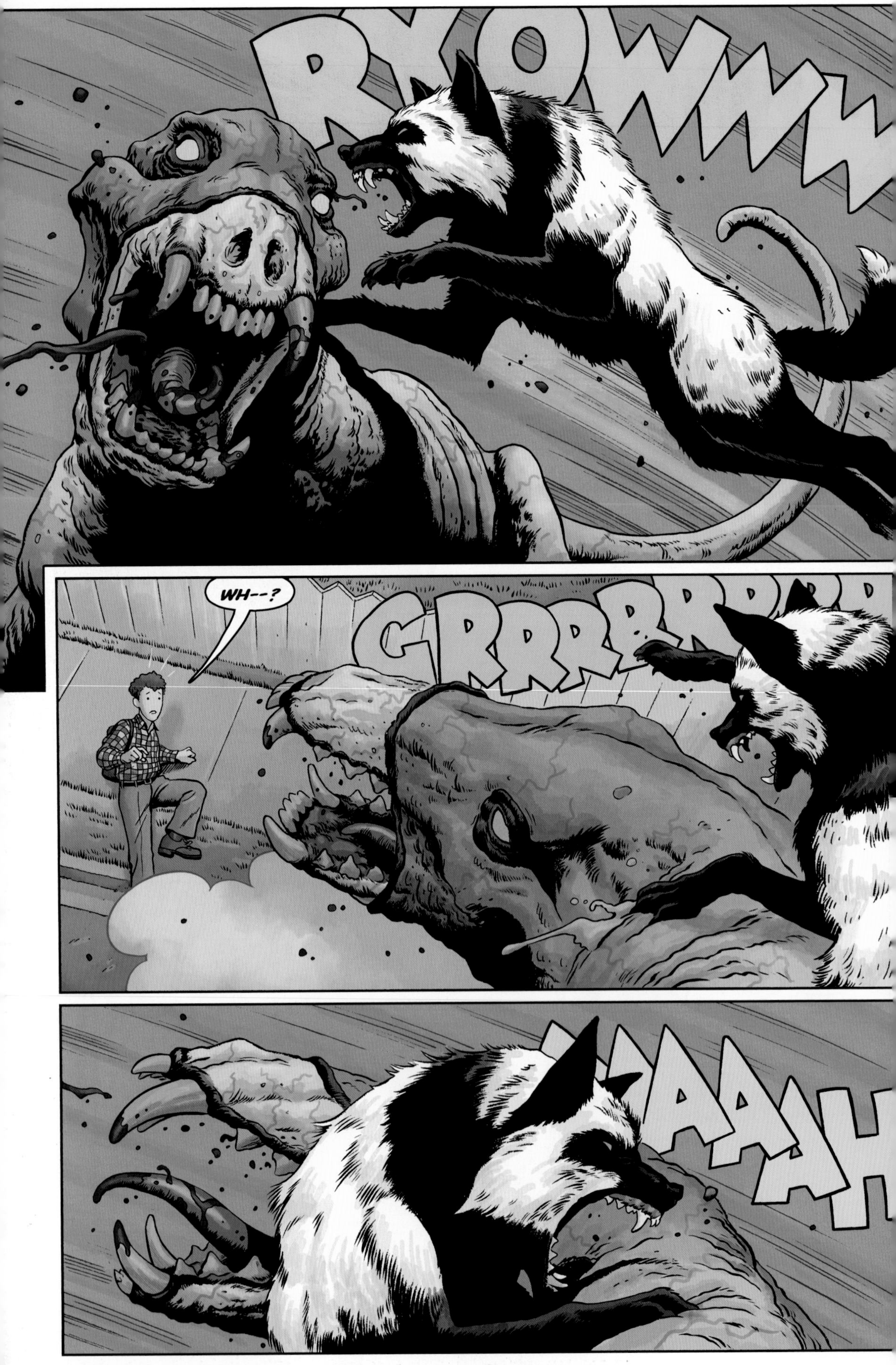
RYOWWW
WH--?
GRRRRRRR
AAAAH

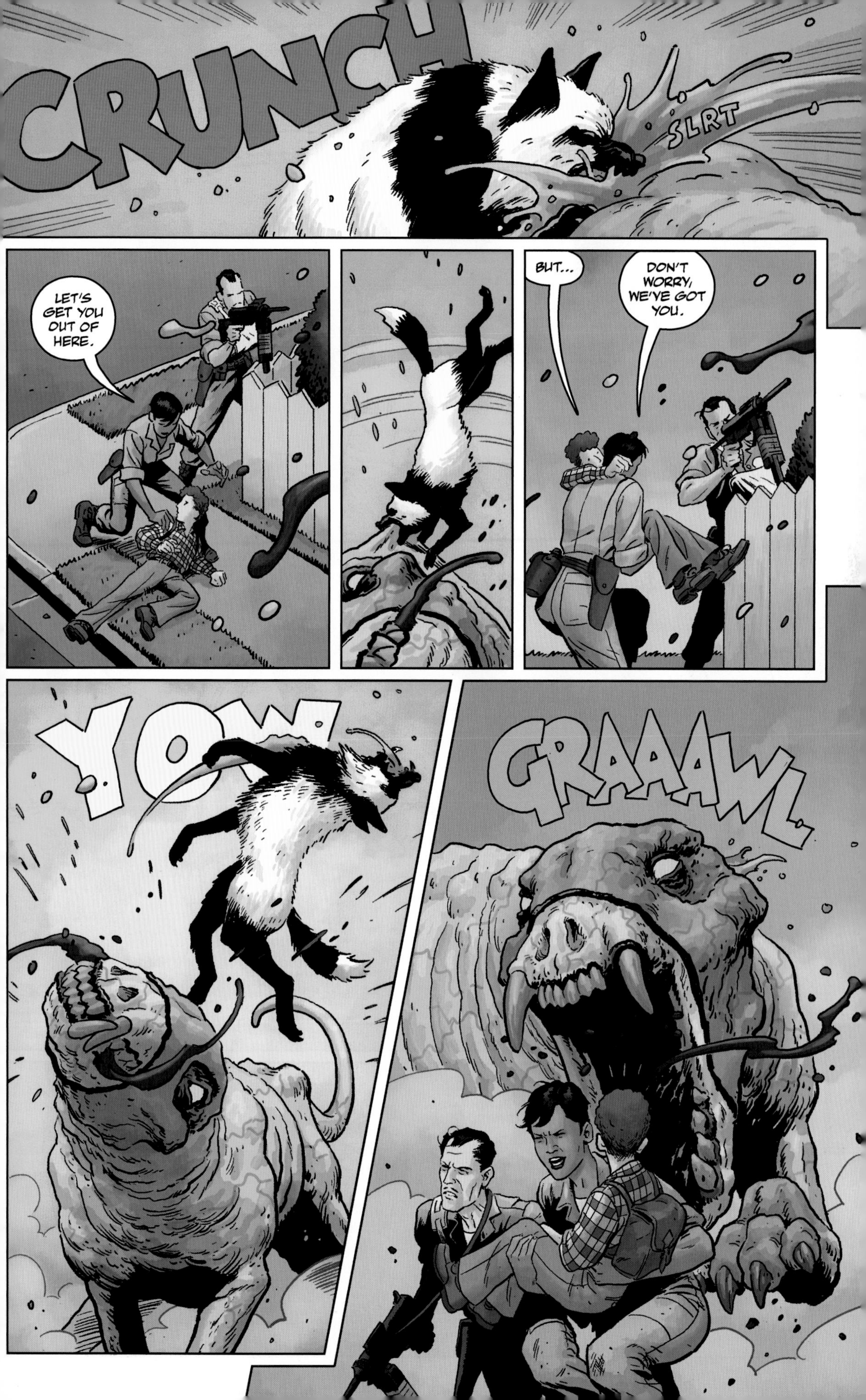
CRUNCH
SLRT
LET'S GET YOU OUT OF HERE.
BUT...
DON'T WORRY, WE'VE GOT YOU.
YOW
GRAAAWL

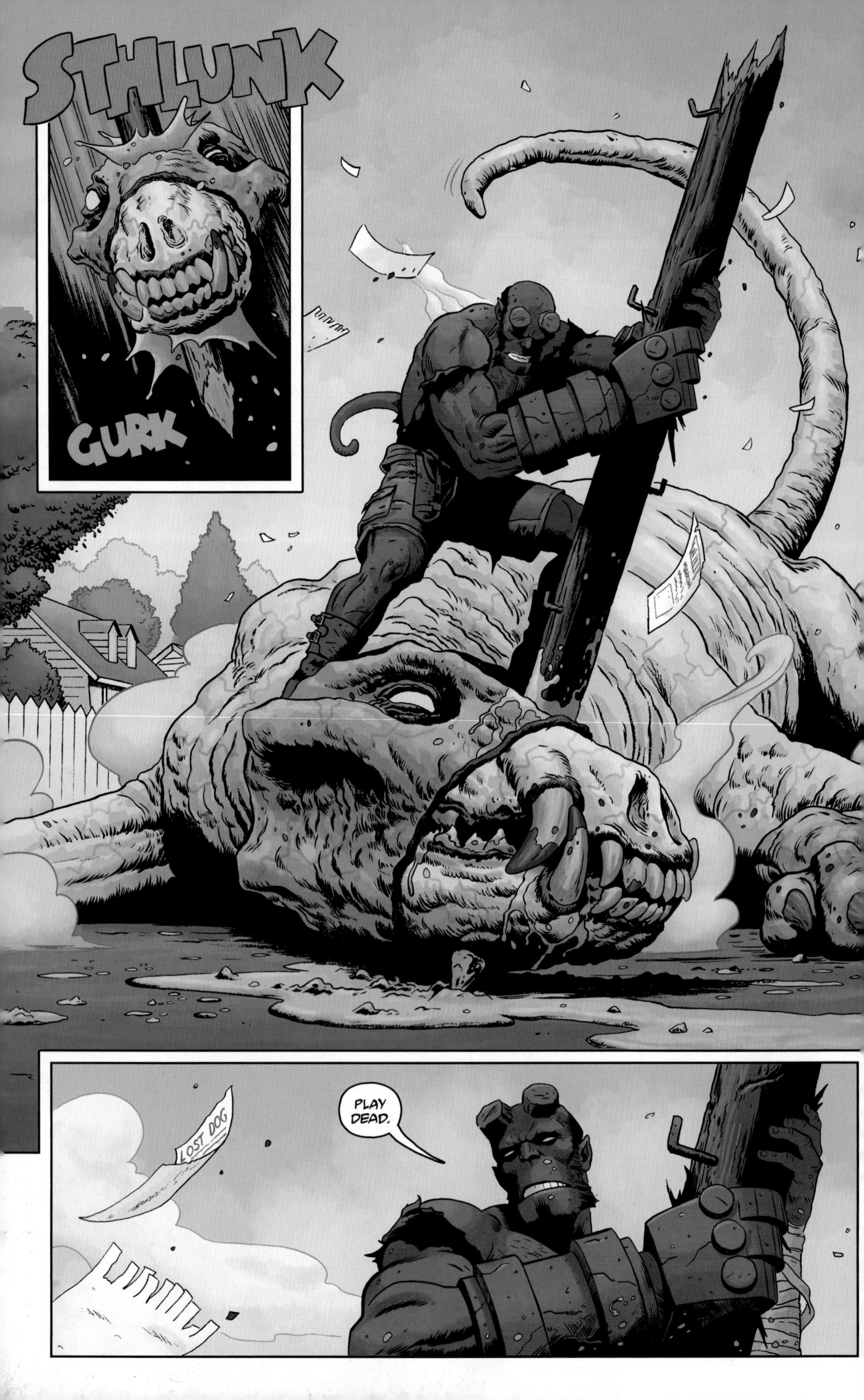
STHLUNK
GURK
LOST DOG
PLAY DEAD.

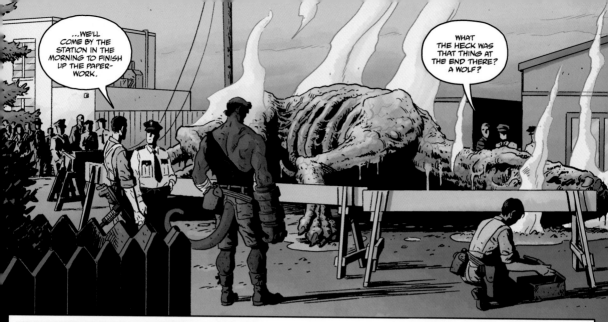

...WE'LL COME BY THE STATION IN THE MORNING TO FINISH UP THE PAPER-WORK.

WHAT THE HECK WAS THAT THING AT THE END THERE? A WOLF?

THE RATE THIS THING IS DECAYING, IT'LL BE COMPLETELY GONE PRETTY SOON.

THE BOYS AT THE LAB WILL KILL ME IF I DON'T BRING BACK A SAMPLE FOR THEM TO--

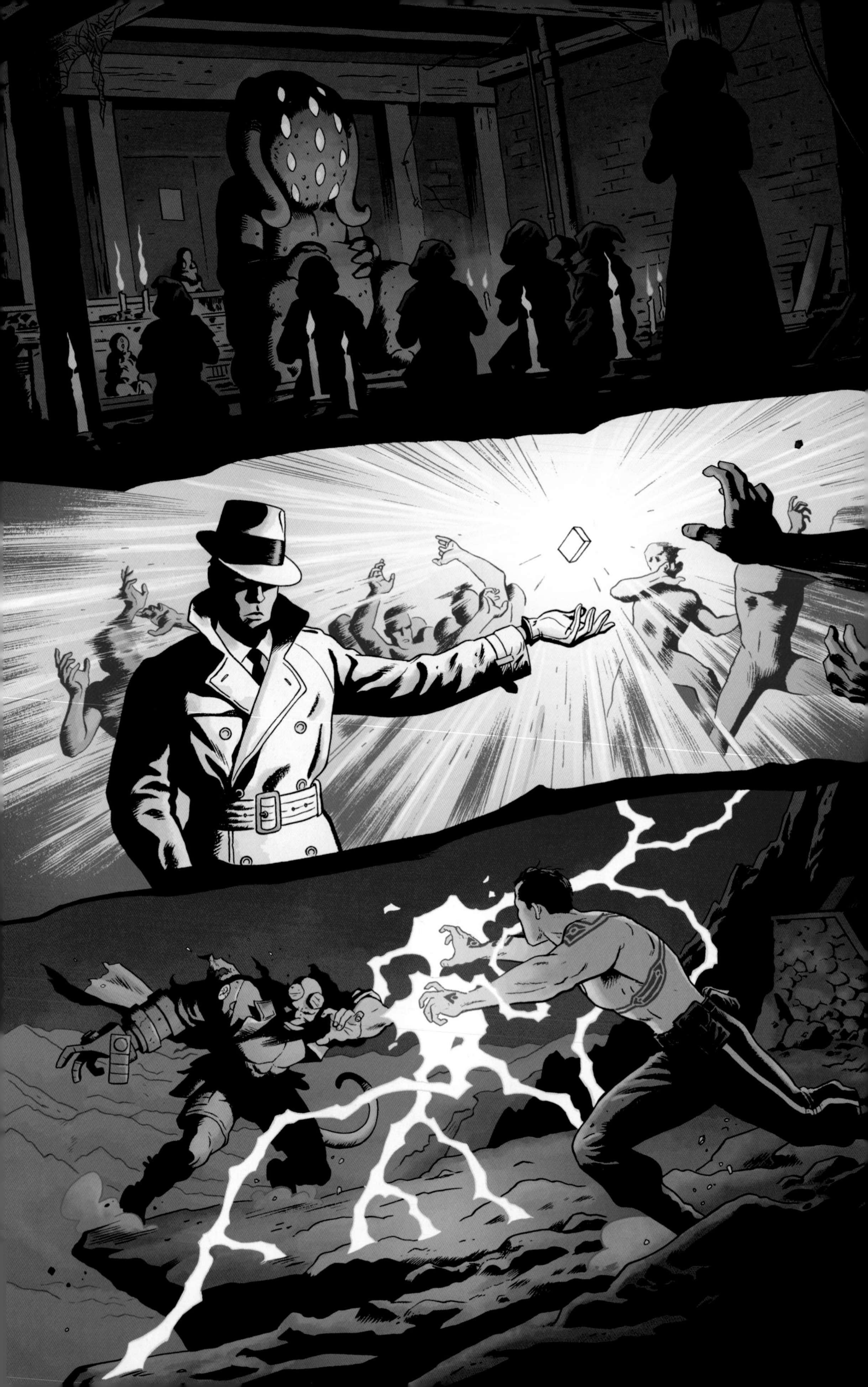

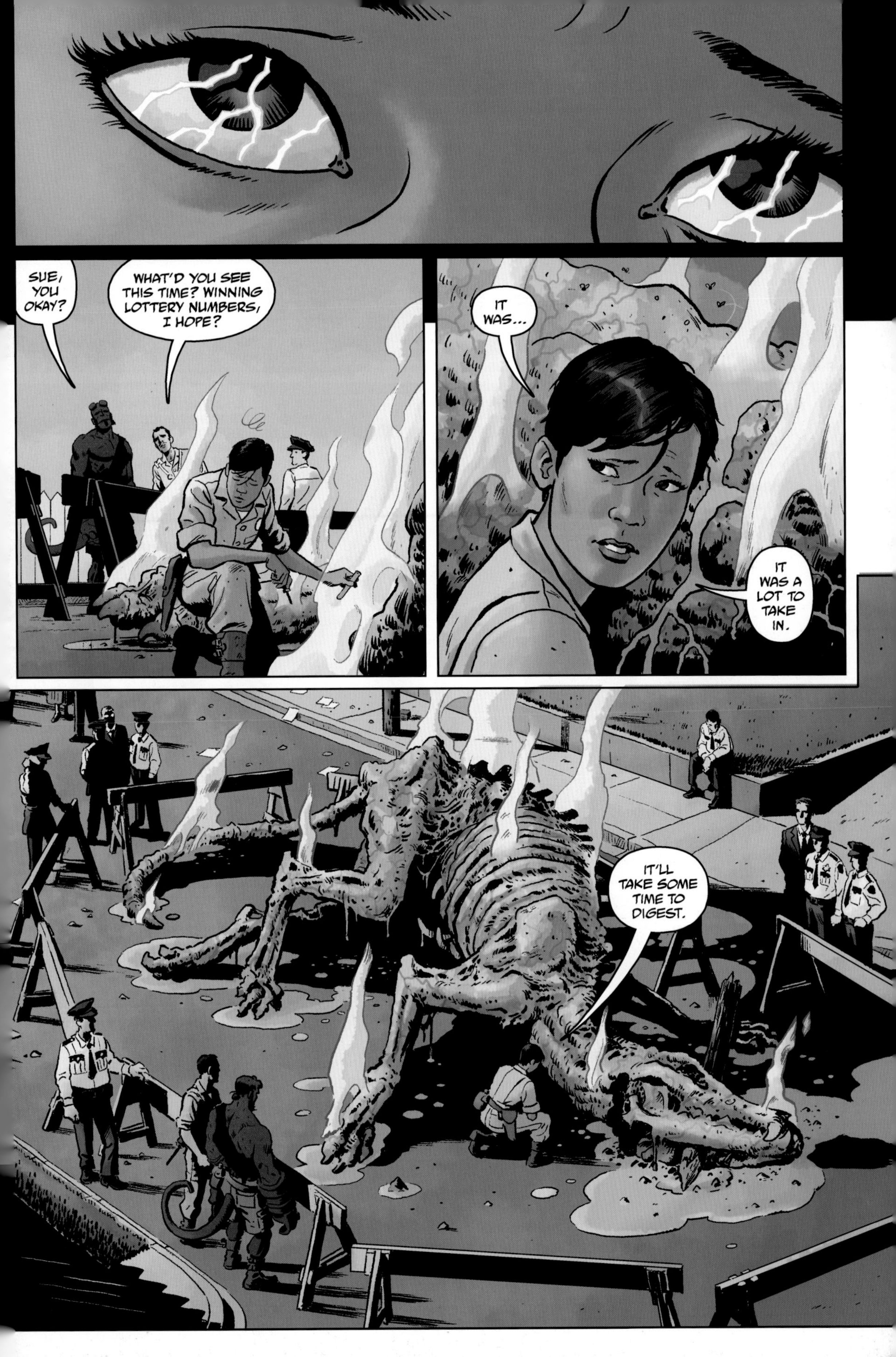
SUE, YOU OKAY?
WHAT'D YOU SEE THIS TIME? WINNING LOTTERY NUMBERS, I HOPE?
IT WAS...
IT WAS A LOT TO TAKE IN.
IT'LL TAKE SOME TIME TO DIGEST.

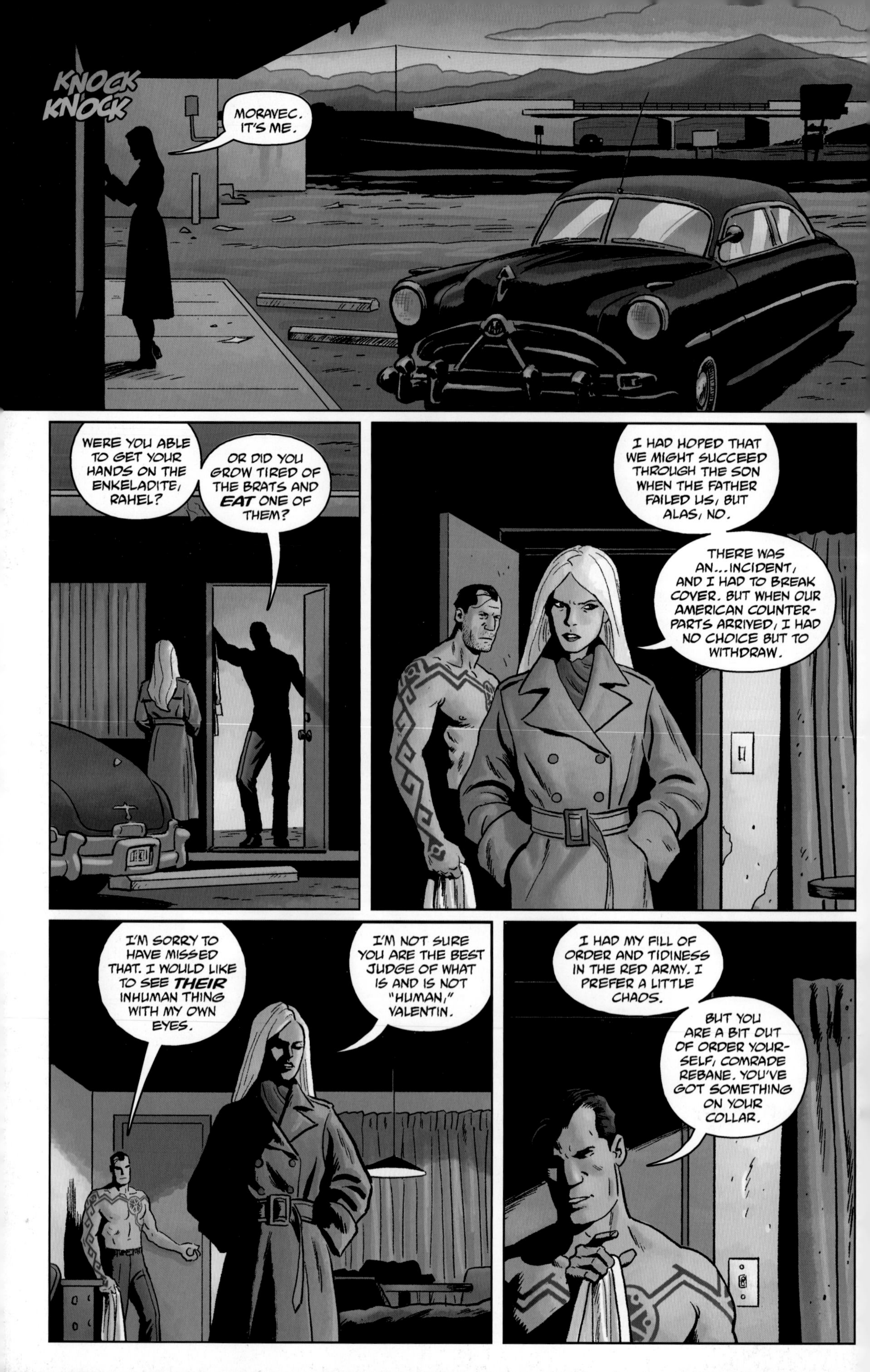
KNOCK KNOCK
MORAVEC. IT'S ME.
WERE YOU ABLE TO GET YOUR HANDS ON THE ENKELADITE, RAHEL?
OR DID YOU GROW TIRED OF THE BRATS AND EAT ONE OF THEM?
I HAD HOPED THAT WE MIGHT SUCCEED THROUGH THE SON WHEN THE FATHER FAILED US, BUT ALAS, NO.
THERE WAS AN... INCIDENT, AND I HAD TO BREAK COVER. BUT WHEN OUR AMERICAN COUNTER-PARTS ARRIVED, I HAD NO CHOICE BUT TO WITHDRAW.
I'M SORRY TO HAVE MISSED THAT. I WOULD LIKE TO SEE THEIR INHUMAN THING WITH MY OWN EYES.
I'M NOT SURE YOU ARE THE BEST JUDGE OF WHAT IS AND IS NOT "HUMAN," VALENTIN.
I HAD MY FILL OF ORDER AND TIDINESS IN THE RED ARMY. I PREFER A LITTLE CHAOS.
BUT YOU ARE A BIT OUT OF ORDER YOUR-SELF, COMRADE REBANE. YOU'VE GOT SOMETHING ON YOUR COLLAR.

AH, YES. AS I SAID, THERE WAS AN INCIDENT. NO MATTER.

BUT *SHE* WILL NOT BE HAPPY TO HEAR OF OUR FAILURE.

PERHAPS. BUT PERHAPS IT WILL NOT MATTER.

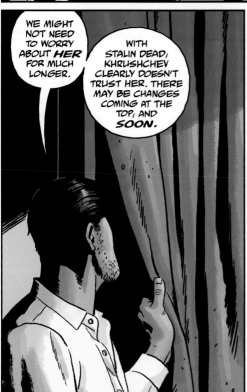

WE MIGHT NOT NEED TO WORRY ABOUT *HER* FOR MUCH LONGER.

WITH STALIN DEAD, KHRUSHCHEV CLEARLY DOESN'T TRUST HER. THERE MAY BE CHANGES COMING AT THE TOP, AND *SOON.*

HAVE A CARE, VALENTIN.

WE STILL HAVE A MISSION TO PERFORM, AND SHE COULD BE LISTENING TO US, EVEN NOW.

Hee hee hee!

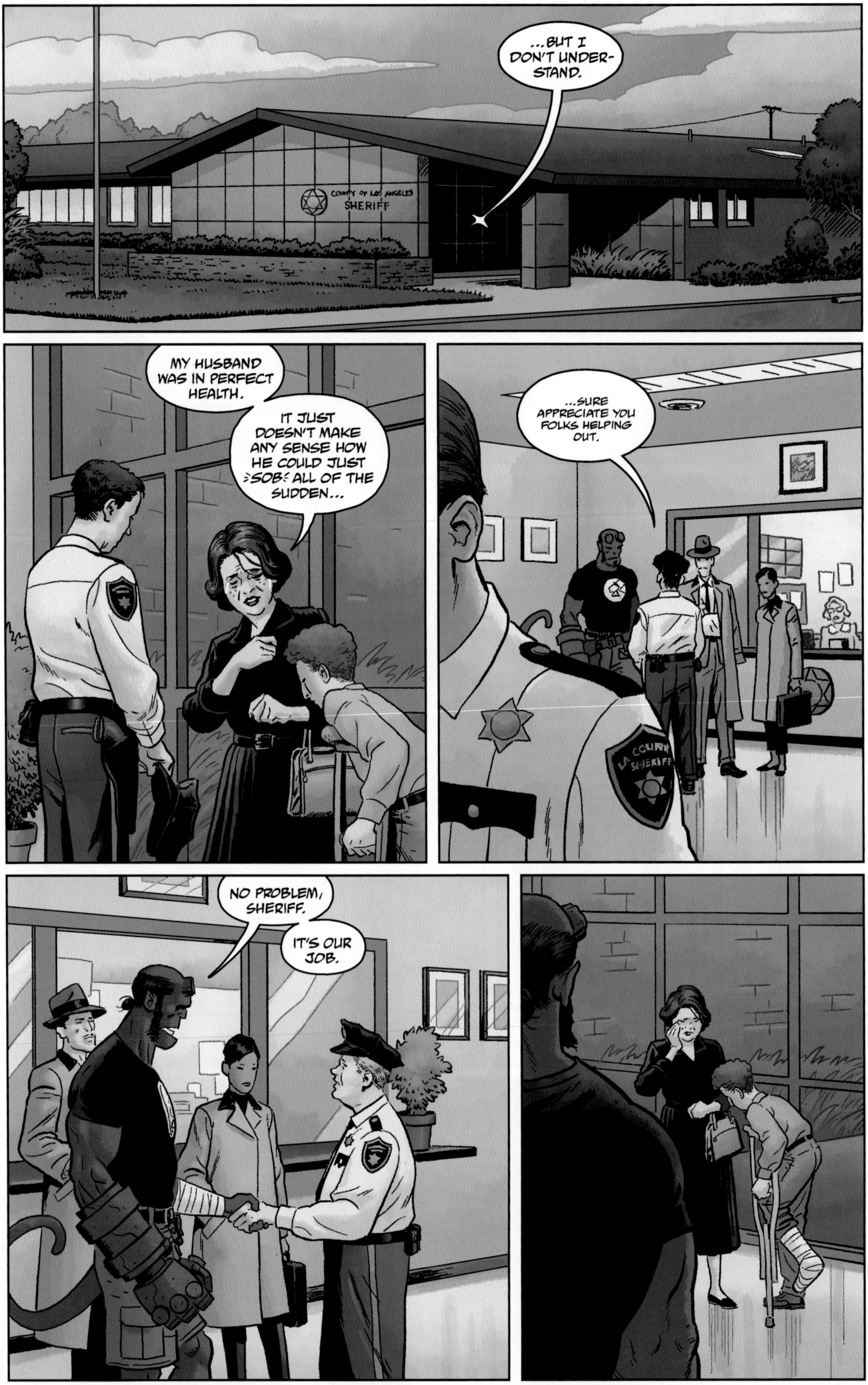
COUNTY OF LOS ANGELES
SHERIFF
...BUT I DON'T UNDERSTAND.
MY HUSBAND WAS IN PERFECT HEALTH.
IT JUST DOESN'T MAKE ANY SENSE HOW HE COULD JUST *SOB* ALL OF THE SUDDEN...
...SURE APPRECIATE YOU FOLKS HELPING OUT.
NO PROBLEM, SHERIFF.
IT'S OUR JOB.

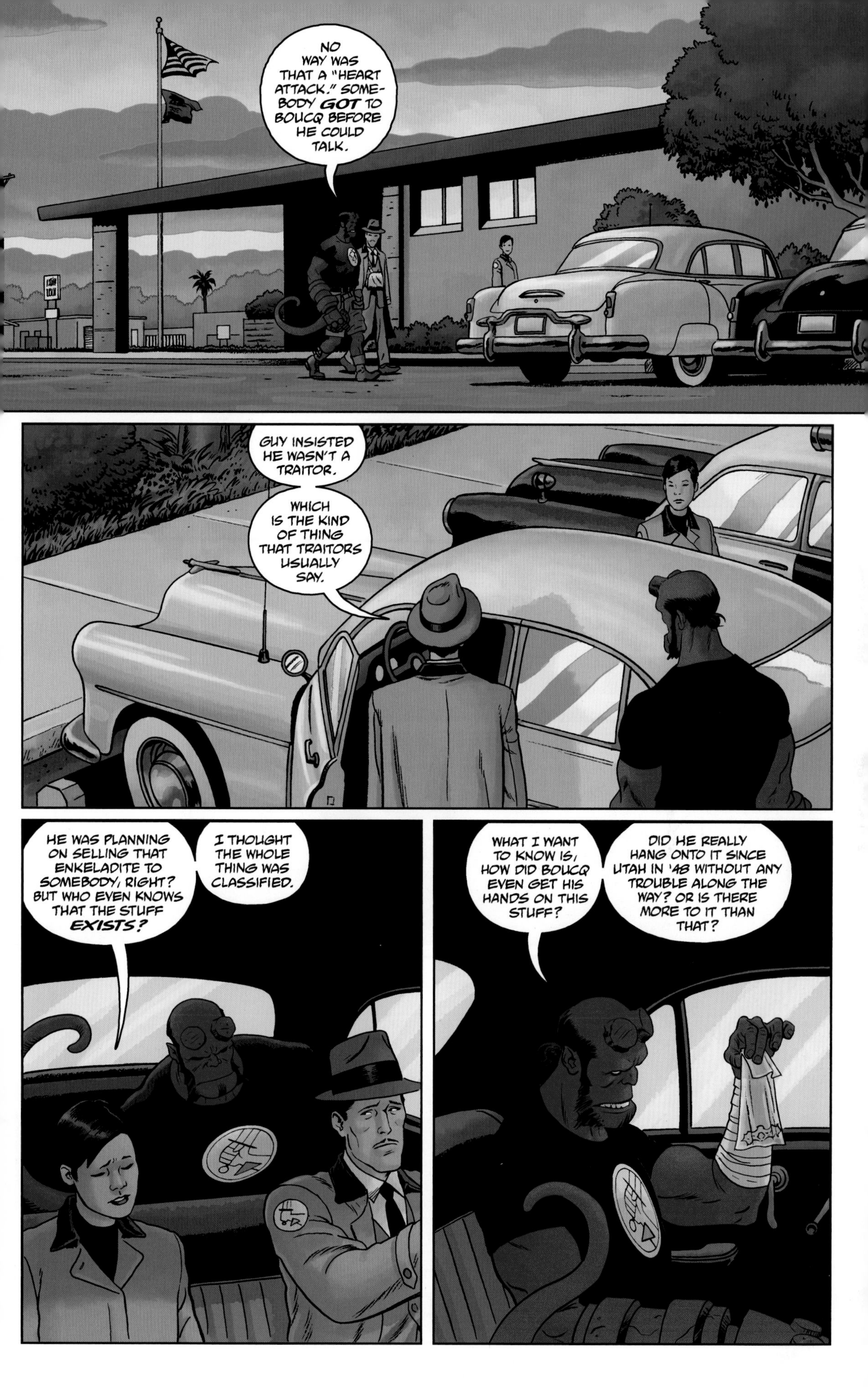
NO WAY WAS THAT A "HEART ATTACK." SOMEBODY **GOT** TO BOUCQ BEFORE HE COULD TALK.
GUY INSISTED HE WASN'T A TRAITOR.
WHICH IS THE KIND OF THING THAT TRAITORS USUALLY SAY.
HE WAS PLANNING ON SELLING THAT ENKELADITE TO SOMEBODY, RIGHT? BUT WHO EVEN KNOWS THAT THE STUFF ***EXISTS?***
I THOUGHT THE WHOLE THING WAS CLASSIFIED.
WHAT I WANT TO KNOW IS, HOW DID BOUCQ EVEN GET HIS HANDS ON THIS STUFF?
DID HE REALLY HANG ONTO IT SINCE UTAH IN '48 WITHOUT ANY TROUBLE ALONG THE WAY? OR IS THERE MORE TO IT THAN THAT?

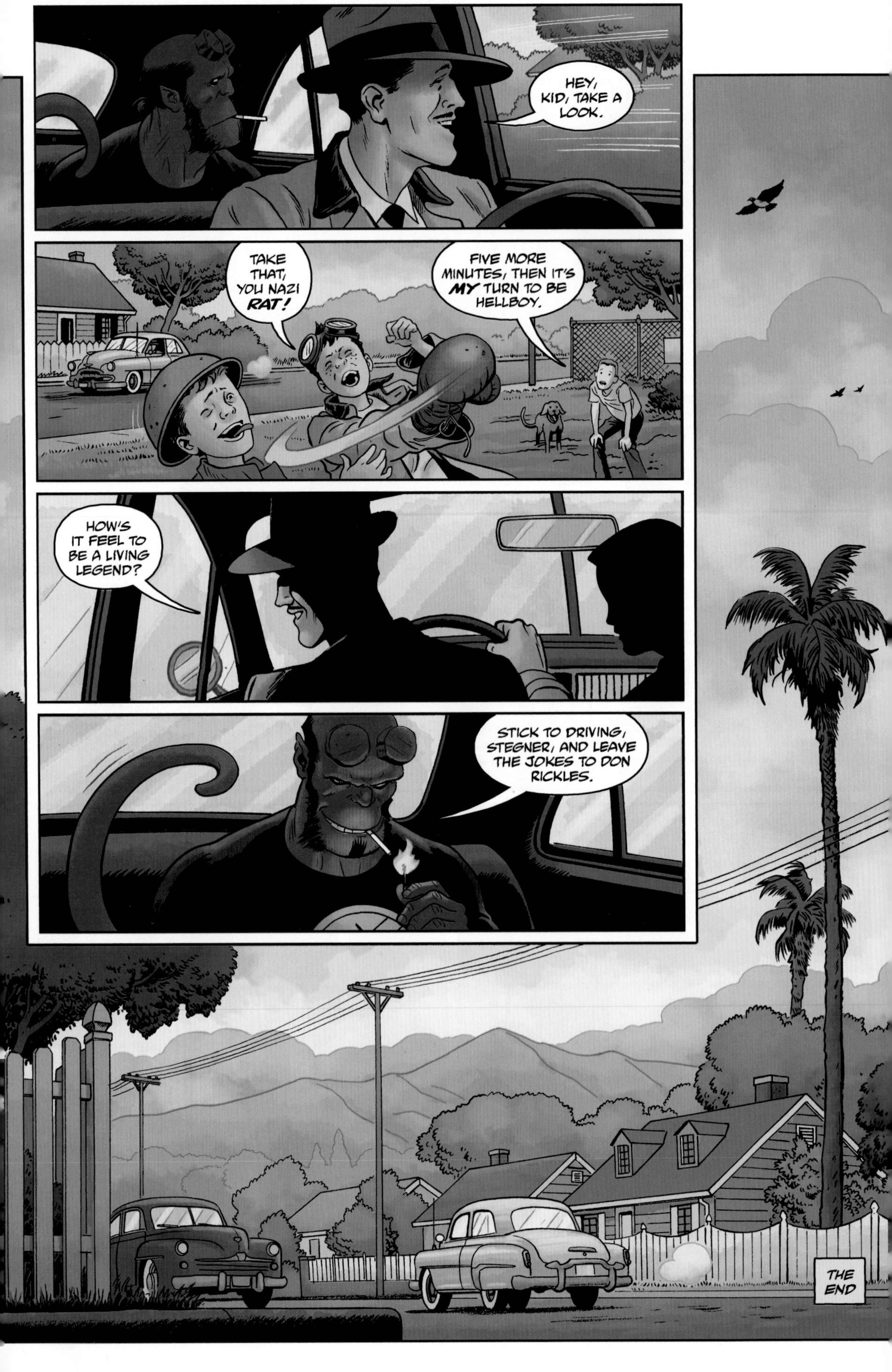
HEY, KID, TAKE A LOOK.
TAKE THAT, YOU NAZI RAT!
FIVE MORE MINUTES, THEN IT'S MY TURN TO BE HELLBOY.
HOW'S IT FEEL TO BE A LIVING LEGEND?
STICK TO DRIVING, STEGNER, AND LEAVE THE JOKES TO DON RICKLES.
THE END

HELLBOY AND THE B.P.R.D. 1953

SKETCHBOOK

Notes by the artists.

wolf Head
(scaled armour)
Boudicca
- wicker chariot -
Pict sword

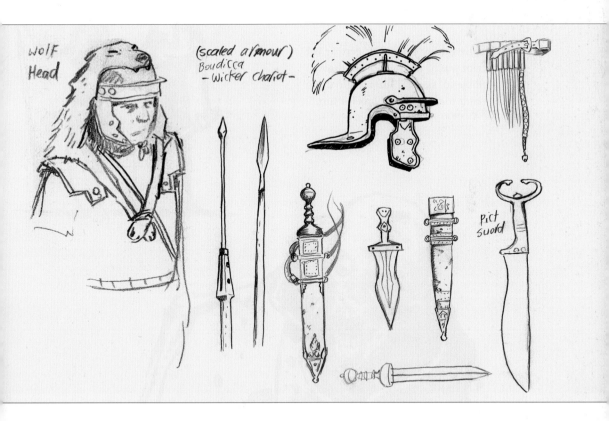

BEN STENBECK: Pencil studies of Roman weapons and armor.

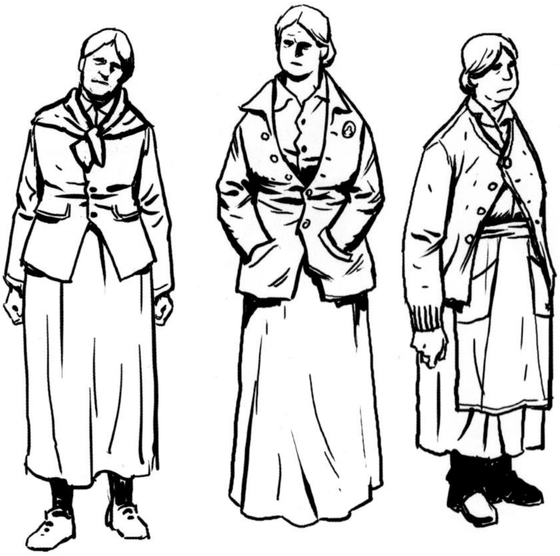

Some ideas for Ann.

The first thing I did after getting the script was to do these quick digital scribbles of skeletal Roman guys. No point to them really, just for fun.

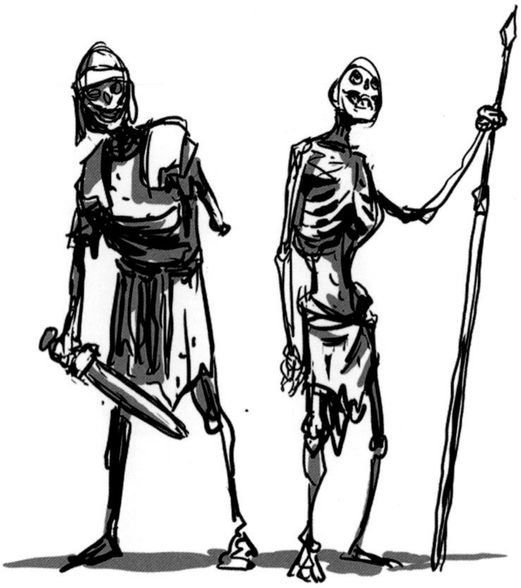

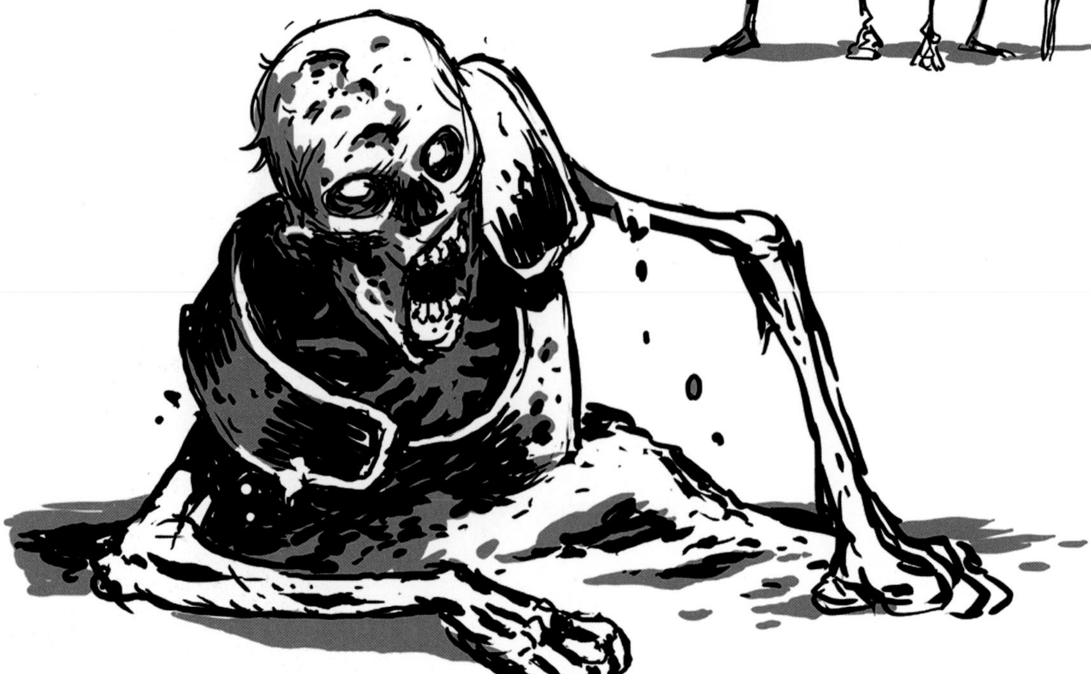

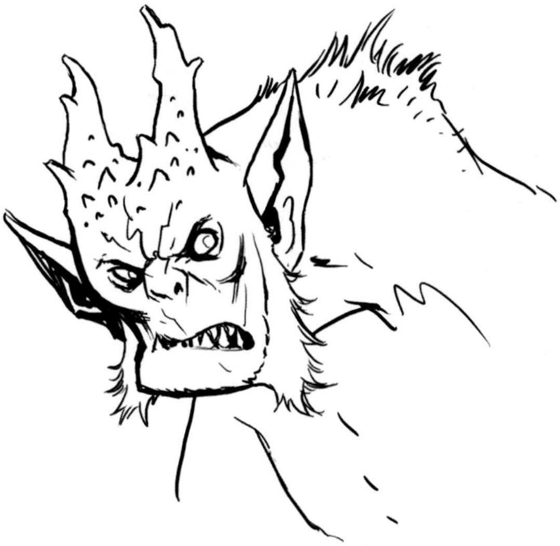

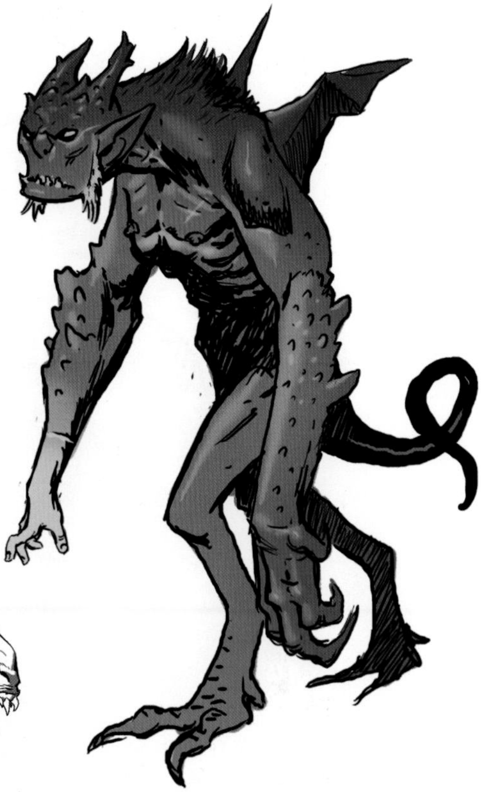

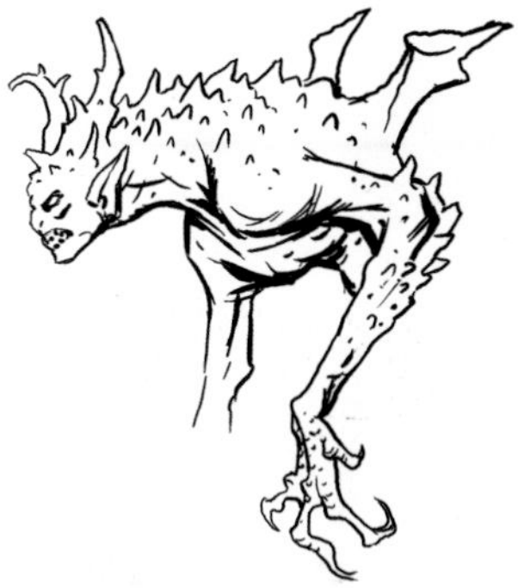

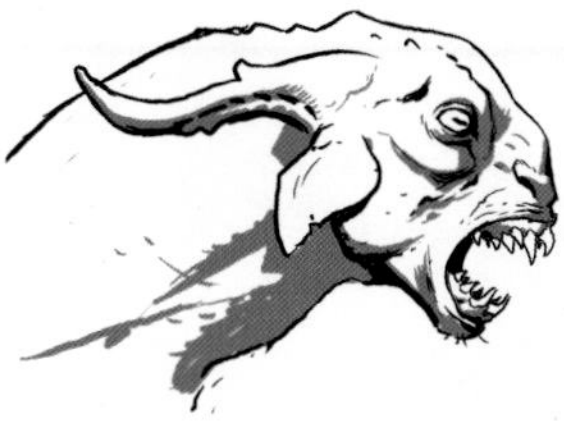

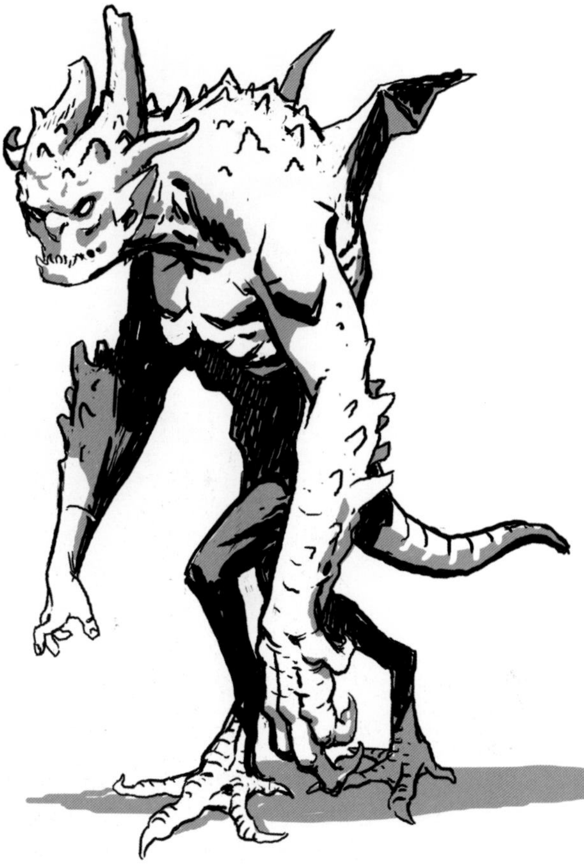

Above are my first passes at the demon from "The Phantom Hand." Mike sent me some sketches he had done of some demons from *Hellboy in Hell* and he wanted this guy to feel similar. I never managed a good shot of his feet in the comic, but he had chicken feet.

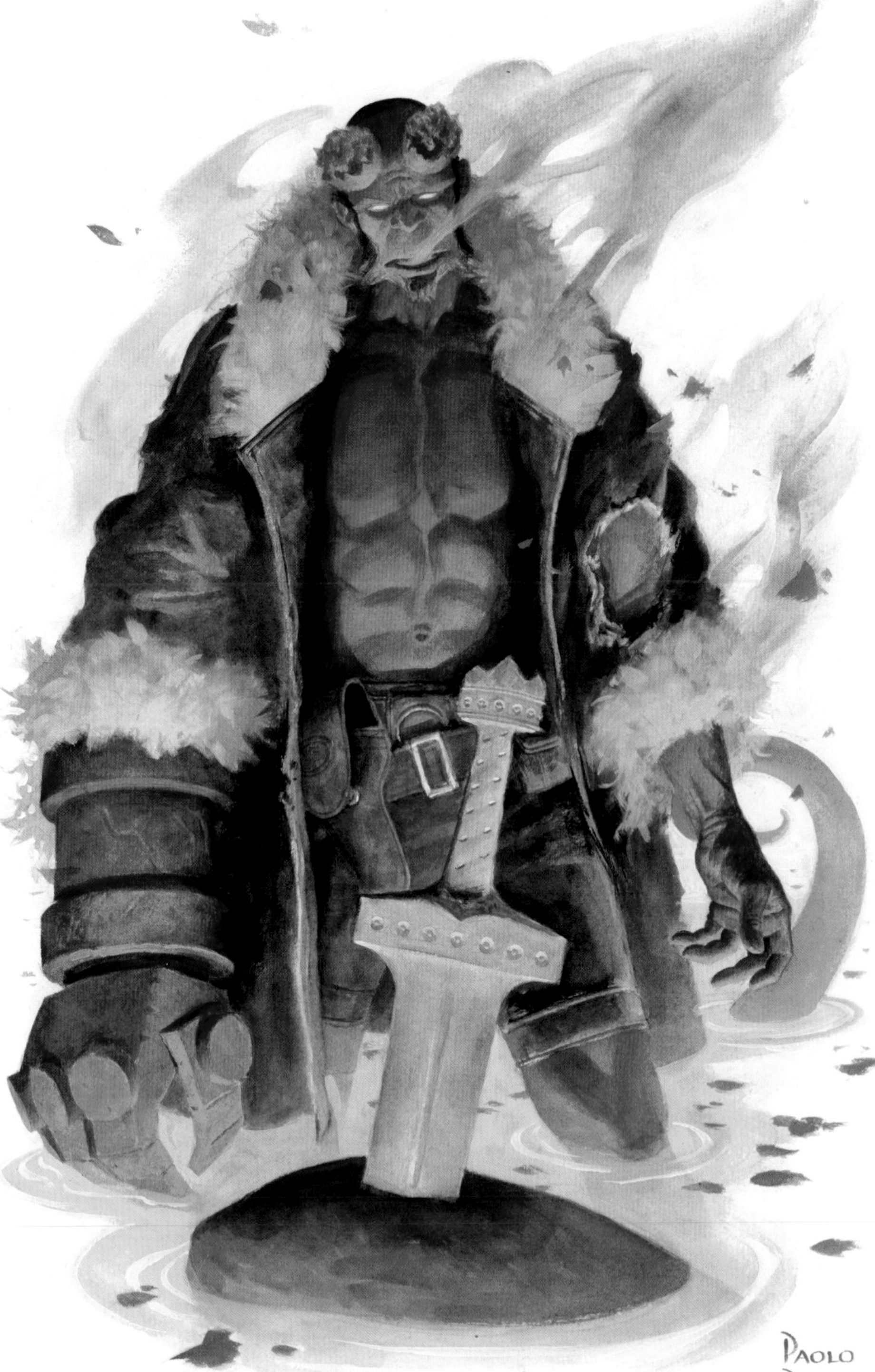
PAOLO
RIVERA
2010

PAOLO RIVERA: This was a private commission done in 2010. It had been a while since I'd read *Hellboy*—I'm a wait-for-the-trade kind of reader—but I had just picked up *The Wild Hunt*. I absolutely loved it, and was inspired to depict this pivotal scene.

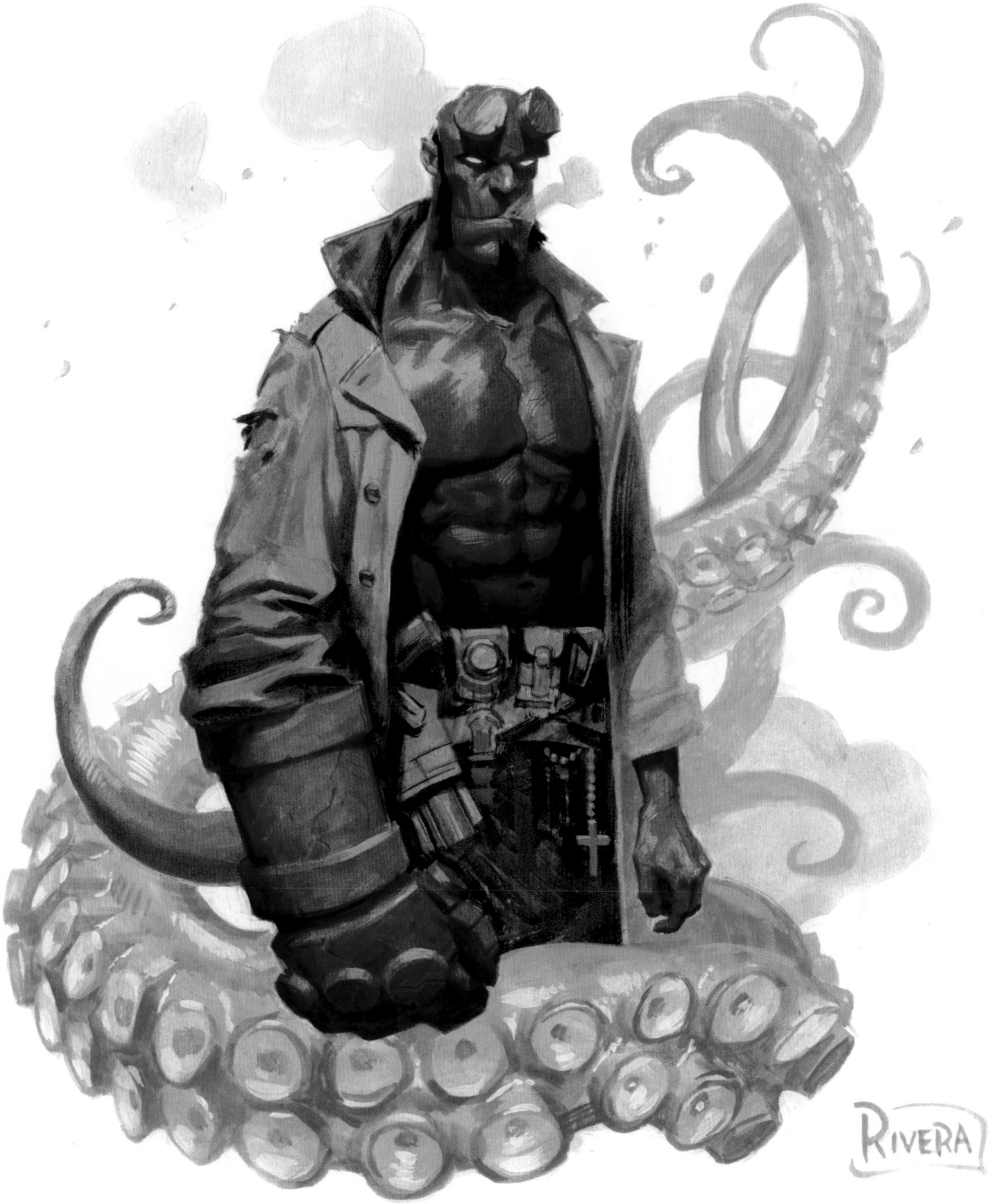
RIVERA

Done for the Hero Initiative charity auction, this piece was painted on a sketch cover in Acryla gouache. I always wondered if Hellboy had a belly button—I have since discovered that he does not. Oh, well.

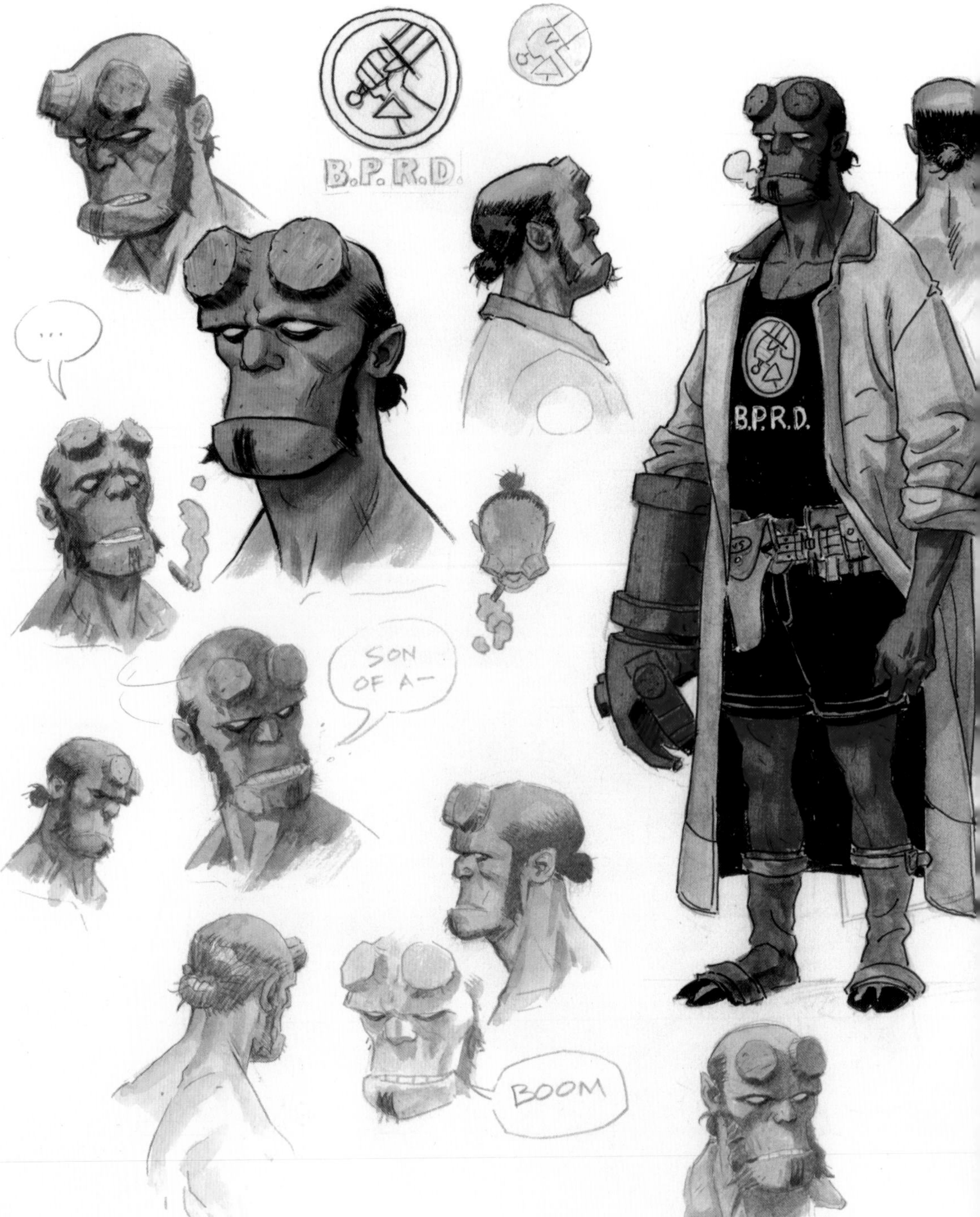
B.P.R.D.
...
SON OF A—
B.P.R.D.
BOOM

Character studies are always my favorite part of any project. No rules, just fun, and once I've sketched them, I'll color a portion each morning as a way to warm up.

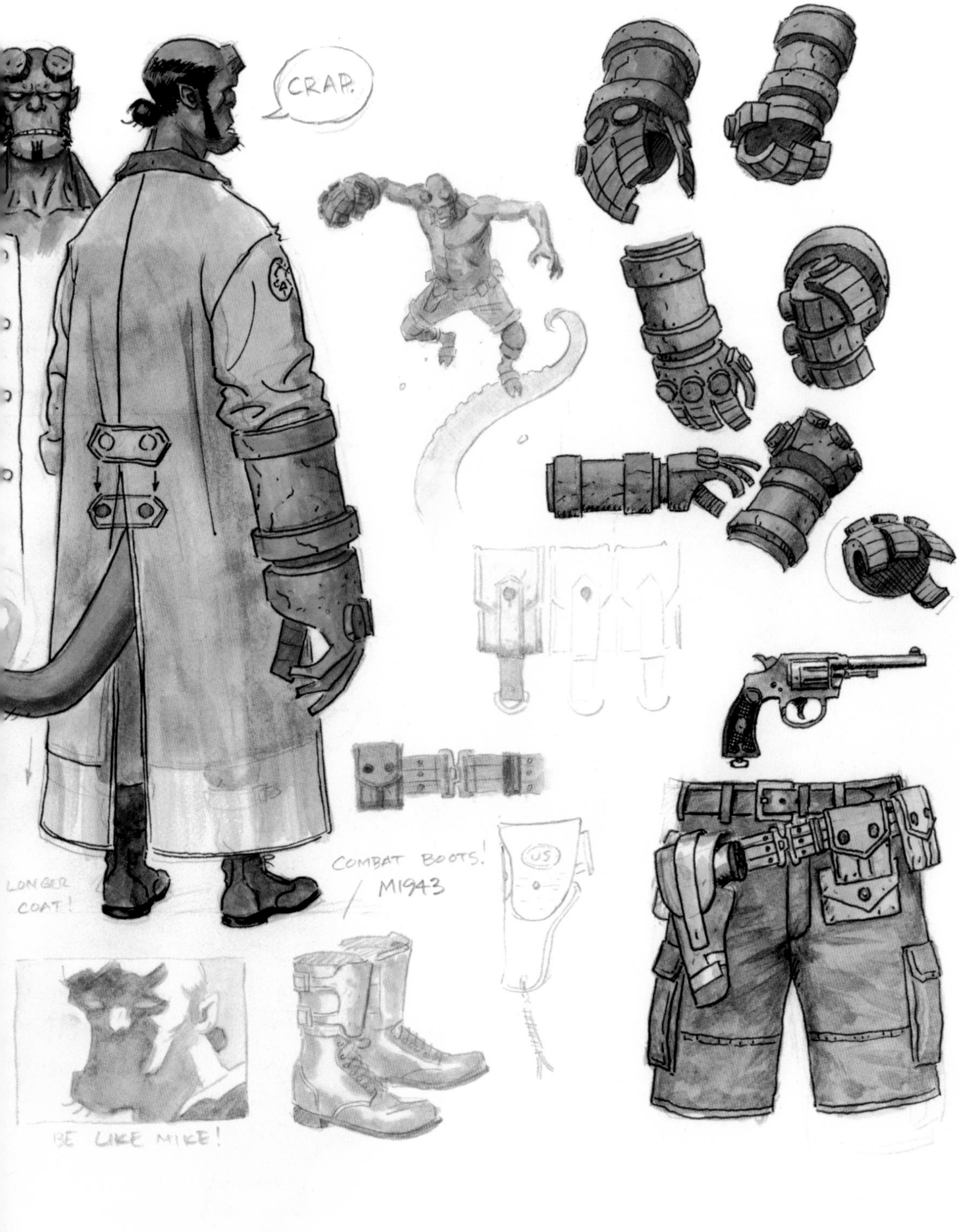
CRAP.
LONGER COAT!
COMBAT BOOTS!
M1943
US
BE LIKE MIKE!

Hellboy is always open to interpretation, but this marks the first time I've drawn the Right Hand of Doom correctly. On the cover to the first issue, I missed a section on the wrist.

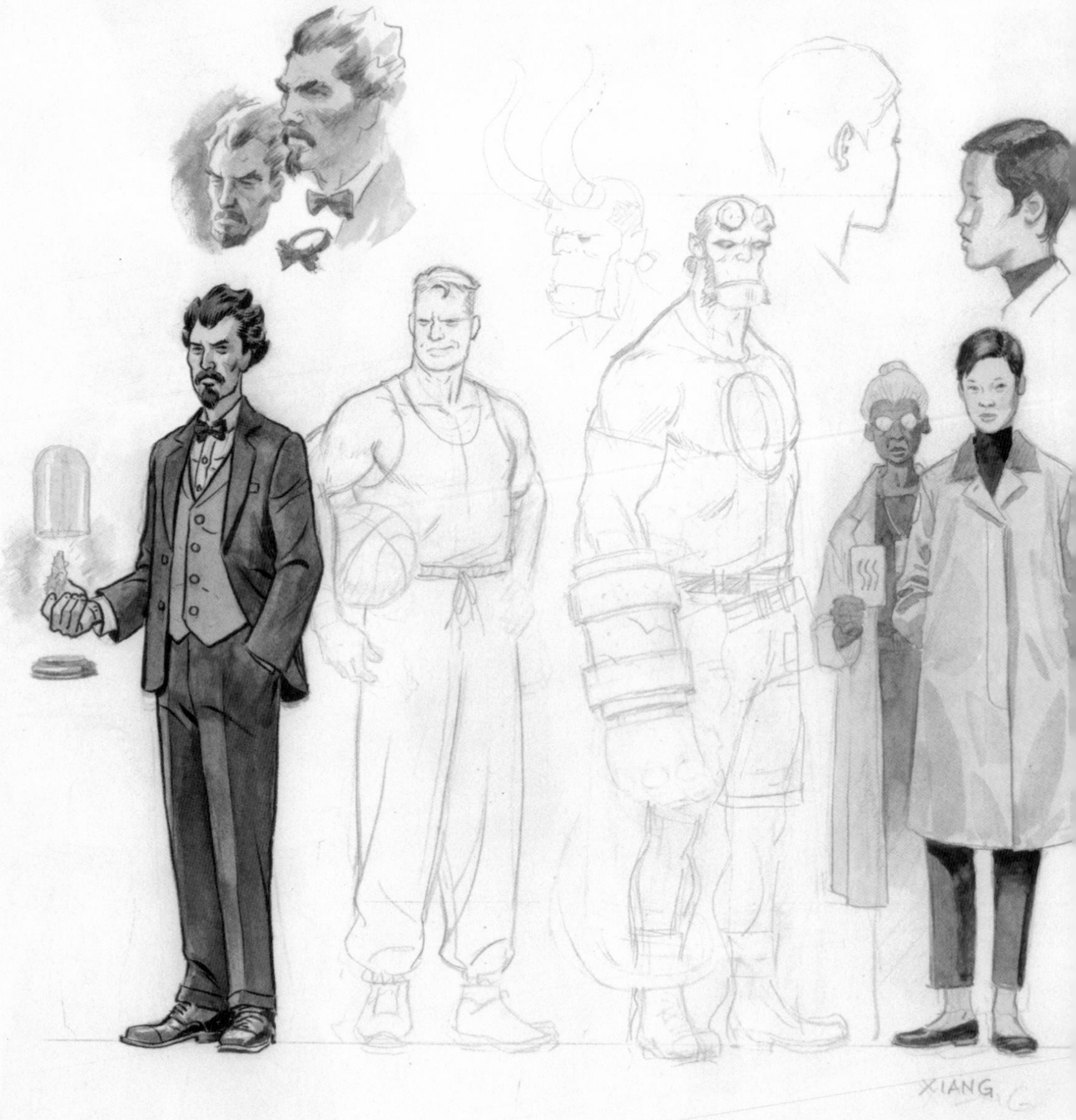
XIANG

Beyond the Fences had many supporting characters, some established, some new, and this is where I worked out my take on them. It was also handy to have them all standing next to each other so I could keep track of their respective heights.

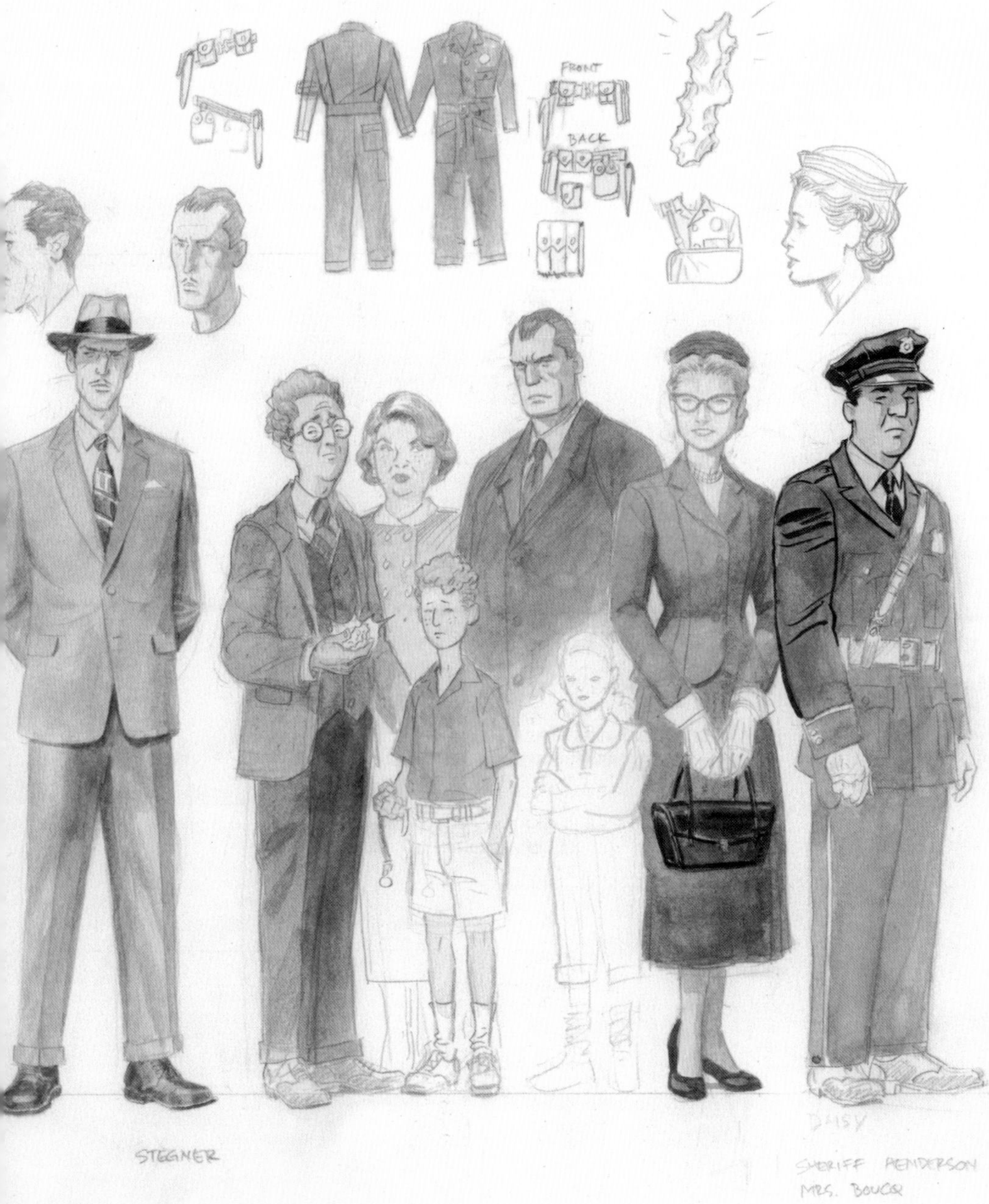
FRONT
BACK
STEGNER
DAISY
SHERIFF HENDERSON
MRS. BOUCQ

I knew Xiang and Stegner would be major players in the tale, but for some reason I thought they'd be in civilian clothes more. I had to make supplemental sketches to show their BPRD uniforms and keep track of what they wore on their belts.

Layouts from the beginning of *Beyond the Fences*.

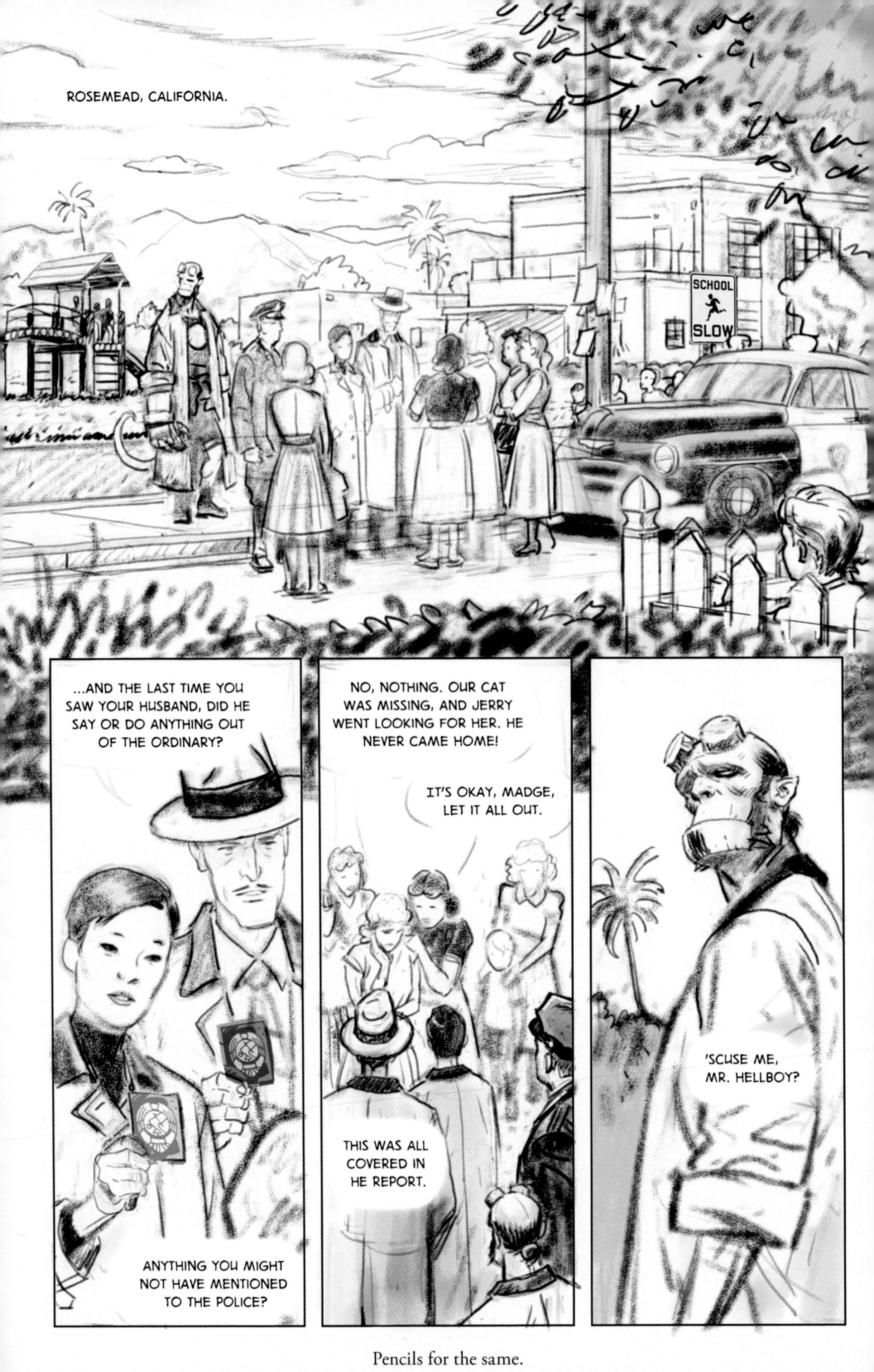
ROSEMEAD, CALIFORNIA.
SCHOOL
SLOW
...AND THE LAST TIME YOU SAW YOUR HUSBAND, DID HE SAY OR DO ANYTHING OUT OF THE ORDINARY?
ANYTHING YOU MIGHT NOT HAVE MENTIONED TO THE POLICE?
NO, NOTHING. OUR CAT WAS MISSING, AND JERRY WENT LOOKING FOR HER. HE NEVER CAME HOME!
IT'S OKAY, MADGE, LET IT ALL OUT.
THIS WAS ALL COVERED IN HE REPORT.
'SCUSE ME, MR. HELLBOY?

Pencils for the same.

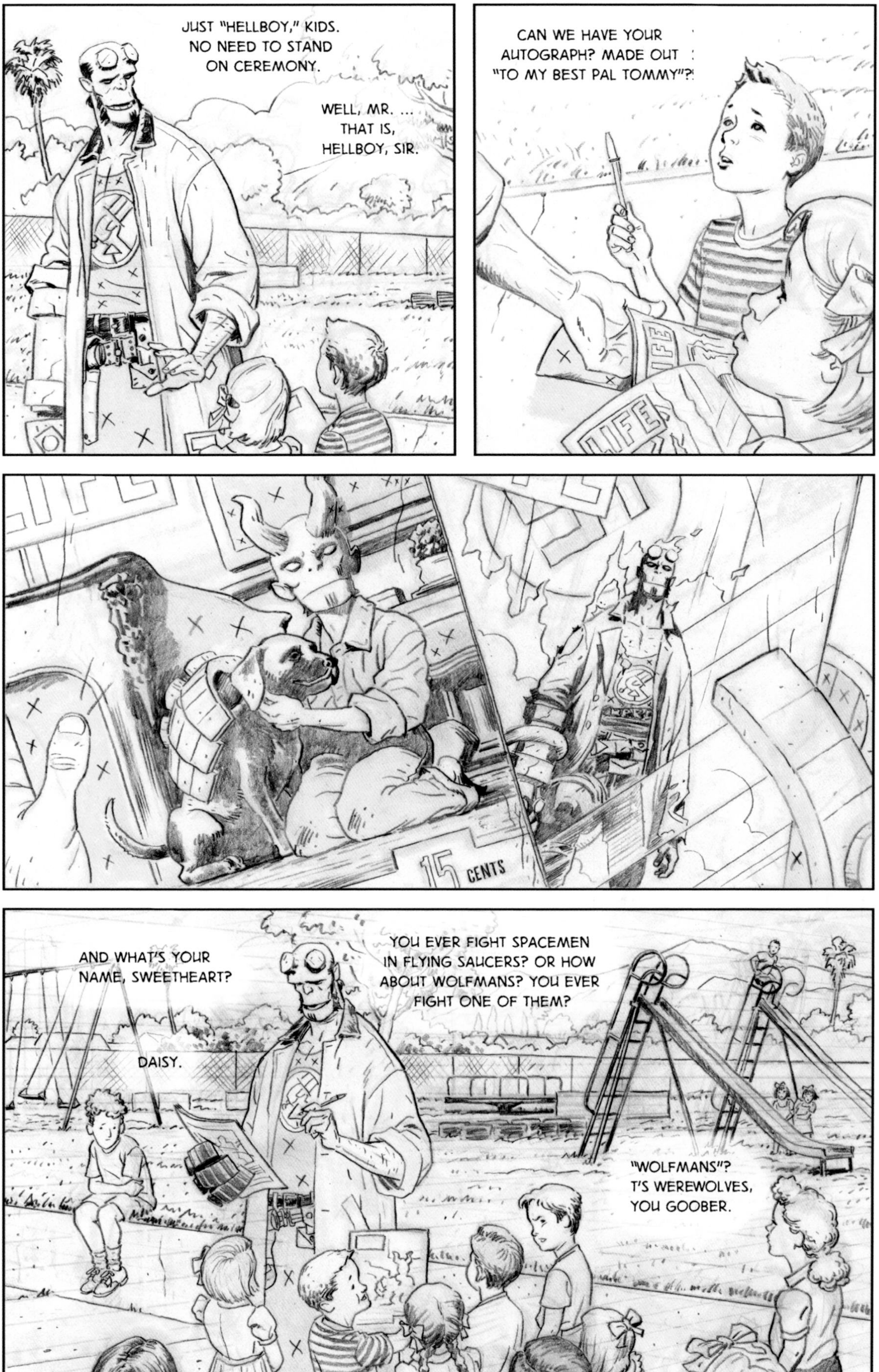
JUST "HELLBOY," KIDS. NO NEED TO STAND ON CEREMONY.
WELL, MR. ... THAT IS, HELLBOY, SIR.
CAN WE HAVE YOUR AUTOGRAPH? MADE OUT "TO MY BEST PAL TOMMY"?!
LIFE
LIFE
LIFE
15 CENTS
AND WHAT'S YOUR NAME, SWEETHEART?
DAISY.
YOU EVER FIGHT SPACEMEN IN FLYING SAUCERS? OR HOW ABOUT WOLFMANS? YOU EVER FIGHT ONE OF THEM?
"WOLFMANS"? T'S WEREWOLVES, YOU GOOBER.

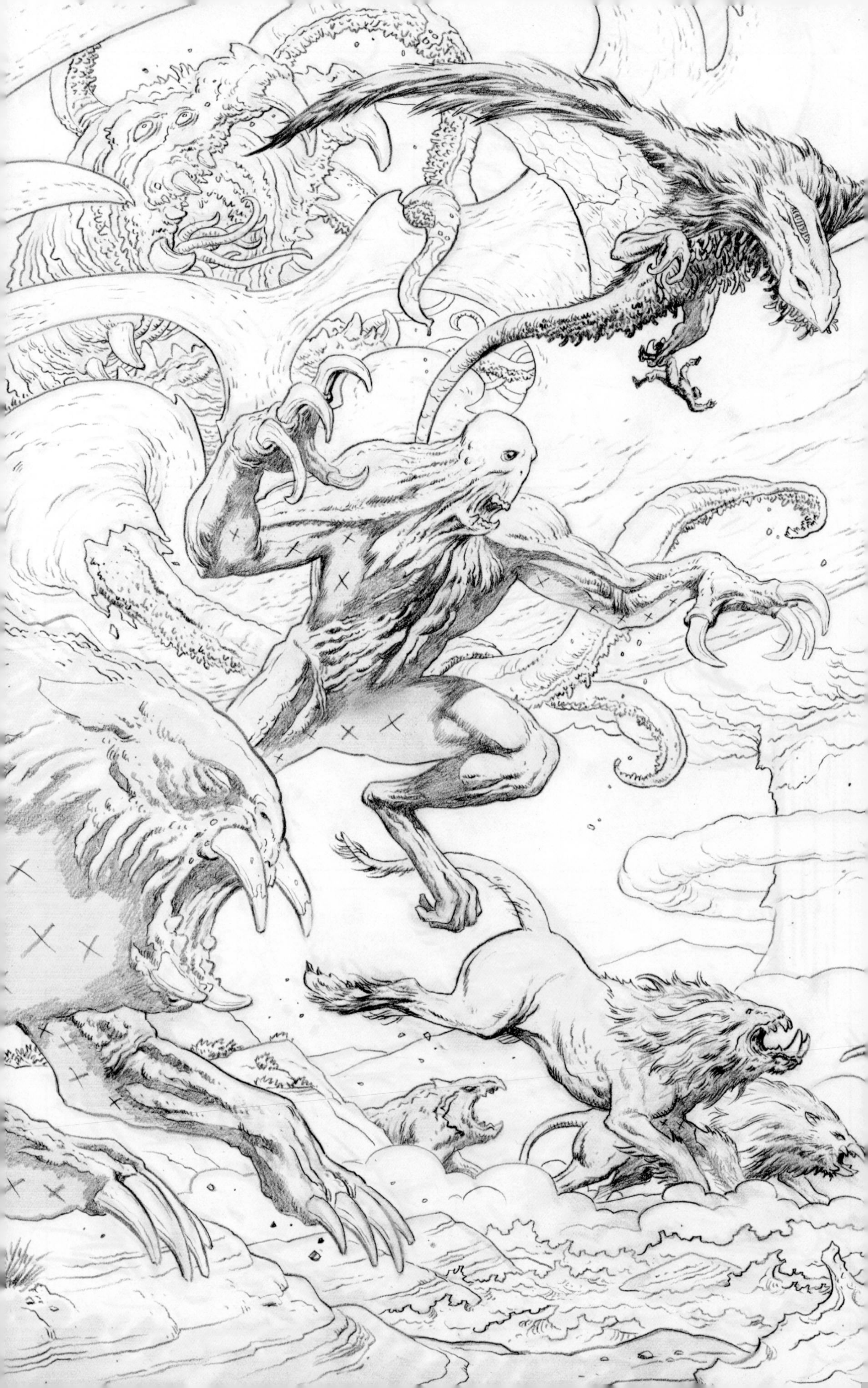

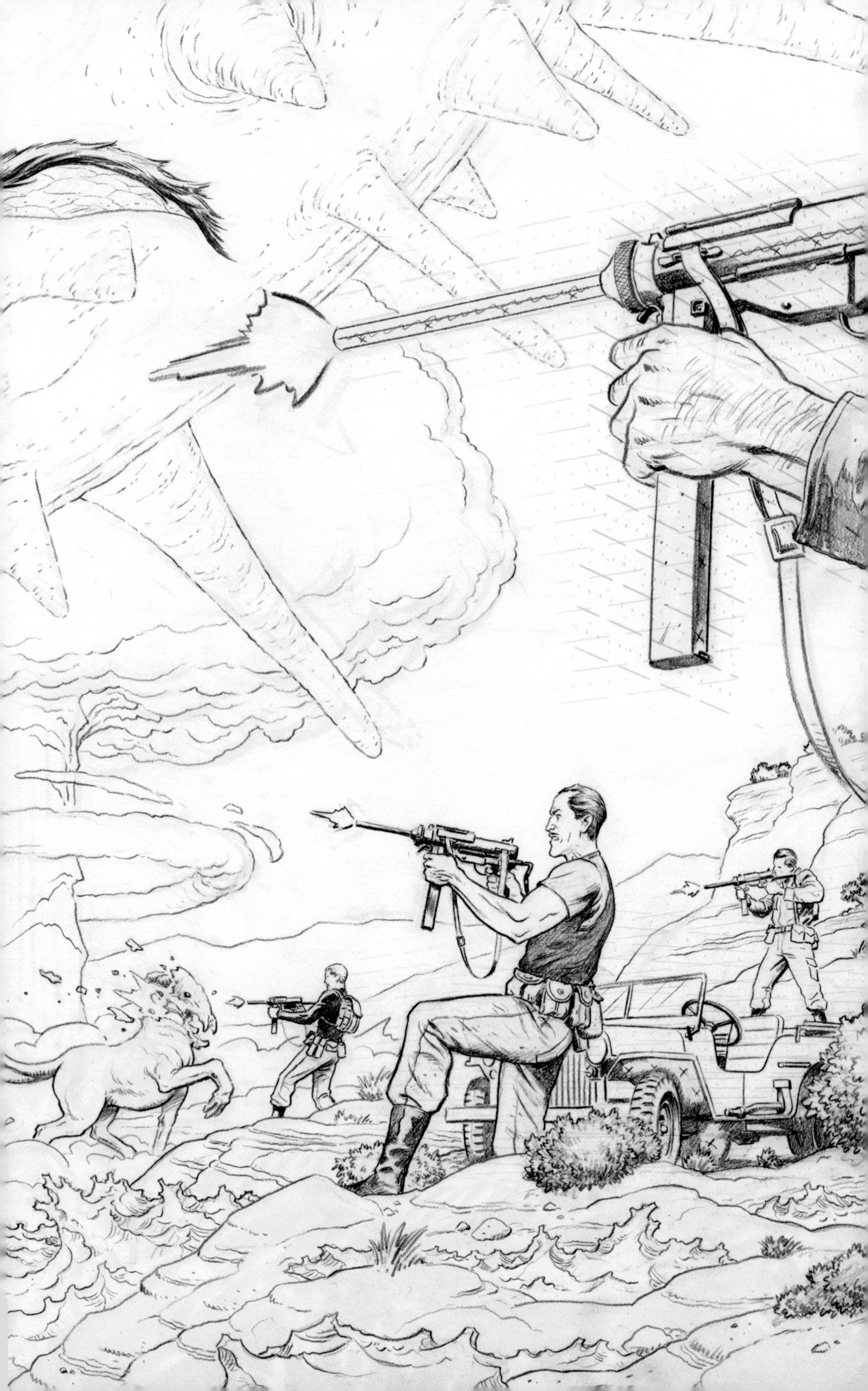

HELLBOY AND THE B.P.R.D.: 1953

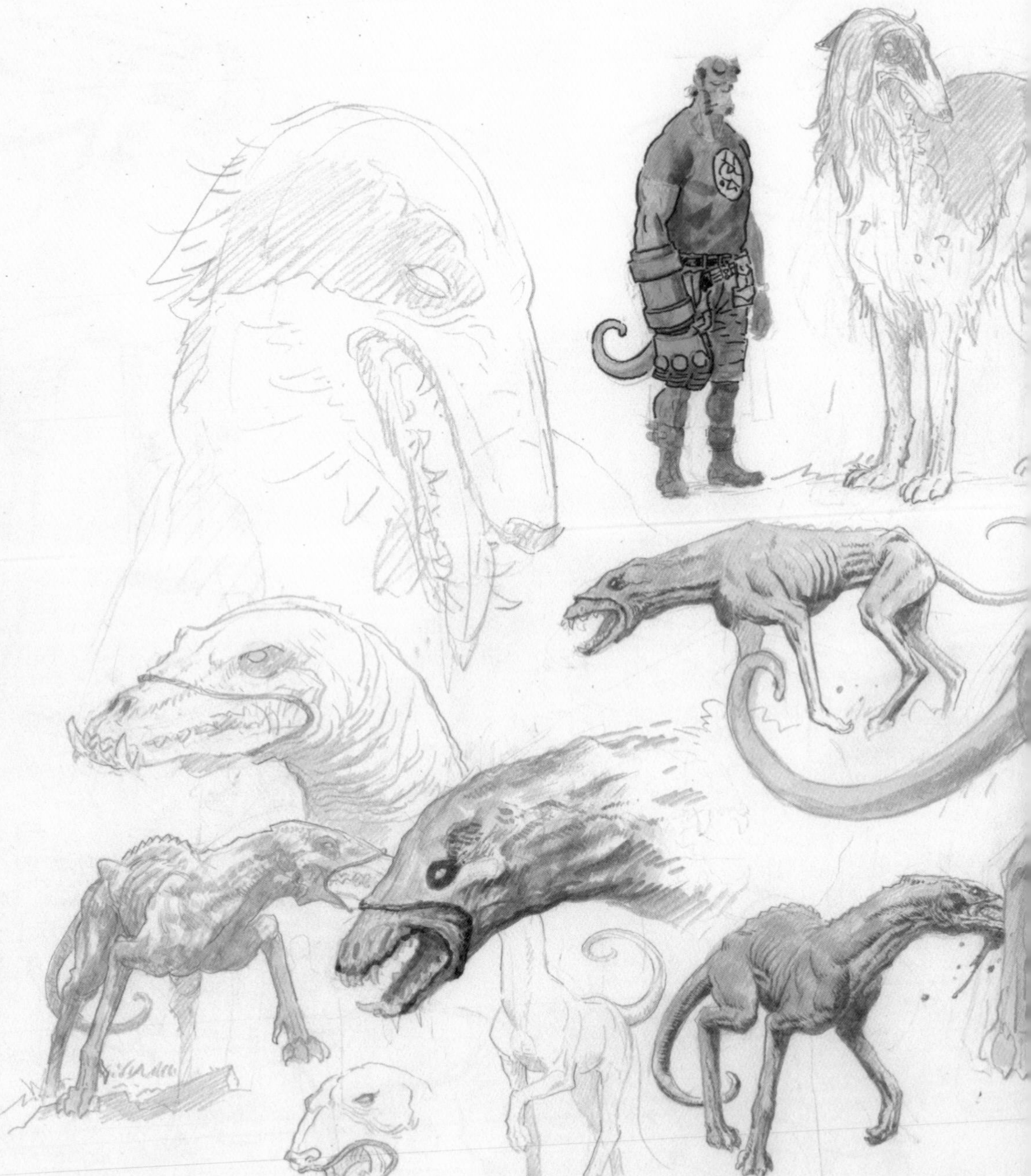

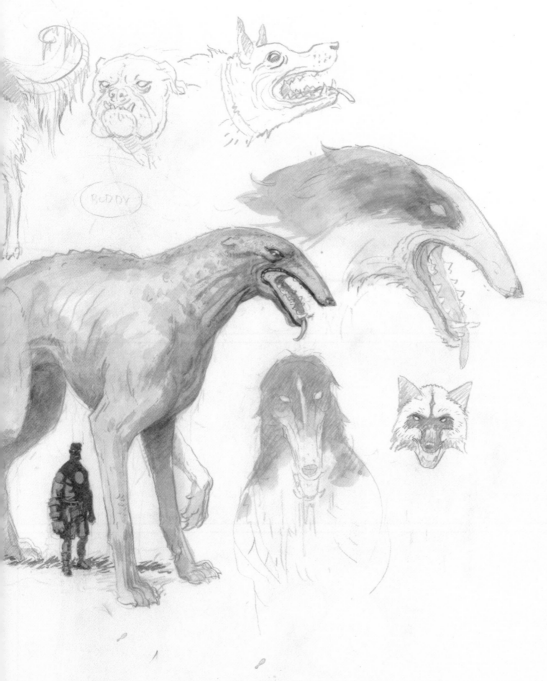

One of my favorite things about drawing comics is all the on-the-job learning that's an integral part of the process. I know nothing about dogs, but as I was searching for reference, I came across a borzoi, which had such an interesting shape. Once I had decided on that, it was just a question of making it super creepy . . . and then even creepier.

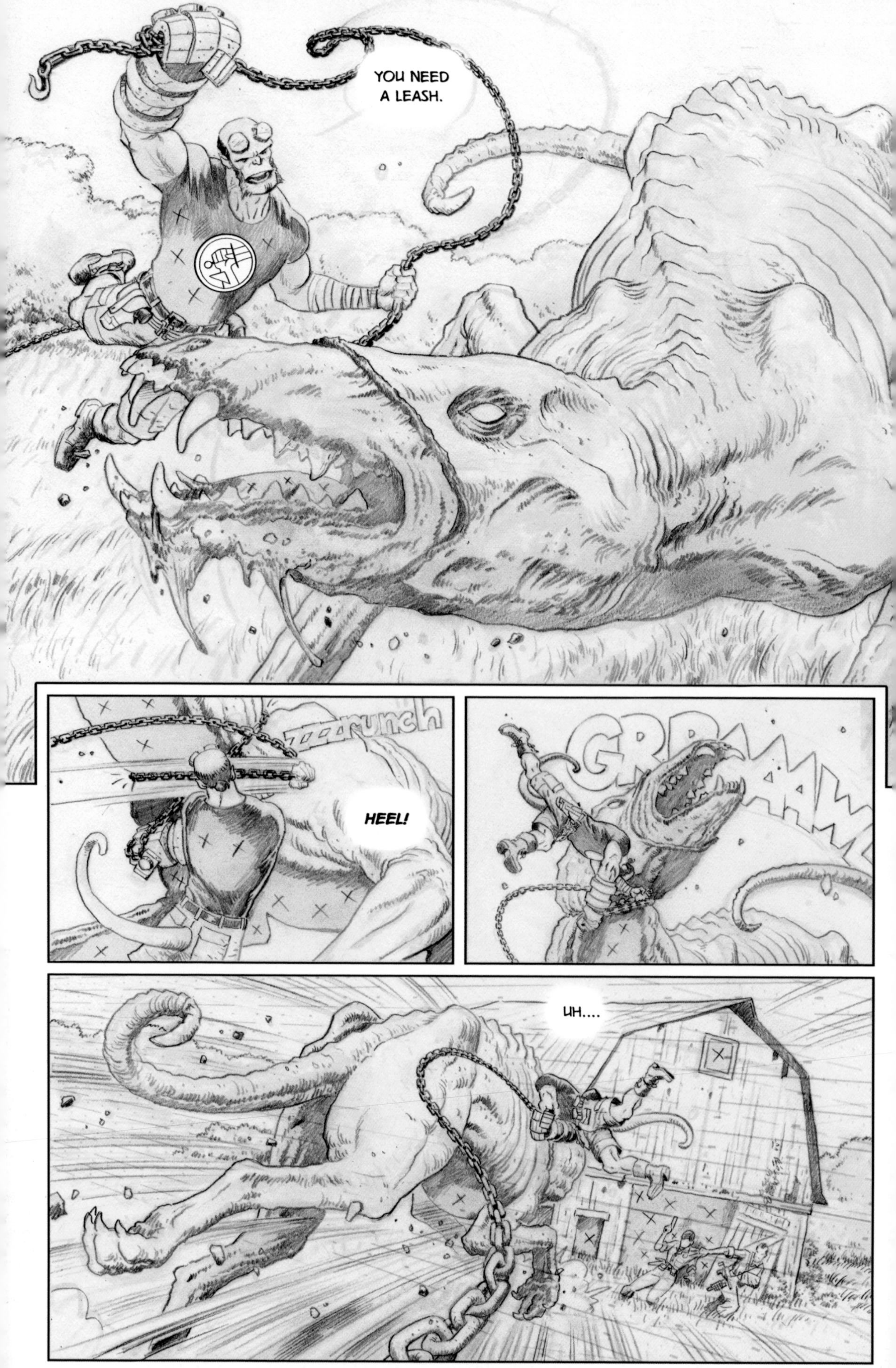
YOU NEED A LEASH.
HEEL!
UH....

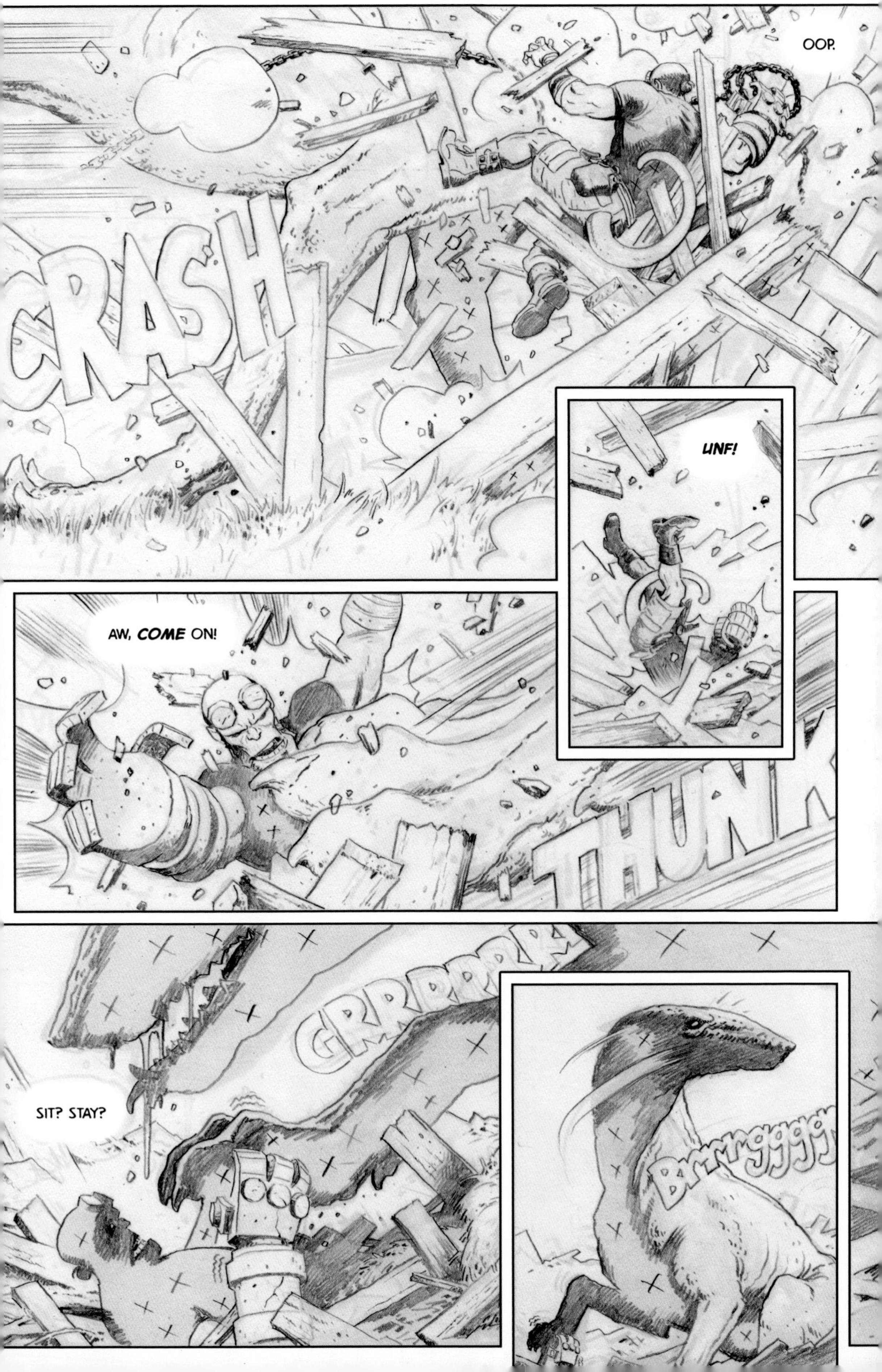
OOP.
CRASH
UNF!
AW, COME ON!
SIT? STAY?

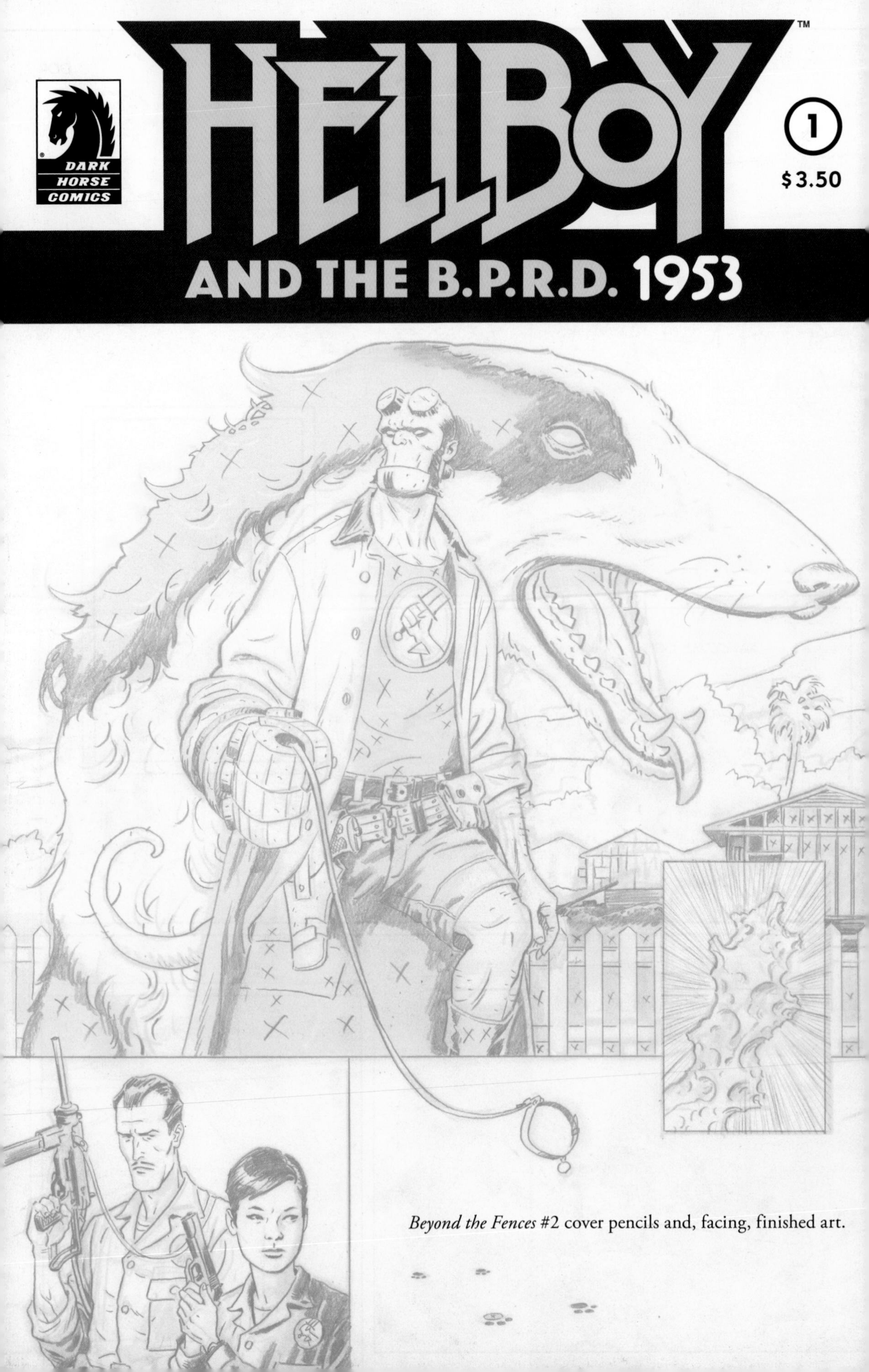
HELLBOY
AND THE B.P.R.D. 1953
DARK HORSE COMICS
1
$3.50

Beyond the Fences #2 cover pencils and, facing, finished art.

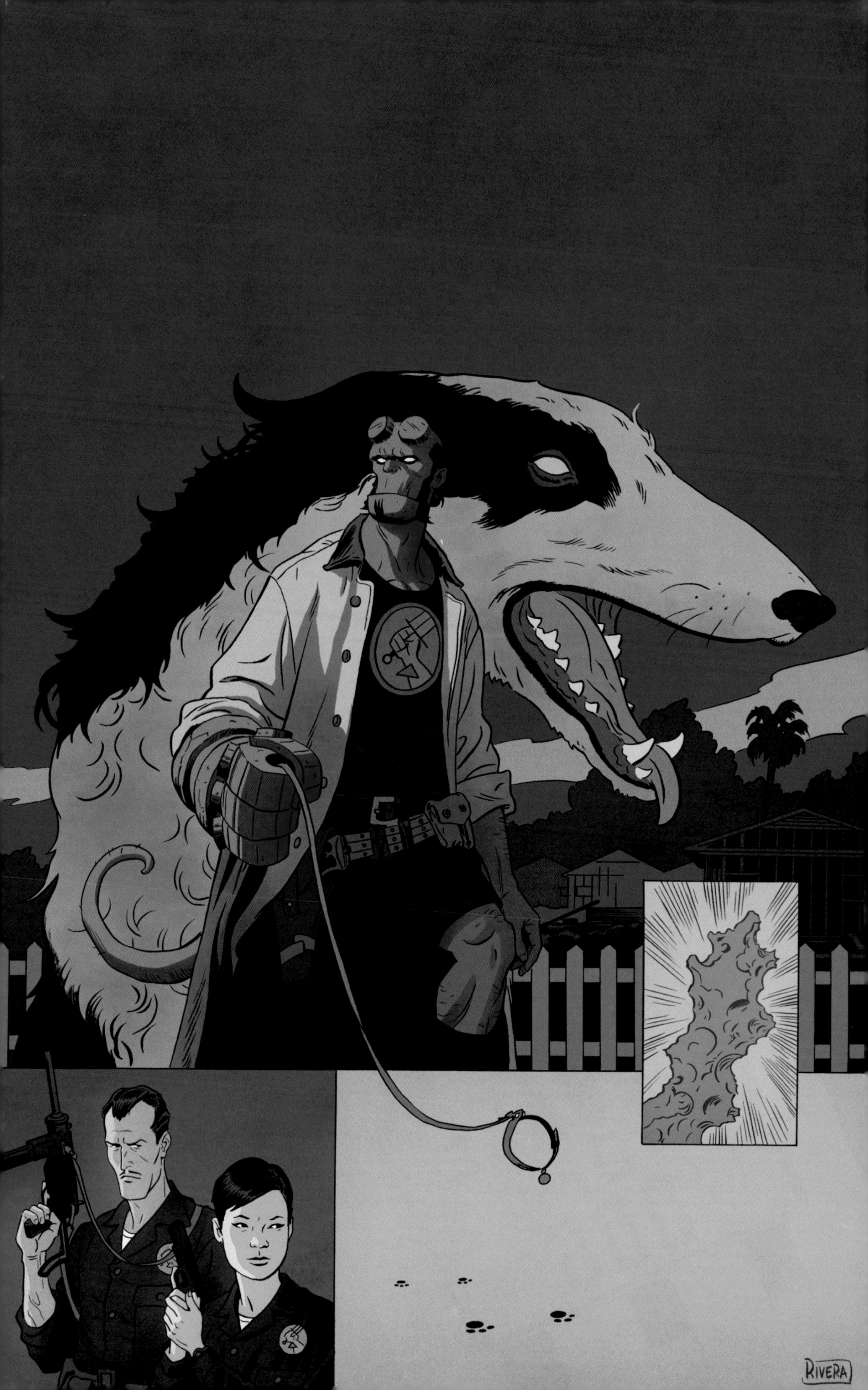
RIVERA

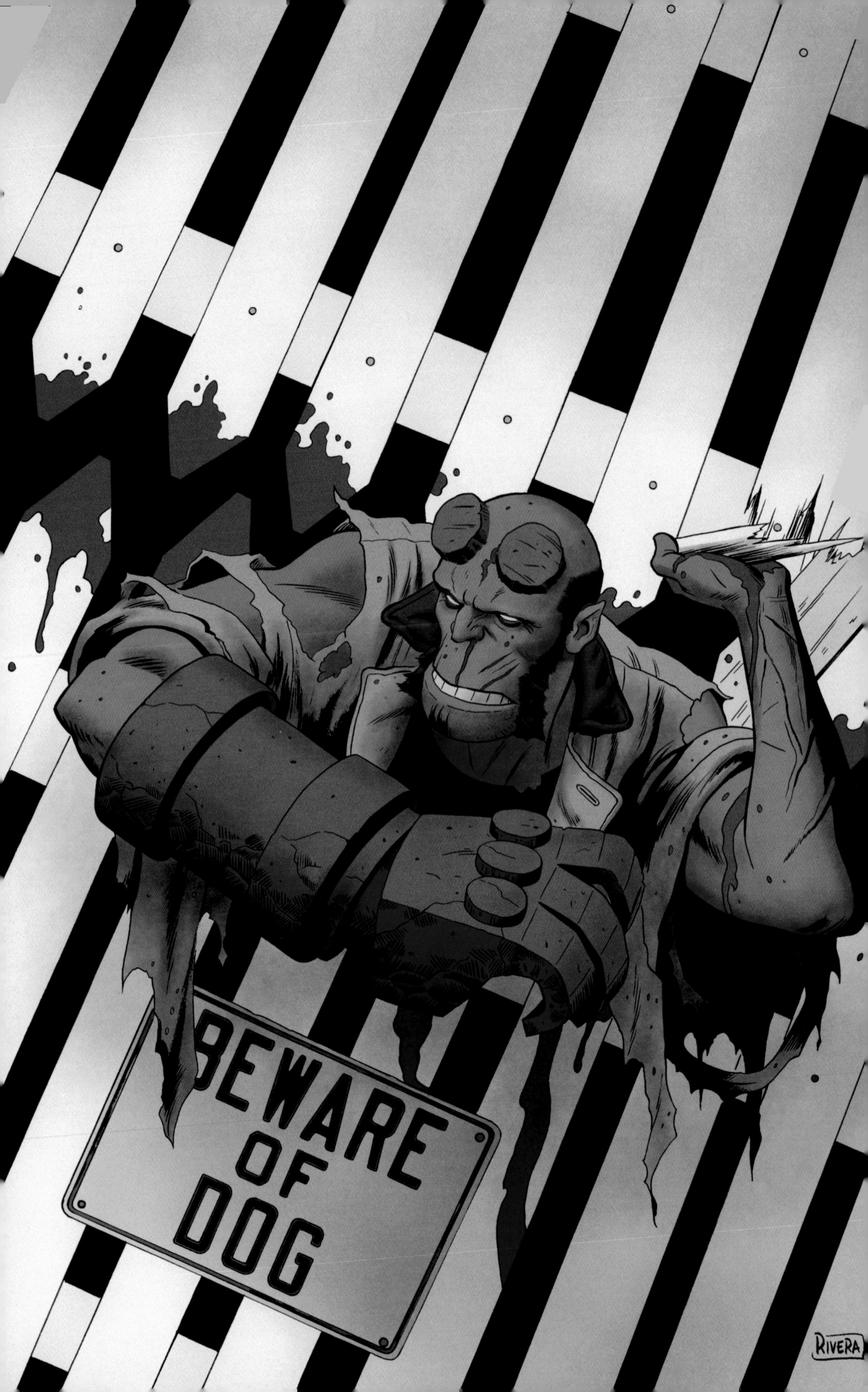
BEWARE OF DOG
RIVERA

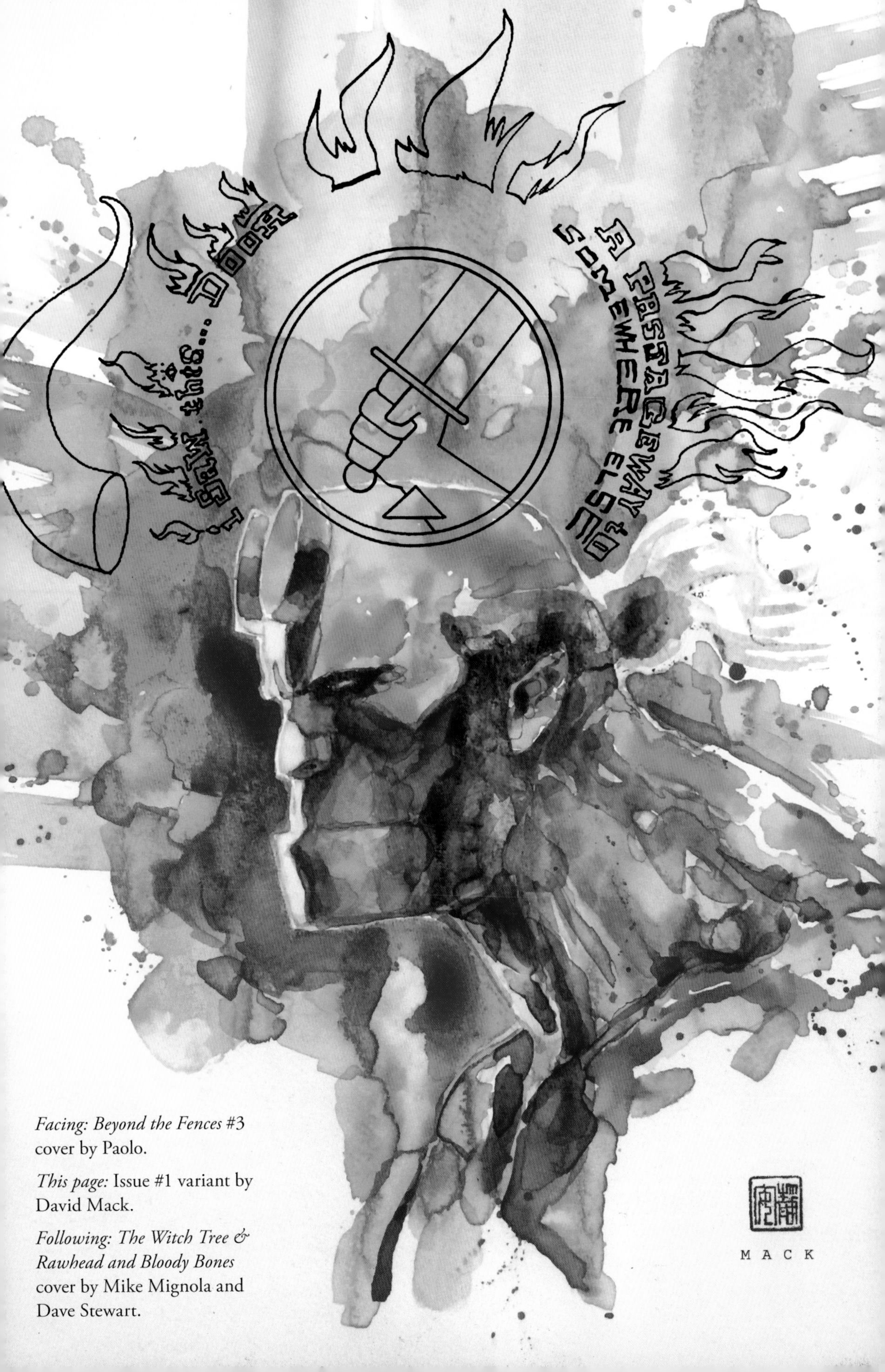
A PASSAGEWAY to SOMEWHERE ELSE
MACK

Facing: Beyond the Fences #3 cover by Paolo.

This page: Issue #1 variant by David Mack.

Following: The Witch Tree & Rawhead and Bloody Bones cover by Mike Mignola and Dave Stewart.

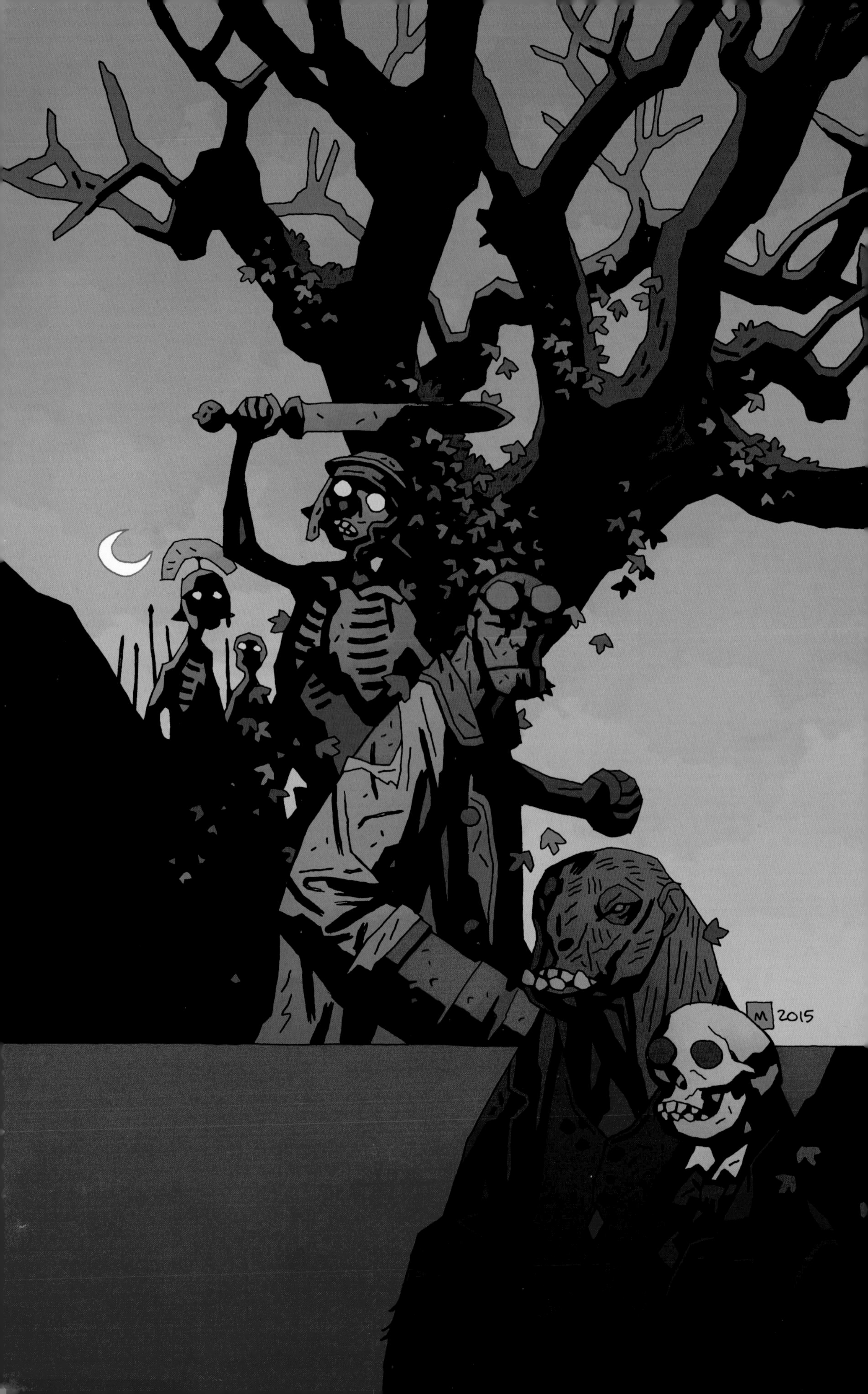
M 2015

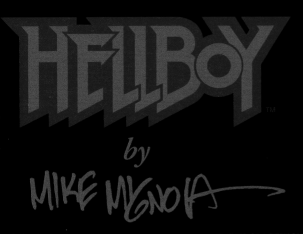

HELLBOY
by
MIKE MIGNOLA

Also by MIKE MIGNOLA →

B.P.R.D.

PLAGUE OF FROGS
Volume 1
with Chris Golden, Guy Davis, and others
HC: ISBN 978-1-59582-609-1 | $34.99
TPB: ISBN 978-1-59582-675-6 | $19.99

Volume 2
with John Arcudi, Davis, and others
HC: ISBN 978-1-59582-672-5 | $34.99
TPB: ISBN 978-1-59582-676-3 | $24.99

Volume 3
with Arcudi and Davis
HC: ISBN 978-1-59582-860-6 | $34.99
TPB: ISBN 978-1-61655-622-8 | $24.99

Volume 4
with Arcudi and Davis
HC: ISBN 978-1-59582-974-0 | $34.99
TPB: ISBN 978-1-61655-641-9 | $24.99

1946–1948
with Joshua Dysart, Paul Azaceta, Fábio Moon,
Gabriel Bá, Max Fiumara, and Arcudi
ISBN 978-1-61655-646-4 | $34.99

BEING HUMAN
with Scott Allie, Arcudi, Davis, and others
ISBN 978-1-59582-756-2 | $17.99

VAMPIRE
with Moon and Bá
ISBN 978-1-61655-196-4 | $19.99

B.P.R.D. HELL ON EARTH

NEW WORLD
with Arcudi and Davis
ISBN 978-1-59582-707-4 | $19.99

GODS AND MONSTERS
with Arcudi, Davis, and Tyler Crook
ISBN 978-1-59582-822-4 | $19.99

RUSSIA
with Arcudi, Crook, and Duncan Fegredo
ISBN 978-1-59582-946-7 | $19.99

**THE DEVIL'S ENGINE
AND THE LONG DEATH**
with Arcudi, Crook, and James Harren
ISBN 978-1-59582-981-8 | $19.99

**THE PICKENS COUNTY
HORROR AND OTHERS**
with Allie, Jason Latour, Harren,
and Max Fiumara
ISBN 978-1-61655-140-7 | $19.99

THE RETURN OF THE MASTER
with Arcudi and Crook
ISBN 978-1-61655-193-3 | $19.99

A COLD DAY IN HELL
with Arcudi, Peter Snejbjerg, and
Laurence Campbell
ISBN 978-1-61655-199-5 | $19.99

**THE REIGN
OF THE BLACK FLAME**
with Arcudi and Harren
ISBN 978-1-61655-471-2 | $19.99

THE DEVIL'S WINGS
with Arcudi, Campbell,
Joe Querio, and Crook
ISBN 978-1-61655-617-4 | $19.99

LAKE OF FIRE
with Arcudi and Crook
ISBN 978-1-61655-402-6 | $19.99

FLESH AND STONE
with Arcudi and Harren
ISBN 978-1-61655-762-1 | $19.99

METAMORPHOSIS
with Arcudi, Snejbjerg, and Julián Totino Tedesco
ISBN 978-1-61655-794-2 | $19.99

END OF DAYS
with Arcudi and Campbell
ISBN 978-1-61655-910-6 | $19.99

THE EXORCIST
with Cameron Stewart, Chris Roberson,
and Mike Norton
ISBN 978-1-50670-011-3 | $19.99

ABE SAPIEN

THE DROWNING
with Jason Shawn Alexander
ISBN 978-1-59582-185-0 | $17.99

**THE DEVIL DOES NOT JEST AND
OTHER STORIES**
with Arcudi, Harren, and others
ISBN 978-1-59582-925-2 | $17.99

**DARK AND TERRIBLE
AND THE NEW RACE OF MAN**
with Allie, Arcudi, Sebastián
Fiumara, and Max Fiumara
ISBN 978-1-61655-284-8 | $19.99

THE SHAPE OF THINGS TO COME
with Allie, S. Fiumara, and M. Fiumara
ISBN 978-1-61655-443-9 | $19.99

SACRED PLACES
with Allie, S. Fiumara, and M. Fiumara
ISBN 978-1-61655-515-3 | $19.99

A DARKNESS SO GREAT
with Allie and M. Fiumara
ISBN 978-1-61655-656-3 | $19.99

THE SECRET FIRE
with Allie, S. Fiumara, and M. Fiumara
ISBN 978-1-61655-891-8 | $19.99

LOBSTER JOHNSON

THE IRON PROMETHEUS
with Jason Armstrong
ISBN 978-1-59307-975-8 | $17.99

THE BURNING HAND
with Arcudi and Tonci Zonjic
ISBN 978-1-61655-031-8 | $17.99

SATAN SMELLS A RAT
with Arcudi, Fiumara, Querio,
Wilfredo Torres, and Kevin Nowlan
ISBN 978-1-61655-203-9 | $18.99

GET THE LOBSTER
with Arcudi and Zonjic
ISBN 978-1-61655-505-4 | $19.99

WITCHFINDER

IN THE SERVICE OF ANGELS
with Ben Stenbeck
ISBN 978-1-59582-483-7 | $17.99

LOST AND GONE FOREVER
with Arcudi and John Severin
ISBN 978-1-59582-794-4 | $17.99

THE MYSTERIES OF UNLAND
with Kim Newman, Maura McHugh, and Crook
ISBN 978-1-61655-630-3 | $19.99

FRANKENSTEIN UNDERGROUND
with Stenbeck
ISBN 978-1-61655-782-9 | $19.99

JOE GOLEM: OCCULT DETECTIVE—THE RAT CATCHER & THE SUNKEN DEAD
with Golden and Patric Reynolds
ISBN 978-1-61655-964-9 | $24.99

THE AMAZING SCREW-ON HEAD AND OTHER CURIOUS OBJECTS
ISBN 978-1-59582-501-8 | $17.99

BALTIMORE

THE PLAGUE SHIPS
with Golden and Stenbeck
ISBN 978-1-59582-677-0 | $24.99

THE CURSE BELLS
with Golden and Stenbeck
ISBN 978-1-59582-674-9 | $24.99

**A PASSING STRANGER
AND OTHER STORIES**
with Golden and Stenbeck
ISBN 978-1-61655-182-7 | $24.99

CHAPEL OF BONES
with Golden and Stenbeck
ISBN 978-1-61655-328-9 | $24.99

THE APOSTLE AND THE WITCH OF HARJU
with Golden, Stenbeck, and Peter Bergting
ISBN 978-1-61655-618-1 | $24.99

THE CULT OF THE RED KING
with Golden and Bergting
ISBN 978-1-61655-821-5 | $24.99

NOVELS

LOBSTER JOHNSON: THE SATAN FACTORY
with Thomas E. Sniegoski
ISBN 978-1-59582-203-1 | $12.95

JOE GOLEM AND THE DROWNING CITY
with Golden
ISBN 978-1-59582-971-9 | $99.99

BALTIMORE; OR, THE STEADFAST TIN SOLDIER & THE VAMPIRE
with Golden and Stenbeck
ISBN 978-1-61655-803-1 | $12.99

DARK
HORSE
BOOKS
DarkHorse.com